Play Therapy with Vulnerable Populations

Play Therapy with Vulnerable Populations

No Child Forgotten

Edited by Eric J. Green and Amie C. Myrick

ROWMAN & LITTLEFIELD
Lanham • Boulder • New York • London

Published by Rowman & Littlefield
A wholly owned subsidary of The Rowman & Littlefield Publishing Group, Inc.
4501 Forbes Boulevard, Suite 200, Lanham, Maryland 20706
www.rowman.com

Unit A, Whitacre Mews, 26-34 Stannary Street, London SE11 4AB

British Library Cataloguing in Publication Information Available

Library of Congress Cataloging-in-Publication Data

Play therapy with vulnerable populations : no child forgotten / edited by Eric J. Green and Amie C.
Myrick.
p. ; cm.
Includes bibliographical references and index.
ISBN 978-1-4422-3252-5 (cloth : alk. paper) -- ISBN 978-1-4422-3253-2 (electronic)
I. Green, Eric J., editor. II. Myrick, Amie C., editor.
[DNLM: 1. Play Therapy. 2. Child. 3. Mental Disorders--therapy. 4. Stress Disorders, Traumatic--
therapy. 5. Vulnerable Populations--psychology. WS 350.4]
RJ505.P6
618.92'891653--dc23
2014039920

∞™ The paper used in this publication meets the minimum requirements of American
National Standard for Information Sciences Permanence of Paper for Printed Library
Materials, ANSI/NISO Z39.48-1992.

Printed in the United States of America

To my devoted parents, Belinda and Gerry, for standing by me, especially during adolescence, and for ensuring I never felt forgotten.

—Eric J. Green

To my beautiful little boy, who serves as a constant reminder of why I do this work. I love you every minute of every day. You are never, ever, forgotten.

—Amie C. Myrick

Contents

Foreword

Nancy Boyd-Webb

Play therapy has always been a dynamic and exciting profession that attracts clinicians from diverse fields. All play therapists, regardless of their professional backgrounds, share a passionate commitment to helping children who are suffering from emotional pain, and they do this by using child-friendly play methods that reflect basic respect for the young person. The field of play therapy has changed greatly since the 1920s when Anna Freud began to use toys and games as a way of building a relationship with her child clients (1926/1946). Since that time numerous models of play therapy have developed, but all share a belief in the power of the therapeutic relationship together with conviction about the child's potential for growth and change as the key to helping (Green & Drewes, 2013; Webb, 2007).

In the past decade there has been increasing emphasis on validating the effectiveness of different approaches to play therapy through controlled research studies. Some of this research has determined that child-centered play therapy and filial therapy are effective in general and for children who experienced crises and trauma. However, most of the research reports conclude that further play therapy studies with children in crisis and trauma need to be conducted, which suggests that there are still many facets of play therapy to explore before definitive conclusions can be drawn about what makes it work. This book does a wonderful job of combining practice wisdom with available evidence-informed research.

Green and Myrick have assembled a dozen chapters that offer examples of a variety of treatment approaches that have demonstrated to be effective with vulnerable and marginalized populations. These include children who have suffered multiple and sometimes ongoing traumas, thereby qualifying them for the diagnosis of "complex trauma." The various chapters present play therapy interventions for sexually abused children, for children following natural disasters, for hospitalized and/or chronically ill children, physically disabled youth, LGBTQI adolescents, and children with obsessive-compulsive disorders. The authors carefully illustrate that no one method is appropriate for all children, and children must be assessed so that treatment methods can be adapted to their individual needs.

The play therapy approaches described in detail in this book include both directive and nondirective methods that demonstrate the use of expressive arts, psychoeducation, and many imaginative and helpful strategies to empower children to control and take charge of their own symptoms. All chapters emphasize engaging the parents as partners with the therapist. Overall, the multi-faceted intervention methods presented here employ a modern, research-supported, integrated philosophy that merges different theoretical orientations and various clinical practices.

The editors, Eric Green and Amie Myrick, who are respectively an associate professor of counseling and a licensed clinical professional counselor, have gathered an impressive group of child therapy authors from the United States and abroad in the fields of psychology, school counseling, clinical social work, nursing, and education. All of these contributors have many years of clinical experience on which they draw as the basis for their informative writing. Whether employing a directive, narrative-based storytelling technique (Prendiville, chapter 4), or teaching children how to externalize and take charge of their obsessive-compulsive symptoms (Myrick and Green, chapter 9), or facilitating the creation of masks that show inside and outside feelings with adolescents who identify with diverse sexual orientation (Goldman, chapter 12)—all of the contributors embody the essence of creativity that they utilize in a playful manner with their child and adolescent clients. Some of the strategies are so appealing I found myself wanting to try them on myself! The incorporation of the parents, and sometimes the entire family, is an ever-present aspect of treating the child in these various models. Many helpful examples of parental coaching are included. Thereby, the systemic view of treatment prevails in this volume, which reinforces the importance of child-family interaction and relational healing.

This book will be a welcome text for colleges and post-master's certificate programs that teach play therapy courses. All the chapters contain rich case examples that demonstrate the use of numerous treatment strategies after the theoretical foundation and appropriate applications have been presented. This clinical emphasis also makes the book highly relevant for practitioners who are looking for new ideas and methods to use in their work with child and adolescent clients who sometimes can be difficult to engage. The authors' emphases on giving the child choices and on building the young person's sense of self-esteem permeate the presentation of strategies that result in stimulating the youth's natural resilience and growth processes.

All these factors combine to make this a very appealing, helpful, and wise book. It manages to meld research findings with useful clinical applications, always keeping the child/adolescent as the focal point. It is a distinct contribution to the field of play therapy and promises to be a solid reference work that practitioners, professors, and students will happily consult and cherish for years to come.

REFERENCES

Freud, A. (1946). *The psychoanalytic treatment of children.* London, England: Imago Press. (original published in 1926).

Green, E. J., & Drewes, A. (Eds.). (2013). *Integrating expressive arts and play therapy with children.* Hoboken, NJ: John Wiley.

Webb, N. B. (Ed.). (2007). *Play therapy with children in crisis. Individual, group, and family treatment (3rd ed.).* New York, NY: Guilford Press.

Introduction

Eric J. Green and Amie C. Myrick

Katy Perry's song, "Firework," is an anthem about self-acceptance and recognizing that our uniqueness is a gift meant to bring us together and not separate. The cover image of the book, a firework sparkler, and the content of this book, both coalesce into one succinct message. Namely, that, children who are vulnerable or identify as different from their more mainstream peers, or are ostracized for being unique, can begin feeling better about themselves and the world around them by first accepting who they are without trying to change what they are. "Firework" celebrates originality and emphasizes the potential that can lie dormant in children who feel they aren't accepted by society. It captures the essence of the message of this book which is for us to acknowledge, through our humanity and compassion, that no child, no matter how different, should ever be left to feel alone or like "wasted space."

This book's idea came about organically from several years of scholarly synergy. Amie was a bright, former student of mine (Eric) from Johns Hopkins University and had initially reached out in 2008 to collaborate on a filial therapy with homeless parents research project (Kolos, Green, & Crenshaw, 2009). I, in turn, invited her to help me with a chapter I was writing for Mary Guindon on facilitating self-esteem in elementary school-aged children using nondirective play therapy (Green & Kolos, 2010). Our styles and clinical practice coalesced, as we started writing extensively on a topic we both were passionate about: play therapy with vulnerable populations. In the spring of 2013, we critically reflected on our work together and reviewed what, if any, next step we could make to possibly contribute something meaningful to the current literature. It was at that point that the "soul" of the book began to take its shape and form.

We recognized that much of our previous research encompassed evidence-informed interventions with vulnerable or marginalized populations within the play therapy paradigm of mental health care. In our clinical work, we acknowledged the extraordinary compassion and resilience when working with children and families from unique and diverse clinical groups that are vulnerable and/or oppressed. Some of these "outliers" are described in this volume, including children affected by obsessive compulsive disorder, complex trauma, and natural disasters. We also recognize that there are many special or unique demographic and pediatric groups that were not described here, but certainly not forgotten, including children affected by blended families, war and terrorism, racism, poverty, psychosis, and so on. The specific populations covered in this book were based on the expertise of the available authors at the time of production of this specific volume and practical editorial decisions from a page limit perspective, and were in no way meant to further marginalize the additional special or unique populations not covered in this volume. We have dedicated our careers to the advocacy of vulnerable children and utilize psychotherapy as a practice to facilitate resilience through woundedness. It is our desire that this volume showcases how any practitioner, with the right tools and training, can further their work with oppressed, wounded, or traumatized children, as well as those affected by unique psychiatric diagnoses. O'Donohue (2004) eloquently described the state of woundedness in others and how it evokes a fundamental empathy and humanity through resilience:

> The beauty that emerges from woundedness is infused with feeling that has suffered its way through the ache of desolation. Where woundedness can be refined into beauty, a wonderful transfiguration takes place. Compassion is one of the most beautiful presences a person can bring to the world and most compassion is born from one's own woundedness. When you have felt deep emotional pain and hurt, you are able to imagine what the pain of the other is like; their suffering touches you. This is the most decisive and vital threshold in human experience and behavior. The beauty of compassion shelters and saves. (pp. 180–181)

Wanting to honor the fundamental resilience in children affected by various unique or exotic conditions, oftentimes warranting specialized treatment, we aimed to assemble a book that was just as unique as the clients we served. Therefore, this volume presents a collection of up-to-date research and practical skill-based play therapy interventions for vulnerable populations relevant to the typical play therapy practitioner. The book is also unique in that many of the chapters include new research developed by expert authors that substantiates the integration of evidence-informed interventions and play therapy. This book's purpose is timely; we have seen an increase in the interest and execution of presentations across the United States, as well as globally, aimed at increasing play therapy clinicians' skills and knowledge.

Our book's focus is not solely on disseminating knowledge about evidenced-based practices, but on balancing research with the need for humanistic psychotherapy and the central importance of the nonjudgmental, warm, therapeutic relationship. We support the notion that soma-psyche, spirit-soul, mind-body connections are equally important and germane for balance in the individual. Competent clinicians must allow children to lead the way to their own healing without necessarily forcing preconceived, manualized treatment approaches. The overarching theme of this book is to provide the clinician with multiple perspectives of integrating research-informed practice with common sense, humanistic paradigms that emphasize the salience of the therapeutic relationship as the central crux for change. Therefore, the book serves as a metamodel of the reflective process of postmodern integration: clinicians must gauge what is most important for their clients, their relationship to their clients (and their families), and the intersubjective field that remains. Finally, the book highlights the symbolism involved in play therapy with children, and how these symbols and symbolic activities help the child's psyche heal. Bachofen, as cited by Campbell (2007), stated:

> The symbol awakens intimations speech can only explain. The symbol plucks all the strings of the human spirit at once; speech is compelled to take up a single thought at a time. The symbol strikes its roots in the most secret depths of the soul; language skims over the surface of the understanding like a soft breeze. The symbol aims inward; language outward. (p. 103)

The contributing authors, with both national and international representation, were chosen for this project based upon their expertise in research-supported protocols and evidence of peer-reviewed scholarship in the play therapy field with special child populations. In the "Foundations" section, the first two chapters cover the research support of integrative practice, as well as the latest evidence in empowering parents through filial therapy, a paradigm that demonstrates a sizeable treatment effect size of change. The second section of the book, "Clinical Applications for Traumatized Populations," details play therapy practices with children made vulnerable through single-incident and repeated, complex traumatic experiences, and with hospitalized and chronically ill children. The third and final section, "Clinical Applications for Psychosocial and Developmental Issues," discusses developmental disruptions in children, including autism spectrum disorders, OCD, and externalizing conditions that interfere and significantly impact children's academic and social functioning. Chapter 11 comprises a rarely covered topic in play therapy, working with children with physical disabilities; and in the final chapter, Linda Goldman provides a heartfelt and culminating account of incorporating play-based support and necessary advocacy with adversely affected adolescents who identify as gay or lesbian.

We want to thank all of the contributing authors on this project for their time, expertise, and selfless contributions to the book, as well as the larger field of play therapy. We could NOT have done this without you. We also want to acknowledge our editor, Amy King at Rowman & Littlefield, for this amazing opportunity. We want to humbly express our gratitude to Nancy Boyd-Webb, an icon in the social work and play therapy fields (and also the person who gave me [Eric] my very first "break" to write a chapter for her book back in 2006), for writing the foreword. Finally, we want to extend our heartiest gratitude to you, the reader and play therapy practitioner, for being in the trenches day after day, doing the difficult, oftentimes arduous, work of caring for children's shattered souls through the science and art of play therapy. We hope this volume will assist you in your own journey and lead you to explore additional resources, training, and supervision to further deepen your meaningful work with special children and increase your advocacy for vulnerable populations.

REFERENCES

Campbell, J. (2007). *The mythic dimension*. Novato, CA: New World Library.

Green, E. J. (2014). *The handbook of Jungian play therapy with children and adolescents*. Baltimore, MD: Johns Hopkins University Press.

Green, E. J., & Kolos, A. (2010). Facilitating self-esteem in elementary school aged-children: Perspectives from child-centered play therapy. In M. H. Guindon (Ed.), *Self-esteem across the lifespan* (pp. 49–61). New York, NY: Routledge/Taylor & Francis.

Kolos, A., Green, E. J., & Crenshaw, D. (2009). Conducting filial therapy with homeless parents. *Journal of American Orthopsychiatry, 79*(3), 366–374.

O'Donohue, J. (2004). *Beauty the invisible embrace: Rediscovering the true sources of compassion, serenity, and hope*. New York, NY: HarperCollins.

I

Foundations

Chapter One

Integrating Play Therapy and Evidence-Informed Interventions with Vulnerable Populations

An Overview

Anne L. Stewart and Eric J. Green

In the current literature, researchers place significant emphasis on mental health clinicians utilizing protocols that maintain fidelity of treatment and demonstrate treatment efficacy with patients (i.e., standardized, manualized, evidence-based treatment protocols). The most current mental health research demonstrates that clinicians adhering to manualized treatment approaches may increase opportunities for children and adolescents to psychologically heal within a posttraumatic growth context and possibly experience symptom remission. Evidence-based treatment approaches are often validated by rigorous control or experimental design studies and typically utilize a manualized approach with patients to reduce specific, psychiatric symptoms at specific, time-informed intervals. Most notably, cognitive behavioral therapy (CBT) has received substantial attention in the mental health field over the past several years as being the "gold standard" in psychotherapy for remediating multiple childhood disorders and associated symptomologies, especially related to traumatization.

In his recent meta-analysis in the *American Psychologist*, Jonathan Shedler (February–March 2010) stated that "insight therapies" (i.e., play therapy), or those approaches that include not only symptom remission but also the distinguishing feature of fostering positive psychological capacities demonstrate moderate treatment effect sizes in multiple mental health disorders in children. Shedler identified multiple factors specific to the insight-based psychotherapies, such as play therapy, that can be integrated within evidence-based treatment approaches (hence the term "evidence-informed treatment"), including (a) focus on affect and expression of emotion, (b) identification of themes and recurring patterns, (c) focus on the therapy relationship, and (d) the exploration of fantasy life.

This first chapter's aim is to provide the most current research-supported and evidence-informed trends in play therapy interventions with special populations so that readers may consider additional training to competently and ethically incorporate them into their current clinical practice. As with the remainder of this volume, this chapter seeks to clearly and practically link current scientific validation with play therapy interventions in a straightforward manner. Within evidence-informed play therapy approaches, clinicians ascribing to an integrative approach utilize the most current effective treatment protocols available, while incorporating developmentally appropriate, insight-based therapy, such as play therapy, into practice.

RESEARCH SUPPORT

Historical and Current Context of Psychotherapy Integration

Psychotherapy, as a specific treatment intervention, is a relative newcomer in the venerable history of healing efforts. In service of alleviating human suffering, the early and innovative models of psychotherapy, developed by Freud, Jung, and Adler, were themselves efforts to integrate information from medicine and philosophy, including epistemology (i.e., the branch of philosophy which questions what constitutes knowledge and beliefs) and ethics (i.e., the branch of philosophy which examines fundamental principles of what is morally right). These first pioneers in psychotherapy developed treatment models that challenged prevailing beliefs and advanced new paradigms regarding the prominence of psychological factors on the etiology of illness and health.

Jackson (1999) reported that the term "psychotherapy" was introduced by Hippolyte Bernheim in the publication *Hypnotisme, Suggestion, Psychotherapie* in the late 1880s. As a professional scientific field, psychotherapy progressed in a manner consistent with Kuhn's (2012) description of the process of scientific inquiry. Seymour (2011) recommended that play therapists apply information from Kuhn's model to better appreciate the recurring issues in the history of psychotherapy and to help inform current efforts in psychotherapy integration. Kuhn's explanation in *The Structure of Scientific Revolutions* posits that information is amassed around an enduring question and area of interest and explanatory models, or paradigms, are created. Over time, the existing models are subject to scrutiny in ways that are consistent with the methods of discovery and knowledge building of the particular discipline and time period. As a result, more supporting evidence for a given model is created or different formulations are put forth, claiming their enhanced explanatory power. Kuhn stated, "assimilation requires the reconstruction of prior theory and reevaluation of prior fact, an intrinsically revolutionary process that is seldom completed by a single man and never overnight" (p. 7).

Kuhn stated that periods of intense dialogue and controversy are to be expected in the process of constructing a scientific field. Saltzman and Norcross (1990) named the periods of active examination in the history of psychotherapy, "therapy wars," an apt name for times where followers of one model waged vitriolic campaigns to demonstrate their ultimate superiority over the other models. Kuhn's examination also showed that the process of scientific inquiry tends to shift focus from one feature to another. In psychotherapy, the debates have coalesced around theoretical orientation, practice and techniques, and the research designs used to validate the effectiveness of a particular approach.

Evidence of enduring interest in the nature of psychological problems and how they can best be treated, as well as interest in psychotherapy integration, appeared as early as 1930 with a comparison of Pavlovian conditioning and psychoanalysis (Arkowitz, 1984); however, single-school psychotherapy approaches predominated through the early 1980s. The most common theoretical allegiance, during this time of rapid proliferation of psychotherapy models, was to psychoanalytic, behavioral, or humanistic schools of thought. A discernable shift began to take place in the 1980s when the field of psychotherapy was characterized by the ascendance of eclecticism. While the time period has been described as chaotic with a confusing array of therapies from which to choose, the interest in eclecticism heralded a shift from the single-school approaches to a less dogmatic and rigid perspective and "more openness to looking at complementary aspects of treatment from different angles" (Henriques, 2011, p. 209).

A significant occurrence in the psychotherapy integration movement was the creation of the Society for the Exploration of Psychotherapy Integration (SEPI) in 1983. SEPI is an international organization whose mission is to "promote the exploration and development of approaches to psychotherapy that integrate across theoretical orientations, clinical practices, and diverse methods of inquiry" (SEPI, 2014). Through the 1990s and 2000s psychotherapy integration grew into a recognized area of research and practice, as the number of articles and presentations forwarding new models increased and textbooks comparing and contrasting integrated models were published.

Along with the researchers and theorists, practitioners and policy makers in child mental health have argued convincingly for an integrated approach to child psychotherapy (Drewes, Bratton, & Schaefer, 2011; Green, 2008; Schaefer, 2003; Shirk, 1999). Shirk noted that many children enter treatment meeting criteria for more than one diagnostic category and present with stressors across multiple levels and multiple settings. For example, a child may be referred for treatment due to behavioral problems at school, display symptoms of depression and inattention, and reside with an overburdened, anxious parent in an unsafe neighborhood. A national study of over 10,000 adolescents reported approximately 40 percent of the participants with one disorder also met the criteria for another disorder (National Comorbidity Survey, 2011). The median age of onset was earliest for anxiety (i.e., six years), underscoring the importance of multifaceted intervention approaches and early intervention.

The use of evidence-based principles in the practice of mental health care has definitely affected the dissemination of health care funds, and not always to the benefit of the clients or the providers. However, promising research findings from filial and parent–child treatment programs and child trauma interventions have added interest, and in some cases, a demand for particular types of evidence-based treatments to be conducted by external funding agencies. Importantly, and of special interest to play therapists, many of the findings support the importance of responding to the child in their familial context, developing strong parent–child relationships and of incorporating cognitive–behavioral and sensory-based and symbolic experiences for optimal outcomes (Brandt, Perry, Seligman & Tronick, 2014). Drewes (2011) stated, "Because psychological disorders, especially for children and adolescents, are multi-layered, complex and multi-determined, a multifaceted treatment approach is needed" (p. 23).

Play therapy enters the integrated psychotherapy conversation at a particularly dynamic time, as the broader field is characterized by intense evaluation of the various integrated models and, at the same time, embroiled in in-depth discussions regarding the benefits of reworking the clinical science foundation for psychology. Henriques (2011) suggested the field is transitioning toward a paradigm shift to unify the clinical sciences, rather than focus on integrating various theoretical models. Play therapists have a great deal to learn and to contribute to the current dialogue.

MODELS OF PSYCHOTHERAPY INTEGRATION AND THE PRACTICE OF PLAY THERAPY

As the psychotherapy integration movement progressed, four different types of integration emerged. The generally recognized integrated models include: technical eclecticism, common factors, integrative assimilation, and theoretical integration (Prochaska & Norcross, 2010; Stricker, 2010). During the time that issues related to integrated research and practice were becoming increasingly prominent in the disciplines of psychology and counseling, the field of play therapy was more focused on the demonstrating the effectiveness of single-school approaches. Examples of many of the current types of integrated child play psychotherapy models, while not always explicitly named by play therapists as "integrated models," are evident in the play therapy literature and outlined in the following section.

Technical Eclecticism

As the name implies, technical eclecticism focuses on selecting and applying techniques to discover what works best for a client within a prescriptive perspective. Followers of this practical model do not focus on the theoretical basis from which a technique was derived. Play therapists may be drawn to apply this model when striving to construct evidence-based treatments for specific disorders or with particular pediatric populations. Given the diversity of clinical profiles addressed in cases of divorce, Kenney-Noziska and Lowenstein (2015) apply an integrated technical eclecticism approach to devise prescriptive, attuned treatment plans, informed by research in current trends and issues. They recommend that play therapists select evidence-based techniques to address the specific symptoms the child is experiencing while adhering to best practice guidelines for therapists providing mental health services to families in court-involved therapy. Kenney-Noziska and Lowenstein encourage play therapists to consult guidelines from the Association of Family and Conciliation Courts to augment their understanding of how the legal system impacts treatment and to provide direction to others regarding their roles and responsibilities. Underscoring the complexity of conducting play therapy when the family court is involved, this approach can aid the therapist in balancing boundaries, roles, confidentiality, and professional objectivity and the child's treatment.

Imagine a play therapist receives a referral to see a socially isolated first grade student diagnosed with an autism spectrum disorder (ASD). First, the therapist would review the literature to determine the appropriateness of play therapy as a treatment for ASD. After finding research support for both nondirective and directive play therapy strategies (Gallo-Lopez & Rubin, 2012; Grant, 2014; Green, 2012; Hull, 2015; Ray, Sullivan, & Carlson, 2012), the play therapist would consider the primary area of concern, in this case, difficulties in making and maintaining friends. Based on the research, the therapist could incorporate the use of picture-filled *social stories*, an evidence-based strategy for children with autism, in play therapy sessions and parent and teacher consultation, to enhance the child's social skills (Wright & McCathren, 2012). As part of a comprehensive approach, the therapist would consult with the child's teacher to devise behavioral strategies to enhance learning and decrease disruptive conduct in the classroom, contact the child's pediatrician to discuss the need for a possible medication trial, and meet with the parents to evaluate the appropriateness of a referral for filial therapy (VanFleet, 2012).

This example shows steps that could be used across a number of referrals. First, determine if there is evidence for play therapy as a primary or supplemental treatment. Next, examine the research for recommended techniques, resources, and strategies to use with the disorder/condition. Include relevant child characteristics such as age, gender, and culture, in addition to other resources or stressors; and, lastly, reach out intentionally to partner with the caregivers and other professionals and resources in the child's life. Other models of psychotherapy integration attend not only to the selective use of techniques from different theoretical orientations, but importantly, to the relationship between techniques and theory.

Common Factors Model

The Common Factors Model grew from research showing that positive and similar outcomes were accomplished across a variety of theoretical models and techniques. Creating a secure therapeutic relationship, engaging in a respectful manner, instilling hope, expecting change, and providing an opportunity for clients to share their narrative were identified as crucial factors for change to occur. Thus, the common factors for change and successful outcomes were associated with the therapist, the client, and the relationship, not with the theoretical orientation or particular technique (Wampold & Budge, 2012).

While the original common factors studies were conducted with adult psychotherapy, research with child and teen clients has also been completed. The research findings, across all age spans, consistently support the importance of a secure relationship for all forms of effective counseling and psychotherapy. Shirk, Karver, and Brown (2011) found the effectiveness of the therapeutic alliance, consisting of the relationship, goals, and decision-making process in therapy, was consistent with adult research findings. Namely, studies with child and adolescent clients demonstrated the alliance predicted therapeutic success across a wide number of clinical issues and modalities. Additionally, their comprehensive meta-analysis of child and adolescent alliance-outcome associations yielded an effect size comparable to the adult individual therapy literature. Estrada and Russell (1999) found a correlation between the quality of the child's cooperative and trusting relationship with the therapist and readiness for therapeutic engagement. The findings highlighted the importance of the positive engagement in the therapeutic relationship, often named as a "curative" factor in the adult psychotherapy literature.

Attachment-informed play therapy provides an example of how results from the common factors model can be used in practice. Focusing on the importance of a secure pattern of relationship development in childhood, Whelan and Stewart (2015) illustrate the relevance of attachment research findings to the therapeutic bond in play therapy. A secure pattern of relationship development is strongly associated with resilience and a broad array of positive outcomes in the school-age years and adulthood (Sroufe & Siegel, 2011; Sroufe, 2005). Whelan and Stewart note the process of play therapy is personal, emotional, and takes place within the relationship of child and therapist. In this regard, the primary goal of play therapy parallels the goal of healthy parenting, namely, to develop a relationship that, through moment-to-moment interactions, will help the child form more coherent internal structures and patterns of thinking, feeling, and behaving. Research demonstrates that development of healthy interpersonal patterns that may not yet be present in the child, or ones that are currently underdeveloped due to experiences of chronic stress or trauma in the child's life, can have a positive influence on a number of relational, academic, and behavioral outcomes. From an attachment perspective, play allows for active engagement of the child in a therapist–child relationship, providing moment-to-moment interactions for the therapist to respond to the child's relationship needs and defenses and to generate adaptive relationship patterns (Green, Myrick, & Crenshaw, 2013).

Assimilative Integration Approach

In an assimilative integration approach, the therapist selects and blends key concepts from various perspectives, at both the theory and technique level. Therapists using an assimilative integration model incorporate techniques and concepts from one model in ways that are congruent and consistent with interusing different theoretical orientation(s). An advantage of this approach is that practitioners trained in a single-school approach can maintain their primary theoretical paradigm and incorporate ideas and strategies to expand and enrich their model. Sweeney (2011) characterizes an assimilative integration approach of valuing theory and techniques in the following quote, "An important reminder is necessary about therapeutic techniques. Theory is important, but theory without technique is merely philosophy. Techniques are valuable, but techniques without theory are reckless and potentially damaging" (p. 236). Sweeney suggests that play therapists consider the following questions when determining whether or not to integrate particular techniques: "Is the technique developmentally appropriate?" "What theory underlies the technique?" and "What is the therapeutic intent of using a particular technique?" (p. 236).

Exemplars of the assimilative integrative approach are beginning to appear in the play therapy literature. McGuinness (2011) examines how eye movement desensitization and reprocessing (EMDR) practices can be adapted and incorporated with a more nondirective play therapy approach for traumatized children. McGuinness asserts a number of commonalities that make the use of the EMDR techniques compatible with play therapy. Play therapy and EMDR both lower anxiety, reveal beliefs that cause pain, and are not dependent on verbalization. The therapist is encouraged to begin by following the format of their typical play therapy sessions. In the second or third session the therapist tells the child that they know a game that can help them with negative thoughts and feelings. A play therapist trained in EMDR can then respond sensitively to the child's interest in engaging in the "game" and include EMDR activities throughout the course of the play therapy treatment.

Another example of assimilative integration can be seen in the use of sand tray to treat disruptive behaviors in preschool children. The case exploration by Green and Gibbs (2010) confirms how effective outcomes can be achieved by applying research findings within a developmentally congruent theoretical approach. Green and Gibbs described how to implement an interdisciplinary, integrated sand tray treatment approach with cognitive–behavioral interventions. The cognitive–behavioral interventions were implemented through consultation with the child's school counselor and teacher over the course of treatment. In addition, periodic consultations with the child's family members were held to facilitate their understanding of the therapeutic process.

Child–Parent Relationship Therapy (Landreth & Bratton, 2005) is an example of an assimilative integrated approach to filial therapy with a strong evidence base. Munns (2011) details how to integrate child-centered play therapy and Theraplay; while Ashby and Noble (2011) illustrate the integration of theoretical and techniques from cognitive–behavioral play therapy and Adlerian play therapy for the treatment of perfectionism. The authors of the latter integrative approach cited the assumptions and types of interventions shared by the theories, such as valuing the importance of a strong therapeutic relationship and also believing that the relationship is not a sufficient mechanism for change but requires directive techniques to help the child think in more adaptive ways.

Theoretical Integration Model

The Theoretical Integration Model blends concepts and principles from two or more schools of thought into a unique innovative and coherent framework. Techniques that are compatible with the new structure are identified, but the focus is on the integration of the underlying theoretical constructs (Norcross, 2005). Interestingly, both longstanding and more recent play therapy models are illustrative of the theoretical integration approach. Ecosystemic Play Therapy (EPT) exemplifies a theoretically focused approach in play therapy, viewing the whole child embedded in ecological contexts of their home, school, and community (O'Connor, 2005; O'Connor & New, 2003). EPT is distinctive in that it articulates a specific integrated philosophical base, namely, humanistic and phenomenological philosophies, which are used to help inform the therapist's goal setting, decision making, and perception of the "problem." EPT explicitly addresses personality functioning as part of conceptualization, defining personality as the "sum of intra- and interpersonal characteristics, attributes, cognition, beliefs, [and] values . . . that make a person unique." Roots of psychopathology for the child, such as disrupted attachments and reduced problem-solving capabilities, are also considered in formulating a conceptualization of the child's functioning. Ecosystemic play therapy builds on these ideas from philosophy, personality development, and psychopathology, and includes key concepts from psychoanalytic, child-centered, and cognitive–behavioral theories to generate strategies for intervention. A discussion exploring the use of EPT with urban First Nations People illustrated how EPT was responsive to cultural considerations (Boyer, 2010). The overarching goal of EPT is for the child to be successful and adaptive across all the ecosystems in which they live.

An excellent example of theoretical integration, the Neurosequential Model of Therapeutics, was developed for treatment of maltreated children by Bruce Perry and is described in Brandt, Perry, Seligman & Tronick (2014). The model incorporates fundamentals of neurobiology and child development to create a useful decision-making framework for assessment and interventions for children growing up in chaotic, unpredictable, and unsafe environments.

Acknowledging the Underlying Therapeutic Powers of Play

Drewes (2011) reported research examining the common factors and noted that over half of the elements were related to change processes (all of which are very familiar to play therapists), including developing the therapeutic alliance, providing opportunities for practicing new behaviors, and holding positive expectations about the therapeutic process. Drewes further reflected that the curative factors identified as the therapeutic powers of play (Schaefer & Drewes, 2014) could be construed as the change mechanisms in play therapy. By becoming more knowledgeable about play-based change mechanisms, such as self-expression, positive emotions, empathy, and resiliency, therapists could select relevant agents of change for a child and incorporate them in a prescriptive, evidence-informed intervention plan. This approach could be applied to any of the integrated psychotherapy models to help children and teens address behavioral, emotional, psychological, and relational challenges.

Integrating Play Therapy with Vulnerable Child Populations

It is cogent for play therapists to become familiarized—through research, professional development, and supervised practice—with how to competently integrate play therapy with children considered outliers of typical child diagnoses in regular practice. This book explores play psychotherapy with some of these unique pediatric populations not regularly found in the current literature, including children affected by obsessive compulsive disorder (OCD), very young children affected by sexual trauma, chronically ill children traumatized by multiple hospitalizations and surgeries, and adolescents coping with overt aggression and violence related to identifying as LGBTQI. As multiculturally competent practitioners, play therapists must acknowledge and be sensitive to diverse clinical groups, especially those living in less urban, more rural areas where access to mental health services is limited for children and families. Further, providing psychotherapy for special or unique populations involves extensive, additional training to competently meet the needs of the specialized population, which often requires some type of social justice advocacy component as these unique groups of children are typically marginalized and oppressed. Integrating a play therapy approach with any unique population first requires an awareness and ethical recognition of one's own therapeutic competence and professional boundaries to work only within areas that one has been trained. For example, if a play therapist is practicing in a small rural town in which an adolescent male is being bullied for being gay and is exhibiting self-injurious behaviors, and this is outside the play therapist's competence, the therapist must recognize the limits of his competence and go about ethically remedying it through supervision and peer/expert support to immediately assist this adolescent in crisis (for more information on this topic, see Goldman's chapter in this volume). Second, play therapists are required to meet the unique child within a specific population wherever they are developmentally and relationally by allowing the child to lead the way toward the healing. Practically, this requires play therapists to invite the child to cocreate the psychotherapeutic encounter and choose the selection of techniques in a collaborative manner. Third, play therapists should be in counseling/supervision/peer consultation regularly to effectively employ evidence-based interventions with child play psychotherapy without activating their own personal psychology within the consultation room.

Adopting a Culturally Attuned and Holistic Integrated Approach

There is evidence that culture and the safety of the environment influence most aspects of the treatment process. There is corresponding concern regarding whether evidence-based treatments are appropriate for groups that do not share same culture or context. As play therapists explore integrated models, it is imperative to view children in their relevant environments, taking into account the cultural, linguistic, and socioeconomic context in which they live and play (Gil & Drewes, 2005; Post & Tillman, 2015). Play therapists are encouraged to talk with the caregiver (and child) about presumed causes and ways to address problems and solutions. This creates the opportunity to discuss a variety of culturally relevant topics and faith-based and spiritual beliefs. Spiritual beliefs and faith traditions can offer explanatory power, comfort, or even contribute to subjective distress.

Because approximately 12 percent of children (about one in nine) in the United States are using some form of complementary or alternative medicine, it is important to inquire about the use of herbal remedies, mind–body work, or other healing traditions and resources used in their family or community. The most common therapies used by children are natural products, chiropractic and osteopathic care, deep breathing, and yoga (Barnes, Bloom & Nahin, 2008). Adopting an integrated health perspective does not mean that play therapists practice beyond the scope of their training in mental health and play therapy. Rather, this approach calls upon us to collaborate closely and consistently with the client's family, pediatrician, nurse practitioner, teacher, and other providers.

INTEGRATIVE PLAY THERAPY TREATMENT PLANNING AND PROTOCOL

In spite of many promising steps and the growing recognition of the relevance of and need for integrated approaches for child play psychotherapy, there is scarce agreement about which model might hold the most explanatory power for a given disorder or population. There is little to no research support of integrated approaches with children, with the exception of selected trauma focused and parent–child interventions. So, how best to proceed?

Current recommendations for all health and human service professionals are to consult with evidence-based practice (and evidence-informed interventions) to determine the most effective procedures. This is good news for play therapists, and demands a high level of engagement, rigor, and professionalism in their decision making. The definition for evidence-based practices is the "integration of the best available research with clinical expertise in the context of patient characteristics, culture, and preferences" (APA, 2006, p. 280). The *best available research* refers to scientific results related to intervention techniques, clinical problems, and diagnostically determined disorders. It is important to be reminded that a credible foundation for the effectiveness of play therapy exists (see Ray, 2015; Bratton, Ray, Rhine, & Jones, 2005). Ray, Bratton, Rhine, and Jones's (2001) meta-analysis of ninety-four play therapy experimental research studies concluded that, "play therapy appears to work in various settings, across modalities, age, and gender, clinical nonclinical populations, and theoretical schools of thought" (pp. 93–94). The best available research also refers to findings from related disciplines and results from laboratory and field settings. Again, this can be construed as good news for the field of play therapy. A positive distinction for play therapy research is the degree to which it is informed by findings of typical and atypical development in children. In addition, play therapy research is noted for a large proportion of research conducted in the field—in schools, clinics, agencies, and hospitals.

Integrating *clinical expertise* to inform best practices encompasses a number of abilities to promote positive therapeutic outcomes. For child therapists important competencies to examine include (a) the ability to establish and maintain a strong therapeutic alliance with the child and caregivers, (b) knowledge of attachment theory and mechanisms of self-regulation, (c) consultation skills with mental preschools and schools, (d) knowledge of parent–child and family-based interventions, and (e) awareness of systemwide mental health prevention programs (Rubinson, Yasik, Mowder, 2011).

There is a growing collection of journals (e.g., *Early Childhood Services: An Interdisciplinary Journal of Effectiveness*; *Clinical Child Psychology and Psychiatry*; *International Journal of Play Therapy*; *Child Development*; *Journal of Early Childhood and Infant Psychology*) and databases (e.g., the National Registry of Evidence-Based Programs and Practices at http://www.nrepp.samhsa.gov, and What Works Clearinghouse at http://www.whatworks.ed.gov) to help play therapists stay well informed to promote positive outcomes for their child clients. Clinical expertise develops over time and from multiple sources, including clinical experience, scientific training, theoretical understanding, self-reflection, knowledge of research, and continuing education and training.

The final element of evidence-based practice is to integrate patient characteristics, culture, and preferences. For play therapists, this involves viewing the child in context; and while it is vital to intentionally explore all the possible relevant dimensions for a child, this is an approach quite familiar to successful play therapists. Examining the interaction of gender, sociocultural and familial factors and stressors (ethnicity, race, social class, religion, disability status, family structure, employment status), and the impact of the institutional and environmental contexts, such as institutional racism, health care disparities, and access to care, are all elements to consider in conducting a comprehensive intake and formulating an effective case conceptualization. The next section comprises a case study describing the integration of evidence-based intervention with play therapy.

CASE STUDY

The following case study describes an evidence-based play therapy treatment with, Luke, a six-year-old boy. The psychotherapy model employed an assimilative integrated approach incorporating attachment and humanistic theoretical approaches to understand Luke's major issues and guide the intervention, with cognitive–behavioral, sensory-based neurobiological, and parent–child relationship techniques incorporated. In addition, this case was guided by concepts from systems theory (boundaries, hierarchy, rules, roles, subsystems, and power, etc.), consultation with the school, physicians, social service department staff, and other allied health professions featured significantly in the child's treatment. Information has been altered to obscure the identity and protect the confidentiality of the child and family.

Luke's adoptive parents sought play therapy services after they had participated in an evidence-based parent education program, the Circle of Security (COS) (Cooper, Hoffman, & Marvin, 2014), sponsored by the Department of Social Services (DSS). During intake the parents reported how beneficial the COS program was in enhancing their understanding of how and why they needed to actively help Luke regulate his emotions so he could better regulate his behaviors. They had modified their previous discipline approach of timeouts and spanking to follow the COS model of moving closer to Luke, coregulating with him, to help him organize his feelings or to be comforted or protected when he was overwhelmed by his emotions.

The parents reported that early in the school year, Luke's teacher had complained about his inability to stay focused, complete assignments, especially writing assignments, and was beginning to talk back to her and refuse to follow directions. His parents stated they occasionally saw Luke act this way at home, but it was not typical behavior. In contrast, their primary concern was Luke's sad and discouraged demeanor. They reported that during the five months of first grade, they had witnessed a dramatic change in his mood. The parents reported, with obvious concern, that his sad affect was quite different from his usual cheerful, if a bit changeable, mood. They noted that he had begun to talk about himself as "stupid" and "dumb." They had been practicing strategies from the COS approach, trying to respond to his sad affect and not just dispute his comments. However, his negative mood was persisting and they understood from the DSS worker that play therapy might be able to help.

The parents reported that they had fostered and eventually adopted Luke, taking him taking him home from the hospital when he was a newborn. The intake revealed that Luke's developmental history was significant for prenatal cocaine exposure and early disruptions in his caregiving. While he was removed from his biological parents at birth and placed with his foster to adoptive parents, his early history was also complicated by over four years of intermittent visitation with his biological parents. During this time, he had sporadic and rather chaotic visits with his biological mother, father, and extended family. This was an attempt, by the then–foster parents, to permit a relationship to develop with the birth parents and the reaching out was endorsed by the DSS. In addition, two years after Luke was removed from his birth home, his biological parents gave birth to a baby girl, Ellie. After fifteen months of complicated and increasing adversarial court proceedings, Ellie was also removed from the biological parents and placed in their home with Luke. Visits had not taken place for the last four months, but were in the midst of being scheduled and rescheduled, usually due to last minute cancellations by the biological parents.

Importantly, discussions about everyday family life revealed many strengths. Luke's father worked full time doing construction and operated a small family farm where the family resided. Luke's mother worked part time at a retail shop where her children could accompany her most days. No other medical issues, trauma, or separations were noted. Luke had attended a small faith-based daycare on occasion and had seemed to enjoy the experiences with no reports of difficulties from the staff. The family had well-established and developmentally appropriate routines, including bedtime and meal times. Luke completed his chores of feeding chickens and horses with parent supervision and with pride.

A flexible approach to treatment was described that included individual play therapy, parent consultation, parent–child sessions, family play sessions, and active consultation with the other people and agencies involved in Luke's life. The parents appeared a bit surprised, but pleased with the description, stating that they could "use all the help they could get" and were ready to have Luke begin play therapy.

When Luke and his mother arrived, he hid his face against her skirt and peeked at the therapist, exhibiting behaviors consistent with a younger child, but illustrating a positive attachment with his adoptive mother. Bringing along a front loader toy vehicle from home, he was able to separate from his adoptive mother and enter the play room. Over the first few sessions, themes of demonstrating competence and exploring independence/dependence through building (with Legos) and construction (working in a sand pile in the office fireplace) predominated. These themes resonated developmentally (for a six-year-old boy to imitate his father's activities) and in terms of his current school difficulties (wanting to feel competent and needing help to manage his strong emotions). The therapist noted how rigid Luke's play was in the first two sessions and that by staying in the metaphor (of working on a construction job), Luke began to integrate problem-solving tasks from the therapist into the play scenarios. For example, a truck might break down and the therapist, acting as the driver, would wonder what to do. The therapist also noted that Luke's grip when playing with the Legos was quite weak and that despite this, Luke persisted building through multiple failed attempts.

In consultation with Luke's teacher, the therapist learned how frustrated the teacher was with Luke's refusal to do his assignments. The teacher acknowledged that his noncompliance was almost exclusively associated with writing tasks, which were, unfortunately, a significant part of the first grade curriculum. However, the teacher was also perplexed with how quickly Luke became upset and how long it took for his to settle down to discuss he would not comply with the teacher's request to do his writing assignment. The teacher noted that the school had a policy of discussing any misbehavior in the moment with the student, including making a plan and having the child promise not to make the poor decision again. While this approach could have some positive elements, from the teacher's description, it was being administered in a rigid and demanding way, further escalating Luke's upset. The therapist shared information regarding the presence of difficulties in regulation for children with prenatal drug exposure and attachment insecurities which might help explain some of Luke's reactivity and his inability to engage in productive problem solving in the midst of being upset. The teacher and therapist also created a straightforward positive reinforcement plan to acknowledge Luke's academic successes and affirm the times he was able to comply with teacher requests. This had the added advantage of helping the teacher note the times Luke was behaving as expected.

The therapist's consultation with the DSS case worker revealed a confusing picture of cross-state jurisdiction and unclear leadership in the management and status of the case. A series of conference calls were completed and the case was clearly assigned to the local department. In addition, using attachment findings, the therapist discussed the purpose of the visits and how confusing and anxiety provoking the chaotic visits and unreliable contact might be for Luke, indeed for all involved. It was determined that subsequent visits would be scheduled with more specific goals and supports in place for the children (Luke and Ellie), and the adoptive and birth parents.

After four weeks of play therapy and the school and DSS consultation, a parent consultation was held. The parents reported that Luke's affect had actually seemed to brighten at home and while he had some good days, he continued to have significant problems at school. The therapist suggested that individual play therapy sessions continue and that Luke be referred for a comprehensive psychoeducational evaluation, including an occupational therapy evaluation (due to the observed fine motor weakness) and that the parents consider consulting with a developmental pediatrician about the appropriateness of a trial of medication for anxiety for Luke. The parents and therapist discussed the reasons and benefits of the assessments and agreed to move forward. Then, over the course of two weeks Luke was suspended twice from school for trying to hit his teacher and two dogs, cherished family pets unexpectedly died, and the shop where the mother worked was robbed.

The collective anxiety was rampant and sense of security in the family fabric was unraveling. The therapist met with the parents to adjust the treatment plan. It was decided to add a series of four family play sessions, beginning with the creation of a family aquarium, followed by the therapist teaching and practicing four square breathing (on counts of four, breathe in, hold, breathe out, rest), reading the *Moody Cow* book to the family and together making glitter jars to depict angry or upset brains (plastic jars with water, glycerin, and flakes of glitter with the lids glued shut). Each family member responded favorably to the information in the *Moody Cow* book about what happens to the brain and how to use meditation with the prop of the glitter jar—both to signal the upset and to help reestablish a sense of calm. The family reported using this technique during times of upset and adding a "family quiet time" to the nightly bedtime routine. The family also completed a family sand tray (Green, 2014), and family puppet show, both of which included themes related to continued processing the loss of the family pets.

The therapist consulted with the mother and teacher to reframe Luke's noncompliance as feelings of being overwhelmed and anxious. This interpretation of Luke's behavior was an unfamiliar notion for the teacher, and it seemed beneficial to let the teacher know the developmental pediatrician had recommended medication for anxiety. With the mother's and Luke's permission, the therapist shared information about how to use the *Moody Cow* and glitter jars with the teacher. The teacher was agreeable, indeed excited, about using the technique as a universal classroom strategy to signal needing time to get calm (not just for Luke).

In this case study, the family presented with many strengths, including a willingness to accept help and be actively engaged. This approach was facilitated by the therapist's attention to integration concepts from a framework of attachment and humanistic theory with selected intervention techniques and the strengths and challenges of the client and family. Using the relationship with the therapist as a secure base the family members were able to receive help to organize their feelings and explore the harsh and unexpected events that occurred in the context of an attuned and empathic relationship.

Case Study Conclusion

An integrated psychotherapy approach argues against adopting a static, narrow, and problem-focused approach to our therapeutic work with children. Instead, integrated models encourage practitioners to conduct their work with children fully informed about the ways in which children are embedded in their family, community (school and neighborhood), and culture. Using a broad ecological and relational formulation, in collaboration with the children's caregivers, teachers, community workers, and health providers, is at the heart of conducting play therapy in an integrated and holistic manner. An integrated and holistic approach acknowledges that health is not just the absence of distress and that health for the whole child includes all aspects of mental health.

PLAY THERAPISTS' ENGAGEMENT WITH INTEGRATED PSYCHOTHERAPY MODELS: MOVING FORWARD

The wisdom, creativity, and clinical acumen demonstrated by play therapists as they develop models of psychotherapy integration and construct integrated treatment plans is encouraging. While issues related to sufficient, rigorous, and relevant research methods continue to plague the larger integrated psychotherapy movement and play therapy's inaugural attempts (specifically a call for evidence-based to be defined broadly and to emphasize the role of the client and of the relationship), there are many promising approaches to be further investigated. Play therapists incorporating evidence-based interventions and research-supported practices seem to be moving to a dynamic and responsive conceptualization of their role. They are actively engaged in adopting a holistic paradigm where they can easily move between nondirective and directive and prescriptive methods, all in response to the client's needs and in their scope of practice. The door seems to be opening for creating a professional identity that embraces both science and humanism.

Play therapists are becoming more active consumers of the broader research community in health and mental health. Therapists are consulting research journals and sites listing empirically supported treatments and programs in their own and other disciplines to find techniques that are supported by research, such as the use of positive self-statements and deep breathing for children with anxiety. The literature shows that play therapists have been using a wide variety of integrated approaches and are now beginning to intentionally invoke this framework, discovering or developing integrated models that are compatible with their theoretical model, client needs, and, importantly, their own expertise. As additional research is completed, play therapists are urged to continue critically examining the existing theoretical and evidence-based information and make thoughtful, well-informed decisions using current research information, to reflect deeply on contributions derived on their own clinical wisdom and that are responsive to the characteristics, culture, and preferences of their client's families.

CONCLUSION

This chapter's aim was to provide the clinician with sensible, balanced psychotherapeutic approaches that incorporate the most current research-supported trends in child psychotherapy and play therapy with vulnerable populations. In honoring both evidence-informed and play therapy approaches, clinicians utilize the most current treatment protocols, while integrating developmentally appropriate, insight-based therapy, such as play therapy, into practice. When encountering vulnerable populations, the play therapist first recognizes professional competence, seeks out supervision/guidance/additional training to competently execute treatment, and remains sensitive to providing a voice or advocating for the child who belongs to a unique demographic that may be marginalized in some way. The second chapter in the "Foundations" section of this book continues the discussion by examining the latest research in integrating play therapy in filial work with parents.

REFERENCES

Arkowitz, H. (1984). Historical perspective on the integration of psychoanalytic theory and behavior therapy. In H. Arkowitz & S. Messer (Eds.), *Psychoanalytic therapy and behavioral therapy: Is integration possible?* (pp. 1–30). New York, NY: Plenum Publishing.

APA. (2006). American Psychological Association Task Force on Evidence-Based Practice. Evidence-based practice in psychology. *American Psychologist, 61,* 271–285.

Ashby, J. S. & Noble, C. (2011). Integrating cognitive behavioral play therapy and Adlerian play therapy into the treatment of perfectionism. In A. A. Drewes, S. C. Bratton, & C. E. Schaefer (Eds.), *Integrative play therapy* (pp. 225–240). Hoboken, NJ: John Wiley and Sons, Inc.

Barnes, P. M., Bloom, B. & Nahin, R. (2008). *Complementary and alternative medicine use among adults and children: United States.* CDC National Health Statistics Report #12.

Brandt, K., Perry, B., Seligman, S. & Tronick, E. (2014). *Infant and early childhood mental health: Core concepts and clinical practice.* Washington, DC: American Psychiatric Publishing.

Bratton, S., Ray, D., Rhine, T., & Jones, L. (2005). The efficacy of play therapy with children: A meta-analytic review of the outcome research. *Professional Psychology: Research and Practice, 36*(4), 376–390.

Boyer, W. (2010). Getting to know O'Connor: Experiencing the ecosystemic play therapy model with urban first nations people. Family Journal: Counseling and Therapy for Couples and Families, *18*(2), 202–207.

Cooper, G., Hoffman, K. & Marvin, B. (2014). *The circle of security intervention: Enhancing attachment in early parent–child relationships.* New York, NY: Guilford Press.

Drewes, A. A. (2011). Integrating play therapy theories into practice. In A. A. Drewes, S. C. Bratton, & C. E. Schaefer (Eds.), *Integrative play therapy* (pp. 21–35). Hoboken, NJ: John Wiley and Sons, Inc.

Drewes, A. A., Bratton, S. C., & Schaefer, C. E. (2011). *Integrative Play Therapy.* Hoboken, NJ: John Wiley and Sons.

Estrada, A. U., & Russell, R. L. (1999). The development of the Child Psychotherapy Process Scales (CPPS). *Psychotherapy Research, 9,* 154–166.

Gallo-Lopez, L., & Rubin, L. (Eds.) (2012). *Play based interventions for children and adolescents with Autism spectrum disorders.* London, England: Routledge.

Gil, E. & Drewes, A. (2005). *Cultural issues in play therapy.* New York, NY: Guilford Press.

Grant, R. J. (2014). *More play based interventions for Autism, ADHD, neurodevelopmental disorders, and developmental disabilities* [workbook]. Nixa, MO: Author.

Green, E. J. (2008). Re-visioning a Jungian analytical play therapy approach with child sexual assault survivors. *International Journal of Play Therapy, 17*(2), 102–121.

Green, E. J. (2012). The Narcissus myth, resplendent reflections, and self-healing: A contemporary Jungian perspective on counseling high-functioning Autistic children. In L. Gallo-Lopez, & L. Rubin (Eds.), *Play based interventions for children and adolescents with Autism spectrum disorders* (pp. 177–192). London, England: Routledge.

Green, E. J. (2014). *The handbook of Jungian play therapy with children and adolescents.* Baltimore, MD: Johns Hopkins University Press.

Green, E. J., & Gibbs, K. (2010). Jungian sandplay therapy for preschoolers with disruptive behavior problems. In C. E. Schaefer (Ed.) *Play therapy* (pp. 223–244). Washington, DC: American Psychological Association.

Green, E. J., Myrick, A. C., & Crenshaw, D. A. (2013). Towards secure attachment in adolescent relational development: Advancements from sandplay and expressive play-based interventions. *International Journal of Play Therapy, 22*(2), 90–102.

Henriques, G. (2011). *Toward a unified theory: A new unified theory of psychology.* New York, NY: Springer.

Hull, K. B. (2015). Play therapy with children on the autism spectrum. In D. Crenshaw & A. L. Stewart. *Play Therapy: A comprehensive guide to theory and practice.* New York, NY: Guilford Press.

Jackson, S. W. (1999). *Care of the psyche: A history of psychological healing.* New Haven, CT: Yale University Press.

Kenney-Noziska, S. & Lowenstein. L. (2015). Play therapy with children of divorce: Using a prescriptive model. In D. Crenshaw & A. L. Stewart. *Play Therapy: A comprehensive guide to theory and practice.* New York, NY: Guilford Press.

Kuhn, T. (2012). *The structure of scientific revolutions: 50th anniversary edition.* Chicago, IL: University of Chicago Press.

Landreth, G. & Bratton, (2005). *Child–parent relationship therapy: A 10 session filial therapy model.* New York, NY: Taylor & Francis.

McGuinness, V. (2011). Integrating play therapy and EMDR with children: A post-traumatic intervention. In A. Drewes, S. Bratton, & C. Schaefer (Eds). *Integrative Play Therapy* (pp. 195–206). Hoboken, NJ: John Wiley and Sons.

Munns, Evangeline (2011). Integration of child-centered play therapy and Theraplay. In A. Drewes, S. Bratton, & C. Schaefer (Eds). *Integrative Play Therapy* (pp. 325–340). Hoboken, NJ: John Wiley and Sons.

National Comorbidity Study. (2011). Lifetime Prevalence of Mental Disorders in US Adolescents: Results from the National Comorbidity Study-Adolescent Supplement (NCS-A). Retrieved from http://www.ncbi.nlm.nih.gov/pmc/articles/PMC2946114/.

Norcross, J. C. (2005). A primer on psychotherapy integration. In J. C. Norcross & M. R. Goldfried (Eds.), *Handbook of Psychotherapy Integration, Second Edition* (pp. 10–23). New York, NY: Oxford University Press.

O'Connor, K. (1997). Ecosystemic play therapy. In K. O'Connor & M. K. Braverman (Eds.). *Play Therapy Theory and Practice. A Comparative Presentation* (pp. 234–284). New York, NY: John Wiley & Sons.

O'Connor, K. (2001). Ecosystemic play therapy. *International Journal of Play Therapy, 10*(2), 33–44.

O'Connor, K. (2005). Addressing diversity issues in play therapy. *Professional Psychology: Research and Practice, 36*, 566–573.

O'Connor, K. & New, D. (2003). Ecosystemic play therapy. In C. Schaefer (Ed.) *Foundations of play therapy.* New York, NY: John Wiley and Sons.

Prochaska, J. O., & Norcross, J. C. (2010). *Systems of psychotherapy: A transtheoretical analysis.* (7th ed.). Belmont, CA: Brooks/Cole.

Ray, D. C. (2015). Research in Play Therapy: Empirical Support for Practice. In D. Crenshaw & A. Stewart (Eds.). *Play therapy: A comprehensive guide to theory and practice.* New York, NY: Guilford Press.

Ray, D., Bratton, S., Rhine, T., & Jones, L. (2001). The effectiveness of play therapy: Responding to the critics. *International Journal of Play Therapy, 10,* 85–108.

Ray, D. C., Sullivan, J. M., & Carlson, S. E. (2012). Relational intervention: Child-centered play therapy with children on the autism spectrum. In L. Gallo-Lopez & L. Rubin (Eds.), *Play-based interventions for children and adolescents with autism spectrum disorders* (pp. 159–175). New York, NY: Routledge/Taylor & Francis Group.

Rubinson, F., Yasik, A. E., & Mowder, B. A. (2011, April). Evidence-based practice in infant and early childhood psychology (Practice Forum). Retrieved from http://www.apadivisions.org/division-16/publications/newsletters/schoolpsychologist/2011/04/evidence-based-practice.aspx.

Saltzman, N, & Norcross, J. C. (1990). *Therapy wars: Contention and convergence in differing clinical approaches.* San Francisco, CA: Jossey-Bass.

Schaefer, C. E. (2003). Prescriptive Play Therapy. In C. E. Schaefer (Ed.), *Foundations of Play Therapy* (pp. 306–320). New York, NY: John Wiley & Sons, Inc.

Schaefer, C. E. & Drewes, A. A. (Eds.). (2014). *The therapeutic powers of play: 20 core agents of change.* Hoboken, NJ: John Wiley & Sons.

SEPI. (2014). Society for the exploration of psychotherapy integration. Retrieved from http://www.sepiweb.com.

Seymour, J. (2011). History of psychotherapy integration and related research. In A. Drewes, S. Bratton, and C. Schaefer (Ed.), *Integrative play therapy* (pp. 3–19). Hoboken, NJ: John Wiley & Sons.

Shedler, J. (2010, February–March). The efficacy of psychodynamic psychotherapy. *The American Psychologist, 65*(2), 98–109.

Shirk, S. R. (1999). Integrated child psychotherapy: Treatment ingredients in search of a recipe. In S. Russ & T. Ollendick (Eds.) *Handbook of psychotherapies with children and families* (pp. 369–384). New York, NY: Plenum Publishers.

Shirk, S. R., Karver, M. S., & Brown, R. (2011). *The alliance in youth psychotherapy.* Psychotherapy, *48*(1), 17–24.

Stricker, G. (2010). A second look at psychotherapy integration. *Journal of Psychotherapy Integration, 20*(4), 397–405.

Sroufe, L. A. (2005). Attachment and development: A prospective, longitudinal study from birth to adulthood. *Attachment and Human Development, 7*(4), 349–367.

Sroufe, L. A. & Siegel, D. (2011). The verdict is in. *Psychotherapy Networker.* pp. 34–39, 52–53.

Sweeney, D. (2011). Group play Therapy. In C. Schaefer (Ed.). *Foundations of play therapy* (2nd ed., pp. 227–252). Hoboken, NJ: Wiley.

VanFleet, R. (2012). Communication and connection: Filial therapy with families of children with ASD. In L. Gallo-Lopez and L. C. Rubin (Eds.), *Play-Based Interventions for Children and Adolescents with Autism Spectrum Disorders* (pp. 193–208). New York, NY: Routledge Taylor & Francis Group.

Wampold, B. E., & Budge, S. L. (2012). The relationship—and its relationship to the common and specific factors of psychotherapy. *The Counseling Psychologist, 40,* 601–623.

Whelan, W. F., & Stewart, A. (2015). Attachment-focused play therapy. In D. Crenshaw & A. Stewart (Eds.). *Play therapy: A comprehensive guide to theory and practice.* New York, NY: Guilford Press.

Wright, L. A., & McCathren, R. B. (2012). Utilizing social stories to increase prosocial behavior and reduce problem behavior in young children with autism. *Child Development Research,* Article ID 357291. doi:10.1155/2012/357291

Chapter Two

The Evidence and Filial Therapy

Effectively Integrating Parents Into Child Psychotherapy

Glade Topham and Cynthia C. Sniscak

Filial therapy (FT) was developed in the early 1960s by Bernard and Louise Guerney (Guerney, 1964). In contrast to the popular treatment approaches during that period, which viewed children's problems as a function of parent *pathology*, the Guerneys believed that a lack of parent knowledge and skills was typically responsible for child and parent–child relationship difficulties. They hypothesized that with education and supportive guidance parents could be trained to conduct child-centered play therapy (CCPT) sessions with their children, with farther-reaching and longer-lasting gains than if the sessions were provided singularly by a trained therapist (Guerney & Ryan, 2013). Several aspects of FT including the competence-oriented, psychoeducational approach, involving multiple family members conjointly in sessions, and the collaborative relationship between therapist and parent were revolutionary at the time of the development of FT.

FT represents an integration of diverse theories including (a) client-centered, (b) attachment theory, (c) family systems, (d) psychodynamic, and (e) cognitive behavioral theories (Guerney & Ryan, 2013; VanFleet, 2013). Client-centered play therapy (CCPT) forms a theoretical foundation for FT, as it is the basis for parent–child interaction (parents utilize CCPT skills in play sessions with their children), and for therapist–parent interaction (with qualities such as therapeutic acceptance, genuine respect, and empathy). A strong parent–child attachment relationship is seen as central to progressing through FT. In learning the play session skills parents develop attunement to their child and demonstrate they are available and responsive through respect for child autonomy and sensitivity to the child's emotional needs. Similarly, the therapist provides a secure psychological base for the parent throughout treatment. The influence of family systems theory occurs within the focus on family relationships and the belief that when one part of the system changes all parts of the system are affected. Attention to the symbolic meaning of children's play and what their play may reveal about their internal world is influenced by psychodynamic theory. Finally, cognitive behavioral theory has large influence on the process of training parents in the FT skills. Therapists use reinforcement, shaping, and vicarious learning and also challenge parent beliefs that may prevent them from responding appropriately to their child (Guerney & Ryan, 2013; VanFleet, 2013). Filial therapists (1) teach parents to conduct special play sessions with their children; (2) supervise the play sessions and engage in postplay discussions with parents to facilitate skill development, parent attunement, and to collaboratively address barriers to improved parent, child, and family functioning; and (3) guide the parents in successfully applying and generalizing the play session skills to everyday family interaction (VanFleet, 2013).

As FT has continued to grow in popularity so has the number of adaptations to the original group FT model. These include an individual model of filial family therapy (VanFleet, 2013), a short-term, ten-session group format (Landreth & Bratton, 2006), a fourteen- to eighteen-week group FT format with foster and adoptive families focused on children who have experienced trauma and attachment problems (VanFleet, Sniscak, & Faa-Thompson, 2013), and a thirteen-week group format for head start families (Wright & Walker, 2003). Although these adaptations have similarities, to avoid confusion, this chapter will focus on VanFleet's individual filial family therapy model. Throughout the following sections, the term refers to the primary caregiver in the family (i.e., foster parent, biological parent, adopted parent, grandparent, etc.). In addition to describing the development, theoretical foundation, and research support for FT, this chapter will outline the treatment process, along with a description of specific interventions used in the approach. Finally, a case study illustrates the flexibility and systemic impact of FT.

RESEARCH SUPPORT

Since the creation of FT, over fifty years of research has demonstrated the effectiveness of FT in addressing a broad range of presenting problems with diverse client populations (see VanFleet, Ryan, & Smith, 2005). In 2005 Bratton and colleagues conducted a meta-analysis of research examining play therapy interventions. As part of the analysis they examined numerous FT research studies and found FT to be highly effective, with a treatment effect size of change higher than that of play therapy interventions with individual children. Research has demonstrated many positive parent and child gains from FT. Some positive parent outcomes include (a) a decrease in parent stress (e.g., Tew, Landreth, & Joiner, 2002); (b) an increase in parent self-confidence (Glass, 1986); (c) an increase in parent acceptance of the child (e.g., Bratton & Landreth, 1995); (d) an increase in parent empathy (e.g., Harris & Landreth, 1997); (e) parents allowing more self-direction for the child (Smith & Landreth, 2003); and (f) overall improvements in the parent–child relationships (Grskovic & Goetze, 2008). Positive benefits to children include (a) an increase in child self-confidence (e.g., Costas & Landreth, 1999); (b) reduction in child depression and anxiety (e.g., Tew et al., 2002); (c) an increase in children's expression of emotion (Glass, 1986); and (d) a decrease in child behavior problems (e.g., Grskovic & Goetze, 2008).

Research has shown FT to be an effective intervention for parents and children from a wide range of backgrounds and presenting issues or complaints (VanFleet, Ryan, & Smith, 2005). FT is effective with two-parent families (Glass, 1986), foster parents (Guerney & Gavigan, 1981), single parents (Bratton & Landreth, 1995), and incarcerated fathers (Landreth & Lobaugh, 1998) and mothers (Harris & Landreth, 1997). Similarly, FT is effective with parents of children with chronic illness (e.g., Tew et al., 2002), conduct problems (Johnson-Clark, 1996), learning difficulties (Kale & Landreth, 1999), and pervasive developmental disorders (Beckloff, 1997). It has also been effective with parents of children who have witnessed domestic violence (Smith & Landreth, 2003) and nonoffending parents of sexually abused children (Costas & Landreth, 1999). Finally, FT is effective with parents from a variety of cultural and ethnic backgrounds including parents who are Chinese (Chau & Landreth, 1997), Native American (Glover & Landreth, 2000), Korean (Jang, 2000), Hispanic/Latino, African American (Sheely-Moore & Ceballos, 2010), German (Grskovic & Goetze, 2008), and Isreali (Kidron & Landreth, 2010).

Typically more severe parent and child problems prior to treatment tend to predict poorer treatment outcomes in parent training and child psychotherapeutic interventions. However, in a study of the predictors of FT outcome, Topham and colleagues (2011) found that higher levels of parent distress and poorer child emotion regulation prior to treatment were predictive of more reductions in child behavior problems across treatment. Similarly, poorer parent regulation of emotion prior to treatment was predictive of greater increases in parent acceptance across treatment. This research suggests that FT is particularly effective with more severe parent and child problems, and also, although not directly tested, provides evidence that FT leads to increases in child and parent emotion regulation.

OVERVIEW OF VULNERABLE POPULATION

As demonstrated in the current literature, one of the strengths of FT is that it can be flexibly used with a wide variety of family forms and presenting problems. Most treatment programs targeting children or the parent–child relationship take an "intervention as intervention" approach with a focus on reducing problem behaviors, while failing to attend to broader relationship issues central to healthy child development and socialization (Cavell & Elledge, 2004). FT takes a "socialization as intervention" approach which focuses on assisting families with presenting problems, while also helping families establish and maintain patterns of interaction that are predictive of healthy development and strong child outcomes (Topham & VanFleet, 2011). The child-centered nature of the intervention, the systemic focus on family relationships, and the theoretical integration of diverse theories in FT make it appropriate for a broad range of presenting issues including abuse, trauma, adoption, divorce, internalizing and externalizing disorders, and problems in the parent–child relationship. FT is appropriate for children as young as two and a half years old and as old as twelve, with some modification for children on either end of the continuum. FT may be contraindicated in cases where parents do not have the intellectual ability to understand the play session skills, where parents are incapable of focusing on their child for any meaningful length of time as a result of being overwhelmed by their own needs, or for treatment of abuse where the parent is the perpetrator. FT can be flexibly integrated with other interventions depending on family needs. For example, parents and/or children may receive some individual therapy concurrent with FT, and sessions with the entire family, including other significant caregivers, may be scheduled during treatment (VanFleet, 2013).

INTEGRATIVE PLAY THERAPY TREATMENT PLANNING AND PROTOCOL

The five phases of FT are (1) assessment, (2) training, (3) supervised play sessions, (4) home play sessions, and (5) generalization and discharge (see VanFleet, 2013 for a detailed description of the FT skills and process). While the length of each phase depends upon the child, parent, and family's needs, the order of the phases is generally not altered, as each phase builds on the work of prior phases. The assessment phase typically includes two sessions. Parents are invited to attend the first session without children to enable the therapist to build a relationship with the parents, to hear unfiltered parent concerns, and to conduct a thorough assessment of child, parent–child, and family relationships/functioning and developmental and social histories. Parents are asked to complete paper and pencil measures and to return them to the second session. All family members are invited to the second session to participate in a family play observation. The therapist briefly meets with the family all together to get to know the children and help them feel comfortable with the therapist and the playroom. Parents and children are then instructed to play together for around twenty minutes while the therapist observes from an unobtrusive position in the room. Following the play observation, the therapist discusses the observed patterns with parents and invites parents to describe how interaction at home is similar and different. If therapists have sufficient information and believe that a FT recommendation is appropriate, they may discuss this with the parents toward the end of the second session.

The training phase typically includes three to four sessions and is focused on teaching parents the play session skills prior to their beginning play sessions with their children. During the first training session the therapist demonstrates the play session skills in brief (ten- to twenty-minute) CCPT sessions with each of the children ages three to twelve in the family while the parent observes. Following the CCPT demonstration sessions the therapist meets with the parents to discuss parent observations and briefly helps the parents connect therapist play session behaviors with the four play session skills: structuring, empathic listening, child-centered imaginary play, and limit setting. Because the idea of using play to help alleviate presenting problems may be initially questioned by parents, it is helpful throughout the training process to continually reference the rationale for the skills and to help parents see how the FT process will lead toward the realization of parent goals.

The *structuring skill* communicates the child-centered nature of play sessions while also establishing the boundaries. The structuring skill is primarily used in introducing the special playtime to the child and in preparing the child for and transitioning out of the special playtime. In introducing the play session parents are taught to say "[Child's name] it is time for our special playtime. You can do almost anything you want to do in this playroom. If there is something you cannot do I will let you know." Prior to ending the play time the parent gives two time warnings, five minutes and one minute prior to the end of the play session. At the end of the session the parent uses a pleasant but firm voice and begins standing up and moving toward the door to reinforce to the child that the session is over. If the child protests, the parent reflects the child's emotions but reaffirms that the play session is over and guides the child out of the room. ("You are frustrated because you are having a great time in here and don't want the play session to be over but our time is up and we have to leave the playroom now.")

In developing the skill of empathic listening parents learn to give their child their undivided attention and to attune to the content and behaviors of the child's play as well as the child's internal experience (i.e., emotions, desires, intentions) and to reflect them to the child. In learning and using empathic listening parents develop an awareness and acceptance of their child's emotions and needs, an ability to label the emotions for the child, and an ability to communicate acceptance and understanding. Children, in turn, develop an increased understanding of their own internal experience, learn that their emotions and desires are valid and valued, and develop an increased sense of safety and security in the parent–child relationship.

In child-centered imaginary play parents join their child in play when invited to do so and take on imaginary roles according to the wishes of the child. Children are the actor-directors and parents are the actors who play out the child's scripts. When it is unclear how and what the child wants the parent to play, the parent tries to discern the child's wishes and needs without asking the child for directions. This requires parents to flex their *attunement muscles* in attending to child nonverbal communication. Through child-centered imaginary play, parents provide a deep level of validation and communicate investment to their child. They develop increased awareness of their child and increased comfort with play and engaging with their child on his/her level.

Limit setting in the play sessions is kept to a minimum to maintain an atmosphere in which children experience a sense of autonomy and control and the freedom to express themselves in variety of ways. Limits are generally reserved for those related to not damaging toys or the playroom and not hurting self or therapist. Additionally, parents may choose to set a limit on a behavior that would interfere with their ability to maintain an accepting attitude with the child. Parents are taught to use a calm but firm voice and to use a three-step sequence: stating the limit, giving a warning, and enforcing the consequence. The first time a child breaks a limit or is about to break a limit the parent uses the child's name and states the limit. ("[Child's name], remember I said I would let you know if there was something you may not do? Toys are not made to throw at the window. But you may do almost anything else.") If the child breaks a limit the parent has already stated (including during a prior session) the parents restates the limit and tells the child if the limit is broken again she or he will have to leave the special playroom. Finally, if the child breaks the limit for the third time that day (or second time if the limit was stated in a prior session) the parent restates the limit and carries out the consequence by ending the play session and guiding the child out of the playroom. The limit-setting skill helps to create a sense of safety and security for the child in the play session and empowers parents to foster child self-regulation.

During the second session of the training phase the therapist provides a more in-depth description of the four play session skills providing examples of each skill. Following this discussion the therapist briefly conducts role-plays with each parent. The therapist and parent typically remain in their seats while the therapist role-plays a child and the parent practices the empathic listening skill. The purpose of this role-play is for parents to practice the skill and to gain confidence that they can successfully learn the skill. The therapist typically chooses one or two toys to play with, plays at a slow pace, and provides obvious demonstration of emotion for the parent. The therapist provides brief coaching for the parent throughout the role-play. Feedback is encouraging and predominantly positive.

The third and fourth sessions of the training phase are primarily devoted to mock play sessions. These are role-plays in which the therapist plays the role of the child and provides in-the-moment feedback while parents practice all of the play session skills. Typically each parent is given the opportunity to participate in two ten- to fifteen-minute mock play sessions, but a third mock play session may be useful in the case where a parent is experiencing significant struggles in learning the skills or if it is anticipated that the child will present significant challenges for the parent in the play sessions (e.g., a child with pronounced oppositionality). In the case where both parents are participating, parents receive the benefit of vicarious learning as they watch the other parent's role-plays. The therapist adjusts his/her play in the role of the child to facilitate parent learning by providing the parent with opportunities to practice all of the play session skills (i.e., break a limit, invite the parent into play), by playing at a pace that allows the parent to be successful, and by providing obvious signals for the need for parents to use the play session skills (e.g., showing obvious emotion, make a comment out loud about intentions to break a rule). The therapist increases the degree of difficulty in the second mock play sessions with particular attention to challenges the child or children are likely to present for the parents.

Following training, parents begin supervised play sessions. The initial parent–child play session is twenty minutes with subsequent play sessions lasting thirty minutes. Ideally both parents conduct play sessions with each child in the family between the ages of three and twelve. Depending on the numbers of caregivers and children involved in play sessions therapists may need to schedule longer sessions and/or alternate between children each week. During play sessions the therapist and the other parent (if participating) observe as unobtrusively as possible. If there is an observing parent he or she is invited to participate in the feedback session by listening and asking questions, but not in providing feedback. The therapist begins the feedback discussion with some brief positive feedback and then elicits the parent's reaction to the play session. Next the therapist offers detailed skill feedback with specific examples of when the parent used the skills appropriately with one or two suggestions for improvement. Following skills feedback the therapist and parent discuss the nature of the child's play with focus on themes as well as developmental issues demonstrated in the play. In earlier play sessions conversation with parents is primarily focused on skill development but as parents improve their skills the balance shifts to increasing time spent on understanding the child and the nature of the play. These discussions help parents develop increased awareness of their child's internal experience and developmental needs and an increasing appreciation for the value of play.

After the parents have become confident and competent in carrying out the play sessions (usually around five to six play sessions), play sessions are transferred to the family's home. The therapist spends some time in earlier sessions guiding the parent on putting together an inexpensive set of toys to be set aside for play sessions. A session is devoted to helping prepare parents for home play sessions before transferring the play sessions to the home. The therapist helps parents establish where and when play sessions will be held and how distractions will be avoided in order to increase the chances of success. If possible parents are encouraged to conduct a thirty-minute play session with each of their children each week.

During the home play session phase therapists meet with parents weekly or bi-weekly to review home sessions and to begin generalizing the FT skills to everyday parent–child interaction. If new problems arise or the therapist perceives that the parent's skills are slipping the parent may be asked to bring the child in for a direct supervision play session. In terms of generalizing the play session skills parents learn to utilize the empathic listening skill with their children by validating the child's experience and emotion and by providing support and guidance while allowing the child to take responsibility for problem solving. Therapists help parents establish appropriate limits and consequences outside of play sessions and encourage parents to use the same three-step limit setting sequence. Parents are taught to generalize the structuring skill by anticipating child needs and struggles and by preparing the child and the environment for his or her success. The child-centered imaginary play skill is generalized in "special times" in which the parent and child engage in an enjoyable child-directed activity (e.g., making cookies together, building something together, etc.). During special times the parent follows the child's lead with undivided attention, taking interest in the child and his efforts and products.

The family is ready for discharge from FT when (a) resolution of the presenting problem occurs, (b) the child exhibits decreased interest in play sessions, (c) there is decreased intensity and thematic play, and (d) parents have achieved a solid understanding of the FT principles and skills and can apply them consistently. Prior to discharge the therapist typically requests one more supervised play session and invites the parent to complete the paper and pencil measures once again to track progress. If possible a phased out discharge process is used to continue to provide support to the family as they implement what they have learned with increasing independence (Van-Fleet, 2013).

RELEVANT INTERVENTION

One of the more influential interventions of FT is *scaffolding* (Wood, Bruner, & Ross, 1976). Scaffolding is a term that describes sensitive, supportive parental behaviors that encourage children to function at a level above their ability when functioning independently. A related concept in understanding child growth and learning is what the sociocultural theorist Lev Vygotsky termed the *zone-of-proximal development* (ZPD). The ZPD highlights the important roles that adults and children play in child-based learning. The ZPD is defined by two levels of child competence: (1) the *lower end*, which represents the child's actual ability and (2) the *upper end*, which represents what a child can accomplish or master with adult assistance (Diaz, Neal, & Vachio, 1991). When parents scaffold their children they enable their children to perform at the upper end of the ZPD while allowing them as much responsibility and independence as they are capable of taking. In this way children develop task mastery more quickly than if they were on their own. For example a two-year-old child might have great difficulty zipping up her coat; but, if the parent starts the zipper, holds the coat closed, and ensures that other clothing and hair are not in the way the child can succeed at zipping the coat. As the child develops confidence with zipping, the parent may provide verbal instructions to the child on how to make sure hair and clothing are out of the way, and then finally instruction on starting the zipper until the child is self-sufficient.

The concepts of scaffolding and ZPD are useful in understanding the FT process both in terms of how the parent facilitates child growth and learning and how the therapist promotes parent growth and learning. Through the use of empathic listening parents help children understand and accept their internal experience and behavior ("You are trying to build that tower but it is frustrating because it keeps falling"), persist in difficult tasks, and celebrate when they master the task (e.g., "At first it was difficult to get those blocks to balance but you worked at it and figured it out and you are so proud!") while respecting child autonomy and not intrusively doing for the child what s/he can do for him/herself. Outside of the playroom the parent's use of empathic listening may be manifested in discussion with a child who was emotional in response to being excluded by other children from an activity at recess. The parent may reflect, validate, and label the emotions of hurt and frustration and through patiently listening and asking thoughtful questions help the child process what was most difficult about the situation and what the child would like to do to address the problem. The parent does not take over problem solving, but may provide scaffolding in the process by helping the child see potential pit falls in the child's solutions (e.g., hitting another child in the nose may not have the desired outcome).

Similarly, through the structuring skill the parent helps scaffold the child by helping the child understand the boundaries of the play session and helping the child through transitions (starting and ending the play sessions and playroom departures). Outside of the play sessions the parent learns to use the structuring skill to scaffold during much of the parent–child interaction. Parents learn to do this at a broad level, such as helping a child anticipate and prepare for transitions, being intentional about where a child does homework, and reserving difficult tasks and chores for times when the child has the energy and focus to succeed. The parent also learns to use the scaffolding skill in supporting children in specific tasks such as tying shoes, putting a model car together, cooking together, chores, and so on.

Much as the parent uses scaffolding to facilitate child growth and learning, the filial therapist relies heavily on scaffolding to foster parent growth and learning. Although the ZPD concept does not translate perfectly to parent development, it is also a useful construct in describing the parent learning process. Examples can be found in the mock therapy process and in feedback sessions after parent–child play sessions. During the mock practice sessions, the therapist regulates the degree of difficulty of the role-plays (speed of play, how obvious displays of emotion are, oppositions of the child, etc.) to the parent's ability. Feedback is focused primarily on parent skills that are in the parent's ZPD, or those that are newly emerging or just past, but within reach for the parent. For example, for a parent who is new to the process and struggling, the therapist may praise the parent for giving the "child" her undivided attention and scaffold the parent so she can learn to reflect child behavior. The therapist may pause from the play and say "Great job of focusing completely on me as the child and what I am doing. It would be good here to also add a reflection of what I am doing. You could say, 'you are driving that car over to the house.' Why don't you try that?" Or if a parent is doing a little better a gentler "nudge" may be sufficient such as "What am I doing right now?" Then as the parent succeeds with the coached behavior the therapist immediately responds with encouragement, helping the parent continue to build upon successes. For a parent with more advanced skills the therapist may spend less time providing feedback on reflections of "child" actions (a skill that may be well established and below the ZPD) and more time on reflections related to the "child's" internal experience (an emerging skill). Again depending on parent ability the therapist may provide more assistance with direct guidance ("You could say 'you are really excited about that puppet show.'") to less assistance in the form of a gentle prompt ("What might I be feeling here?").

The skills feedback following supervised play sessions follows a similar pattern, with the praise being overwhelmingly positive, particularly focused on emerging skills with a few suggestions for skills that are just within reach for the parent. The therapist also scaffolds the parent's understanding of the child and the child's play in discussion with the parent. For example, for a parent who has a lower level of awareness of the child and has difficulty reflecting on the child's play, the therapist might do more of the work in "shining the light" on specific meaningful behaviors. For instance, the therapist might say, "Did you notice the expression on his face when you played the role of the weaker dinosaur and let him win? What do you think that was like for him? He seemed to be excited and to feel so powerful!" Similarly, the therapist may need to do extra work to scaffold the parent toward themes in play such as the following: "He seemed to do lot of arranging and organizing things. Did you notice that?" Following this the therapist may help the parent understand the possible significance of this for the child, pushing the parent to do as much of the reflecting/hypothesizing as he or she is able. Whereas, for a parent who has a more developed awareness of the child the therapist may push the parent to do the "shining of the light" with questions such as, "What stood out to you from Ben's play?" "What do you think the significance of that was for him?"

The orientation of the filial therapist to focus only on what is within the parent's ZPD helps alleviate potential therapist frustration as a result of low levels of parent skill. The filial therapist avoids getting overwhelmed by the distance a parent has between current functioning and skills mastery because the immediate focus is only on what is within reach for the parent, the next step in his/her development. This allows the therapist to be patient, warm, and supportive and to celebrate parent progress with genuine enthusiasm regardless of current skill level.

CASE STUDY

The following case study illustrates the FT process. All details have been altered to protect client confidentiality. Diana, a single parent and full-time professional, adopted Rico from the Honduran foster care system at ten months of age. She was unable to attain information about his biological family's medical or psychosocial history. She took several months of parental leave at the time of Rico's homecoming, and she had many friends and her parents to offer support. Diana, herself, was adopted as an infant.

She requested therapeutic assistance at the request of Rico's daycare when Rico was four and a half years old. Rico had been asked to leave two previous daycare settings due to aggression and oppositional behaviors; and the director of the current daycare program was becoming impatient with Rico's aggressive behaviors. Rico hit her and others and was reported to be intense, impulsive, and oppositional.

Diana presented as thoughtful, quiet, and introverted. She described Rico as loving and affectionate. However, she reported that he was busy, loud, and talked incessantly. He would not play by himself and wanted to be by Diana's side constantly including when she was sleeping. Diana was overwhelmed by the demands of single parenthood and Rico's behavioral difficulties. She acknowledged feeling resentful and inadequate as a parent. Diana was terrified that she would not be able to find an appropriate daycare setting for Rico that would last if he were asked to leave again, and she asked for help in managing the stress of this situation. She identified her therapeutic goals as wanting to help Rico learn appropriate behaviors and successfully navigate his school day and to assist her in developing some additional parenting skills to manage Rico's problematic behaviors.

After conducting the psychosocial assessment with Diana, a family play observation was scheduled. Rico presented at the second session as energetic and enthusiastic, and he was eager to enter the playroom with Diana. During the play observation the therapist observed that Diana would not allow aggressive themes or physical play. Rico was visibly discouraged and responded by engaging with mom in "acceptable" play. Following the family play observation the therapist talked with Diana about the representativeness of Rico's interaction with her during play. The therapist then provided a summary of the assessment process and discussed with Diana the three types of play therapy: CCPT, directive play therapy, and family play therapy. The therapist suggested that Diana consider FT as the primary intervention in an integrated treatment approach. The therapist briefly presented the primary benefits of FT and invited her to ask any questions or raise any concerns she might have throughout the process. The therapist helped Diana see how the FT process could help reduce Rico's anxieties, increase his self-regulation, reduce her frustrations with him, and strengthen her relationship with him. The training sequence was discussed and the collaborative nature of FT was emphasized, noting that Diana was the expert regarding her son, and because of her importance to him she was in a position to play a key role in the treatment process.

Diana liked the idea of FT although she expressed great anxiety regarding play. She indicated that her parents never engaged in play with her. She remembered being a quiet child who spent most of her time alone reading in her room. She had no fond memories of any imaginative or creative play of her own, and the idea of practicing mock sessions with the therapist raised her anxiety. The therapist used empathy and humor with Diana, normalizing that this was not something parents are typically asked to do, and can be a little uncomfortable at first. With some reluctance, Diana agreed to give it a try. During the next session the therapist taught Diana the play session skills utilizing brief role-plays to help Diana begin to develop a sense for the skills and some confidence so she could be successful.

Early in the third session the therapist conducted a twenty-minute play demonstration while Diana observed. Rico's play was rich and engaging. He created an imaginary world in the sand that was inhabited by some timid and some fierce animal characters. The characters were engaged with one another while busily trying to manage the dangerous and surprising occurrences in this special land. His play was thematic and sequential, imaginative and creative. No obvious developmental delays or immaturity were evident in his play. The play themes were related to power/control, good/evil, danger/safety, rescue/protection, and nurturance/aggression. It appeared as if Rico had considerable issues related to anxiety. Following the play demonstration, Diana reflected and commented on what she observed. Although Diana did not mention it, it seemed apparent to the filial therapist that Diana was uncomfortable with the nature of Rico's play. The therapist asked Diana if the aggressive themes during Rico's dinosaur play was uncomfortable for her. She acknowledged being concerned with the level of aggression in his imaginary play because he was "so aggressive" in general. The therapist wondered aloud whether some of Rico's play might be related to anxiety and pointed out how the play sessions could help Rico gain some understanding and mastery over his anxieties.

Although Diana struggled at first in the mock sessions, she quickly began to learn the skills. In the second mock session role play the therapist included several aggressive imaginary play scenarios and some limit testing to prepare Diana for what she would likely get from Rico in the play sessions. While the training sessions were taking place, the family moved to a new home and Rico began a new preschool resulting in many transitions. During these early sessions, in addition to providing the training, the therapist discussed developmental age and stage issues and made some structuring and limit-setting suggestions to help with immediate difficulties that were overwhelming Diana at home.

In the first play session with Rico, Diana gave an introductory message; she engaged in imaginative play; her attention and affect were exactly right; and she did fairly well in reflecting Rico's behaviors and feelings. Rico's play focused on the sand tray. He used dinosaurs that were the "meanest and scariest" dinosaurs. He started by giving Diana another dinosaur and letting her know that T-Rex wanted to fight her Triceratops. Diana was able to allow the fighting, and she participated in the imaginary play, much to Rico's delight. Dragons and haunted houses entered the play. These elements even scared the powerful dinosaurs. Rico enlarged the play area from the sand tray to the floor and eventually used the whole room. In the middle of the first play session, he stepped outside of the play and said to Diana, "I really like you." Then danger themes began. Water began filling the haunted house, and the animals hid from the water. There were catastrophic events in the lives of the dinosaurs. Before the first session ended, a snake and a rat family were added, including a mommy, daddy, and a baby. The parents were busy catching food for the babies and caring for them. The mommy snake was asked to save the baby snake from the dragon.

During the feedback session the therapist validated the skills Diana utilized. Diana was surprised that Rico engaged in this level of complex play with her, and the therapist guided her in identifying some of the play themes including that of strong family ties and providing care and protection and safety in a dangerous world. A suggestion for improvement was to notice and reflect the emotions of the characters and to speak through them.

From that session through the next three sessions, Rico entered the playroom ready to work. He continued similar themes and used the entire floor and expanded upon the number of characters and events. Consistent themes included family, danger, relationship, safety, protection, and rescue. Play frequently involved Diana as the mommy snake rescuing Rico as the baby snake from predators. Much to Rico's satisfaction Diana became quite skillful at playing her role as the rescuing, protective mother. All of the families had mommies who were looking for their babies and trying to find them and keep them safe. At one point the baby snake could not see the mommy but could hear fighting and stated that mommy was dead forever. Now the dragon would take care of the baby, but then the mommy snake came alive and there was a big battle between the snake and dragon mommies. It was evident that some significant attachment and adoption work was being done in this session.

In the third play session, play began with the baby being "lost and mommy is very far away." Another snake came and told the mommy, "That is really not your baby, it belongs to someone else." Diana reflected from within the role, "Don't take away my baby!" A special house was constructed for safety, which Rico named, "Our house." He then enacted play themes around danger and threat with the baby snake regressing into baby talk. Diana reflected the baby snake's fears and spoke for the mommy snake, "We are safe in this house, we will stay together and Mommy will protect you." Later another baby came to the door and the mommy welcomed the baby. Again, the adoption themes were apparent in the play.

In the postplay feedback session the therapist and Diana discussed play themes. Diana saw the parallels between Rico's play and his fears and anxieties that were driving some of his behaviors at home and at school. This awareness decreased Diana's sense of frustration with Rico and increased her compassion and patience with him. She also began to recognize the important role of the FT play sessions for Rico and even commented that she was beginning to enjoy the play sessions. This session in particular raised issues for Diana in relation to her own adoption and the role of play in her childhood. The therapist helped Diana briefly process these issues in relation to how she viewed and responded to Rico.

In the fourth play session the same themes continued, this time with the dinosaur family. Rico mentioned that they were looking for a spot for a baby to hatch. The new dinosaur said to the mommy dinosaur, "I can be your new baby to protect. You are the mommy and I am the baby. Don't be rough with the baby and don't go too far Mama; not near the volcano because you might die." Diana reflected, "You are worried I might go away and not protect you." Rico responded, "The baby died and is bleeding forever." Diana as the mommy dinosaur expressed her great sadness and Rico exuberantly announced, "I am back!" Throughout the first four sessions Rico played the same themes. Each time he seemed to be moving toward some kind of resolution, working out the anxious attachment issues and moving toward mastery. At the end of the fourth session Rico moved away from his story and began to focus on mastery play by counting things. During the feedback discussion Diana reported she had seen some meaningful improvements in Rico both at home and at school. Based on Diana's growing comfort with the skills, the therapist and Diana decided to go ahead and transition the play sessions to Diana's home. The therapist also worked with Diana to help her identify ways to take some time to take care of herself.

Home play sessions continued to go well with similar themes related to relationships, power/control, good/evil, danger/safety. During this time the therapist met bi-weekly with Diana to discuss home play sessions and to continue to discuss generalizing the play session skills to everyday interaction with Rico. Diana quickly caught on to generalizing the skills and was doing quite well with Rico at home. Rico's behavior continued to stabilize, and Diana continued to gain confidence and to find increasing pleasure in their relationship. After initiating the home play sessions the therapist met with Diana six more times before services were discontinued. Three months after discontinuing services Diana called with concerns about resurgence in some of Rico's problematic behaviors. It became evident in the conversation that Diana had not continued to hold regular play sessions with Rico. At the therapist's encouragement home play sessions were resumed and the behavior problems once again quickly abated.

CONCLUSION

FT is a strength-based approach that brings the parent into partnership with the therapist in addressing child and family presenting issues and complaints. Furthermore, FT is unique in that the process is designed to go beyond the presenting problem to foster family relationships that most effectively promote the positive development of family members. FT is a structured, yet flexible, intervention that can be effective in treating a broad array of presenting problems and issues. A wealth of research demonstrates its effectiveness across vulnerable client populations and cultural and ethnic groups. Another strength of FT is that because it is structured and straightforward, with proper training it can be learned by play therapists and family therapists alike with little difficulty.

REFERENCES

Beckloff, D. (1997). Filial therapy with children with spectrum pervasive developmental disorders. *Dissertation Abstracts International: Section B. Sciences and Engineering, 58*(11), 6224B.

Bratton, S., & Landreth, G. L. (1995). Filial therapy with single parents: Effects on parental acceptance, empathy, and stress. *International Journal of Play Therapy, 4,* 61–80. http://dx.doi.org/10.1037/h0089142.

Cavell, T. A., & Elledge, L. C. (2004). Working with parents of aggressive, school age children. In J. Briesmeister & C. Schaefer (Eds.), *Handbook of parenting training: Helping parents prevent and solve problem behaviors* (3rd ed., pp. 379–423). Hoboken, NJ: Wiley & Sons.

Chau, I. Y., & Landreth, G. L. (1997). Filial Therapy with Chinese parents: Effects on parental empathic interactions, parental acceptance of child, and parental stress. *International Journal of Play Therapy, 2,* 75–92. doi.org/10.1037/h0089409.

Costas, M., & Landreth, G. L. (1999). Filial therapy with nonoffending parents of children who have been sexually abused. *International Journal of Play Therapy, 8,* 43–66. http://dx.doi.org/10.1037/h0089427.

Diaz, R. M., Neal, C. J., & Vachio, A. (1991). Maternal teaching in the zone of proximal development: A comparison of low- and high-risk dyads. *Merrill-Palmer Quarterly, 37,* 83–107.

Glass, N. M. (1986). Parents as therapeutic agents: A study of the effects of filial therapy. *Dissertation Abstracts International: Section B. Sciences and Engineering, 47*(7–A), 2457.

Glover, G. J., & Landreth, G. L. (2000). Filial therapy with Native Americans on the Flathead Reservation. *International Journal of Play Therapy, 9,* 57–80. doi.org/10.1037/h0089436.

Grskovic, J. A., & Goetze, H. (2008). Short-term filial therapy with German mothers: Findings from a controlled study. *International Journal of Play Therapy, 19,* 39–51. doi.org/10.1037/1555-6824.17.1.39.

Guerney, B. (1964). Filial therapy: Description and rationale. *Journal of Consulting Psychology, 28,* 303–310.

Guerney, L. F., & Gavigan, M. A. (1981). Parent acceptance and foster parents. *Journal of Clinical Child Psychology, 10,* 27–32.

Guerney, L., & Ryan, V. (2013). *Group Filial Therapy: The complete guide to teaching parents to play therapeutically with their children.* Philadelphia, PA: Jessica Kingsley.

Harris, Z. L., & Landreth, G. L. (1997). Filial therapy with incarcerated mothers: A five week model. *International Journal of Play Therapy, 6,* 53–73. doi.org/10.1037/h0089408.

Jang, M. (2000). Effectiveness of filial therapy for Korean parents. *International Journal of Play Therapy, 9,* 21–38. doi.org/10.1037/h0089435.

Johnson-Clark, K. (1996). The effect of filial therapy on child conduct behavior problems and the quality of the parent-child relationship. *Dissertation Abstracts International: Section B. Sciences and Engineering, 57*(4), 2868B.

Kale, A. L., & Landreth, G. L. (1999). Filial therapy with parents of children experiencing learning difficulties. *International Journal of Play Therapy, 8,* 35–56. doi.org/10.1037/h0089430.

Kidron, M., & Landreth, G. (2010). Intensive child parent relationship therapy with Israeli parents in Israel. *International Journal of Play Therapy, 19,* 64–78. doi.org/10.1037/a0017516.

Landreth, G., & Bratton, S. C. (2006). *Child parent relationship therapy (CPRT): A 10-session filial therapy model.* New York, NY: Routledge.

Landreth, G., & Lobaugh, A. F. (1998). Filial therapy with incarcerated fathers: Effects on parental acceptance of child, parental stress, and child adjustment. *Journal of Counseling and Development, 76,* 157–165. doi.org/10.1002/j.1556-6676.1998.tb02388.x.

Sheely-Moore, A. I., & Ceballos, P. L. (2010). Empowering Head Start African American and Latino families: Promoting strengths-based parenting characteristics through child parent relationship training—an evidence based group parenting program. *National Head Start Association Dialog, 14,* 41–53. doi.org/10.1080/15240754.2010.541567.

Smith, N., & Landreth, G. L. (2003). Intensive filial therapy with child witnesses of domestic violence: A comparison with individual and sibling group play therapy. *International Journal of Play Therapy, 12,* 67–88. doi.org/10.1037/h0088872.

Tew, K., Landreth, G. L., & Joiner, K. D. (2002). Filial therapy with parents of chronically ill children. *International Journal of Play Therapy, 11,* 79–100. doi.org/10.1037/h0088858.

Topham, G. L., & VanFleet, R. (2011). Filial therapy: A structured and straightforward approach to including young children in family therapy. *Australian and New Zealand Journal of Family Therapy 32,* 144–158. doi.org/10.1375/anft.32.2.144.

Topham, G. L., Wampler, K. S., Titus, G., & Rolling, E. (2011). Predicting parent and child outcomes of a filial therapy program. *International Journal of Play Therapy, 20,* 79–93. doi.org/10.1037/a0023261.

VanFleet, R. (2013). *Filial therapy: Strengthening parent-child relationships through play* (3rd ed.). Sarasota, FL: Professional Resource Press.

VanFleet, R., Ryan, S. D., & Smith, S. K. (2005). Filial therapy: A critical review. In L. A. Reddy, T. M. Files-Hall, & C. E. Schaefer (Eds.), *Empirically-based play interventions for children* (pp. 241–264). Washington, DC: American Psychological Association.

VanFleet, R., Sniscak, C. C., & Faa-Thompson, T. (2013). *Filial Therapy groups for foster and adoptive parents: building attachment in a 14 to 18 week family program.* Boiling Springs, PA: Play Therapy Press.

Wright, C., & Walker, J. (2003). Using Filial Therapy with Head Start families. In R. VanFleet & L. F. Guerney (Eds.), *Casebook of Filial Therapy* (pp. 309–329). Boiling Springs, PA: Play Therapy Press.

Wood, D., Bruner, J. S., & Ross, G. (1976). The role of tutoring in problem solving. *Journal of Child Psychology and Psychiatry, 17,* 89–100.

II

Clinical Applications for Traumatized Populations

Chapter Three

Simple Interventions for Complex Trauma

Play-Based Safety and Affect Regulation Strategies for Child Survivors

Janine Shelby, Brenda Aranda, Lisa Asbill, and Jenny A. Gallagher

Children treated in community mental health settings often have histories of recurrent maltreatment or trauma exposure, but treatments specifically designed for the full complement of complex trauma symptoms have been slow to emerge, are not yet widely available, and often overlook survivors in the middle childhood years. The childhood complex trauma literature provides some degree of guidance to inform clinicians' work; but knowledge about complex trauma treatment for young survivors is incomplete, ambiguous, and sometimes contradictory. Here, we review several facets of the prevailing understanding of childhood complex trauma, identify common challenges faced by play therapists, and conclude with pragmatic suggestions, play-based interventions, and other clinical tools to link play therapists' treatment approaches to current best practice recommendations.

The literature on childhood trauma has historically emphasized youth who survive single or relatively short-term traumatic events. The child trauma treatment literature includes many therapies that are supported by rigorous research, but the clinical needs of chronically traumatized youth may not map well onto treatments designed for less pervasively traumatized children and adolescents. Therapies designed to target the full array of complex trauma symptoms have been slow to emerge, are not yet widely available, and often overlook survivors who are in middle childhood (i.e., focusing instead on either young children or adolescents). As a result, there is limited guidance to inform clinicians' work with young complex trauma survivors, despite the relatively common presentation of complex trauma in community-based clinical settings.

In the following pages, we will describe several issues that commonly arise in clinical work with young complex trauma survivors treated in community outpatient settings. To provide a foundation for the discussion, we will first briefly describe complex trauma and the research-informed and play therapy treatment approaches in the prevailing literature. Then, we will identify common challenges faced by child-focused clinicians in the provision of complex trauma treatment. Along with these issues, we will provide pragmatic suggestions, play-based interventions, and other clinical tools for therapists who undertake the multifaceted, complicated work of delivering complex trauma-informed therapy in the context of an emerging but incomplete and sometimes ambiguous literature. Based upon our work in an urban, underserved community clinic and teaching hospital, as well as on recommendations articulated by the National Center for Child Traumatic Stress Network (NCTSN)'s Complex Trauma Task Force (Cook et al., 2005), our comments are directed toward clinical work with young survivors in the middle childhood years—a particularly underexplored area of the literature.

RESEARCH SUPPORT

Complex Trauma

The term complex trauma encompasses several related concepts and terms. Complex trauma, according to Briere and Lanktree (2008), is a "combination of early and late onset, multiple, and sometimes highly invasive traumatic events, usually of an ongoing, interpersonal nature" (p. 9). Complex trauma refers to both exposure to traumatic events and the effects of these exposures. These incidents may be sequential or simultaneous, and include experiences such as sexual abuse, physical abuse, emotional abuse, neglect, and exposure to family and community violence. Complex trauma survivors commonly experience repeated episodes of trauma, and many have also been exposed to different types of traumatic events, called polyvictimization (e.g., physical abuse, witnessing domestic violence, community violence). Because of this pattern of exposure, they may develop cumulative trauma reactions (i.e., the amplified impact of experiencing repeated, accumulated adverse events over time). In complex trauma, the traumatic exposure is typically of longer duration and usually involves more deficits in caregiver psychological support than is the case for youth who survive limited or single traumatic events.

The term *complex trauma* has been known by many monikers: Terr (1991) differentiated type II trauma from single-incident, type I traumatic events; Herman (1992) labeled the phenomenon Complex Posttraumatic Stress Disorder (C-PTSD). Disorders of Extreme Stress Not Otherwise Specified (DESNOS) has been a proposed diagnosis for more than two decades (Herman, 1992; Van der Kolk, Roth, Pelcovitz, Sunday, & Spinazzola, 2005; Van der Kolk, 2005) and Developmental Trauma Disorder (Van der Kolk, 2005; Van der Kolk et al., 2009) was proposed to conceptualize the disorder as it manifests in children and adolescents. Several short- and long-term sequelae associated with complex trauma have been identified, including the following: (a) affect dysregulation, disruption in relationships and attachment, and identity, anxiety, and affective disorders; (b) addictions; (c) dissociation; (d) somatization and somatic symptoms; (e) sexual disorders; (f) revictimization and repetition of harm in interpersonal relationships (e.g., aggression toward one's significant other, or maintaining an intimate relationship with a perpetrator of violence); as well as possible (g) dangerousness to self (e.g., self-injurious behavior, suicide attempts). The NCTSNC Trauma Workgroup (i.e., Cook et al., 2005) condensed the domains of traumatic impairment as follows: (a) attachment; (b) biology; (c) affect regulation; (d) dissociation; (e) behavioral regulation; (f) cognition; and (g) self-concept.

Caregiver–child attachment difficulties and caregiving styles (e.g., inappropriately invasive, harsh, or detached) are early etiological factors associated with the development of complex trauma. That is, when development involves significant deficits in the child's stability, nurturance, and safety as well as repeated exposure to severely adverse events—particularly those of an interpersonal nature—complex trauma responses may ensue. During early childhood, these symptoms are sometimes diagnosed as Reactive Attachment Disorder (RAD)—which must ensue before the age of five—whereas in older teenagers and adulthood, the diagnosis of Borderline Personality Disorder (BPD) may be most commonly used to describe the same or a similar phenomenon. Despite the diagnostic vacuum for elementary school-age children and young adolescents (cf., Briere & Hodges, 2008), this is a critical period in which to address complex trauma symptoms before youth enter teenage years, when they are at an elevated risk of dangerous or lethal behaviors such as cutting, suicide attempts, substance abuse, and unsafe sexual conduct.

Treatment Approaches

Relative to the proportion of complex trauma-exposed youth in clinical settings, treatments designed *specifically* for these issues have been understudied. Several treatments have been rigorously supported by research for children and adolescents with trauma-related symptoms, but most complex trauma-focused treatments have not been studied using highly powered randomized control trials

(RCTs). Table 3.1, Complex Trauma Treatments, lists some of the most widely known therapies described as complex trauma treatments by either their authors or organizations tasked with the compilation, rating, or categorization of evidence-based treatments. Several additional treatments have been proposed by their authors to be suitable for use with complex trauma survivors (e.g., Trauma-Focused CBT, Cohen, Mannarino, & Deblinger, 2006; Alternatives for Families CBT, Kolko & Swenson, 2002), though they were developed for either a single type of traumatic event (i.e., sexually abused children, or physically abused children) or for single or limited episodes of traumatic exposure. Complex trauma treatments differ from other trauma treatments in terms of their breadth, inclusion of multiple modalities, emphasis on stabilization, and their in-depth focus on complex trauma symptoms, such as dissociation, emotion dysregulation, somatization (Saxe, MacDonald, & Ellis, 2007; Vickerman & Margolin, 2007), and harm from self and others. A particularly comprehensive treatment and one of the few for children of middle childhood age is Integrative Treatment for Complex Trauma for Children (ITCT-C; Lanktree & Briere, 2008). In this treatment, play therapy, collateral, family, and group therapy may be offered as part of the protocol. The therapy for youth eight to twelve years of age (with modifications for both younger children and adolescents; Briere & Lanktree, 2008) includes modules on affect regulation training, titrated exposure, cognitive therapy, and relationship processing, which are differentially utilized according to each child's specific problems or issues.

OVERVIEW OF VULNERABLE POPULATION

According to research findings, about one-fifth of youth in the United States have been exposed to more than one type of victimization (Grasso, Greene, & Ford, 2013; Turner, Finkelhor, & Ormrod, 2010), and most survivors of a traumatic event have experienced prior traumatic incidents (Kessler, 2000). The National Center for Child Traumatic Stress Network's survey of twenty-five sites (Spinazzola et. al., 2003) reveals that the vast majority of children served by the network (78 percent) had been exposed to multiple and/or prolonged trauma, with a modal number of three trauma exposure types. Findings further indicated that initial exposure typically occurred early, with the average age of onset being five years old. Thus, rather than a rare or unusual occurrence, it may be that the most common scenario for youth seeking trauma-focused mental health services is that they have experienced repeated and varied forms of maltreatment and adversity.

Table 3.1. Complex Trauma Treatments

Treatment	Study Details
ITCT	
Authors	Lanktree & Briere, 2008
Ages	2–21
Modality	Individual, family, systems
No. of sessions	Flexible
Research	1 clinical trial (no control group)
Research populations	Children and adolescents exposed to at least 1 traumatic event from which they experienced significant psychological symptoms
SPARCS	
Authors	DeRosa et al., 2006
Ages	12–18
Modality	Group
No. of sessions	Average of 16; short-term model of 5–6
Research	3 clinical trials
Research populations	Youth in foster care with histories of trauma
TARGET	
Authors	Ford & Russo, 2006
Ages	10–18+
Modality	Individual, group, family, systems
No. of sessions	Group intervention range from 3–10 sessions; individual intervention were 12 sessions
Research	4 clinical trials (only 1 with children/adolescents in juvenile delinquency settings
Research populations	Adolescent girls involved in delinquency
Attachment, Self-Regulation, and Competency	
Authors	Blaustein & Kinniburgh, 2010
Ages	2–21
Modality	Individual, family, systems
No. of sessions	12–52+
Research	3 pilot trials (no control groups)
Research populations	Child welfare involved; Child/adolescent girls in residential treatment; children and adolescents in pre/post-adoptive placements

Child–Parent Psychotherapy	
Authors	Lieberman & Van Horn, 2008
Ages	0–5
Modality	Dyadic, collateral
No. of sessions	Approximately 52
Research	2 RCTs
Research populations	Infants and young children exposed to domestic violence

Note. The table is drawn on data related to treatments designed specifically for young complex trauma survivors from the following sources: International Society for Traumatic Stress Studies, Child Welfare Information Gateway, California Evidence-Based Clearinghouse for Child Welfare, and National Child Traumatic Stress Network. The table shows the most rigorous research that has been conducted, rather than all research conducted. The population described is the most commonly studied population rather than all populations.

INTEGRATIVE PLAY THERAPY TREATMENT PLANNING AND PROTOCOL

There is general recognition that complex trauma warrants a *complex* approach to treatment, involving multiple modalities (Lanktree & Briere, 2008; Cook et al., 2005), but there is little consensus as to what treatment modalities or combinations of treatments are most beneficial for this population. There is ambiguity as to which, if, and when evidence-based child trauma treatments designed for single-incident or single-type traumatic events are helpful to survivors of multiple or repeated adverse events. Until additional research is conducted and treatments specifically designed for complex trauma are more widely available, most clinicians will likely continue to use a blend of existing research, anecdotal accounts, and clinical experience to select a treatment approach for young complex trauma survivors. For example, some clinicians adapt the trauma-focused evidence-based treatments (EBTs) designed for single incidents so that they are more suitable for complex trauma survivors (e.g., using some—but not all—components of the treatment protocols, or significantly prolonging some modules to focus on relaxation, affect regulation capacity, and coping skill enhancement). A second clinical approach is to deliver an EBT that targets one of the child's symptoms or symptom clusters—although the treatment may not be designed to address the full amalgam of symptoms associated with complex trauma. In this approach, the therapist eventually delivers successive EBTs sequentially in effort to target additional areas of impairment in a stepwise manner (e.g., targeting disruptive behaviors first if they jeopardize home or classroom placements and then providing trauma-focused therapy to address posttraumatic distress after these symptoms have been successfully managed; or delivering a trauma-based therapy, while disruptive behaviors are not targeted directly until after the trauma-specific symptoms have abated).

As a third approach, play therapy is a widely practiced, readily accepted method used by many child-focused therapists to treat complex trauma because of play's inherent relationship-enhancing qualities, affect-regulating properties, and developmental sensitivity. However, there is disagreement about play therapy for the treatment of complex trauma. In a nationwide survey sponsored by the National Child Traumatic Stress Network [Spinazzola et al., 2003] involving sixty-two clinicians across twenty-five sites and representing 1,699 children, play therapy ranked separately as both the third *most effective* modality by twenty-one (i.e., 33.9 percent), of clinicians and also as the second *least effective* modality by fourteen clinicians (i.e., 22.6 percent) of therapists.

Despite its long tradition, decades of small-scale studies, and popularity, opinions of play therapy have remained divided for several reasons including: (a) play therapy's overly broad scope (i.e., *play therapy* is actually several distinct play therapies, each with a unique level of research support); (b) lack of clarity as to which treatments constitute play therapies (i.e., Are other therapies involving play, such as Parent–Child Interaction Therapy [PCIT; Eyberg et al., 2001] and Child–Parent Psychotherapy [CPP, Lieberman & Van Horn, 2008] play therapies?); (c) lack of awareness of play therapy's emerging evidentiary base among nonplay therapy practitioners— which ranges from therapies that have not yet been studied to those with more sound empirical support; and (d) play therapy's dearth of highly powered RCTs specifically for complex trauma treatment (cf., the meta-analysis of Bratton, Ray, Rhine & Jones, 2005; and the review of Shelby, Ellingsen, & Schaefer, in press). There is a rich base of empirical support, however, for the use of caregiver–child dyadic play therapies for many areas of childhood psychopathology, trauma, and complex trauma (e.g., Child–Parent Psychotherapy [CPP; Lieberman & Van Horn, 2008]; Parent–Child Interaction Therapy [PCIT; Eyberg et al., 2001]; Theraplay [Jernberg, 1979; Munns, 2000]; and Child–Parent Relationship Therapy [CPRT; Landreth & Bratton, 2006]) have continued to accrue research support for the treatment of issues such as attachment and child behavior problems (cf. Bratton et al.'s [2005] meta-analysis in which filial therapy studies showed a significantly larger treatment effect than therapist-led play therapy). As for individual play therapy approaches, Perry (2006) provides a well-articulated rationale for a neurosequential approach integrating play therapy and complex trauma treatment. Myrick and Green (2014) also contribute creative complex-trauma-informed, safety-based play therapy techniques to the discussion of this topic.

Despite the ambiguity related to current practice standards for childhood complex trauma, some guidance exists in the literature. The National Child

Traumatic Stress Network's Complex Trauma Workgroup (i.e., Cook et al., 2005) identified six core components of intervention:

Safety: Creating a home, school, and community environment in which the child feels safe and cared for

Self-regulation: Enhancing a child's capacity to modulate arousal and restore equilibrium following dysregulation of affect, behavior, physiology, cognition, interpersonal relatedness, and self-attribution

Self-reflective information processing: Helping the child construct self-narratives, reflect on past and present experience, and develop skills in planning and decision making

Traumatic experiences integration: Enabling the child to transform or resolve traumatic reminders and memories using such therapeutic strategies as meaning making, traumatic memory containment or processing, remembrance and mourning of the traumatic loss, symptom management and development of coping skills, and cultivation of present-oriented thinking and behavior

Relational engagement: Teaching the child to form appropriate attachments and to apply this knowledge to current interpersonal relationships, including the therapeutic alliance, with emphasis on development of such critical interpersonal skills as assertiveness, cooperation, perspective taking, boundaries and limit setting, reciprocity, social empathy, and the capacity for physical and emotional intimacy

Positive affect enhancement: Enhancing a child's sense of self-worth, esteem and positive self-appraisal through creativity, imagination, future orientation, achievement, competence, mastery seeking, community building, and the capacity to experience pleasure.

These domains provide a useful base from which child-focused therapists can focus their clinical interventions, despite the ambiguities present in the literature and until additional research-supported approaches emerge.

Play-Based Applications of Complex Trauma Treatment Guidelines

Play therapy's long tradition of widespread use for attachment-related issues, accumulating research (i.e., particularly for attachment issues), high index of acceptability among child-focused therapists, and inherent qualities lead many to conclude that some forms of play therapy hold practical value as a means of or vehicle for achieving the therapy components put forth by the NCTS Complex Trauma Workgroup. Based on these core components, we now propose several play-based interventions that allow play therapists to integrate best practice parameters with developmentally sensitive techniques. Though not intended as a treatment protocol, and not derived from empirical research, these evidence-informed interventions are intended to bridge a gap between research and common practice until evidence-based treatments are developed and broadly disseminated for this population. Here, we will focus on the first two components described by the NCTS work group (i.e., safety and self-regulation) because of their prominence in the environmental and psychological conditions related to the development and maintenance of complex trauma symptoms.

Safety

Unfortunately, maltreatment episodes recur for many youth despite their child protective services or mental health treatment involvement, and youth with prior maltreatment events are at greater risk of additional traumatic exposures. Therefore, many clinicians deliver treatments while ongoing—though undisclosed or unsubstantiated—incidents of child maltreatment occur. In these cases, a trauma-focused approach addressing past traumatic events is unlikely to be effective given the higher-order child maltreatment issue and such a focus may, in fact, be iatrogenic. In complex trauma cases, therapists must remain attentive to the possibility of child safety and maltreatment issues and invest additional attention to ongoing or potential trauma exposure at the outset of treatment, with consistent assessment and monitoring of additional traumatic exposures throughout the course of the therapy. This approach may be unfamiliar to clinicians who view safety-related issues as the domain of child protective services and law enforcement, or to those who are accustomed to relying solely on caregivers' reports and goals to determine the treatment focus. Nevertheless, it falls largely upon therapists to discern the family's highest-order needs related to the child's mental health issues. In complex trauma cases, diagnosing the child's symptoms accurately involves the therapist's regular and flexible hypothesis making about whether or not maltreatment accounts for the child's clinical presentation, so that the best interventions can be provided.

In families of youth who experience complex trauma, past experiences, family and cultural values, and fears about the consequences of disclosure commonly pose barriers to communication between family members and therapists. By discussing this issue directly with caregivers, and then asking caregivers to provide explicit statements during sessions that the child should tell the therapist about "anything, even if it has been a secret in the past," parents model the ability to trust and to speak bravely about their realities, struggles, and successes. In one safety-focused intervention described by Shelby & Maltby (in press), a jack-in-the-box toy is shown to the family. After the child and parent look at the clown, the lid is closed and the therapist describes how everyone in the family knows that a clown is in the container, even if no one sees it at the moment or discusses it. The family is asked to remain silent for a few seconds and then asked whether the silence makes the clown disappear or whether they remain aware that the clown can emerge imminently. As the therapist begins to turn the crank, the family is encouraged to speak about the experience of waiting for something known to spring forth at any moment (e.g., anticipation, excitement, or anxiety). After the clown ejects from the box, the therapist notes the sense of relief or positive emotion that usually accompanies the experience and then uses this activity to provide psychoeducation about the importance of open communication.

In a different intervention proposed by the same authors, families are asked to participate in a game based on the idiom "to spill the beans" by carrying several large bags of raw beans from one side of the therapy room to the other without spilling any beans. Unbeknownst to the family members, the bags have holes in them. With a sense of surprise and amusement, family members soon discover that beans fall to the floor when they attempt to transport the bags. After the activity, the therapist discusses how much work it is to try to keep beans inside a bag that will inevitably leak the beans. Because these interventions are enjoyable, play based, and unlikely to rouse defensiveness, family members are oriented to the notion of open discourse in a pleasant and appealing manner. As a third intervention related to communication (Shelby & Maltby, in press), the therapist asks a child to hide something in the sand while the therapist looks away. As the therapist then tries to find the item, the clinician discusses how he or she would like to help find the hidden object. The therapist then describes how the child's help is needed to uncover the item more quickly than would be the case if the therapist were to search on his or her own. In response, the child gives the therapist clues and works collaboratively with the therapist to uncover the object. This intervention is helpful in both building the therapeutic alliance, but also in teaching the child reluctant to disclose his past experiences that therapists are neither all-knowing nor oblivious to the presence of hidden material.

In a different intervention focused on familial patterns, the caregiver is asked to create a family genogram in which the intergenerational pattern of trauma exposure, child maltreatment, domestic violence, substance abuse, and other pertinent issues are depicted within the family tree. This is used to highlight the fact that these experiences often occur across multiple generations. If the parent's family history is positive for these risk factors, there are often opportunities to highlight the parent's courage in seeking support and progressing beyond chronic patterns of victimization or risk factors. In fact, caregivers are encouraged to share with their children (i.e., in an age-appropriate manner) how they are working toward breaking familial patterns. Children are encouraged to create certificates of appreciation for their parents and present them as awards for parental courage during a conjoint therapy session.

Other safety-based interventions include Hewitt's (1999) therapeutic management safety contract in which each family member independently creates a list of inappropriate contact, privacy boundaries, and exposure. The therapist ultimately compiles these lists into a single safety contract. The family members agree to uphold the contract and to inform the therapist and others of violations to the contract. At each session, the therapist assesses adherence to the terms of the contract. In Alternatives for Families-CBT (Kolko & Swenson, 2002), paper-and-pencil forms are used on a weekly basis to inquire about safety-related events and experiences. As an additional intervention, Shelby and Maltby (in press) suggest the use of stimulus cards with either labels or illustrations of typical safety-related issues (e.g., "someone hit someone else," "someone came into a room while I was undressed") used for safety and privacy assessment during each session.

Safety is also enhanced as caregivers develop stronger attachments to and enjoyment of their children. Dyadic treatments, such as those described earlier, hold value in both elevating the caregiver–child bond and decreasing child maltreatment risks.

Self-Regulation

Affective and behavioral regulatory skills are important to many areas of functioning. Yet, the capacity to regulate affect and tolerate distress is typically underdeveloped in complex trauma survivors, who often have difficulty identifying the chain of events, emotions, and behaviors that lead to affective and behavioral dysregulation. Youth with dysregulated affect are at greater risk of current and future self-harm behaviors and suicidal ideation (Miller, Linehan, & Rathus, 2006), and often engage in coping behaviors similar to those of younger children (Berk, Neece, & Combs-Ronto, 2013; Perry, 2006). In order to enhance affect regulation skills, we propose the use of a trimodal approach. First, the triggers to and/or patterns of dysregulation are identified and interventions emphasize the alteration of environment, parental, or other unnecessary stressors that may limit a child's affect regulation abilities (i.e., affect regulation is enhanced by reduction of environmental stressors). Second, the caregiver's affect regulatory abilities are assessed and strengthened so that caregivers are able to model their use of effective coping and distress tolerance skills. Finally, the child's self-regulatory ability is enhanced via a number of strategies and techniques. Several such techniques will now be proposed, including techniques to identify the chain of events related to the incident of dysregulation, coping, mindfulness, and relaxation following physiological arousal.

Based upon Linehan's (1993) chain analysis, used to assess the triggers and vulnerabilities that lead to affect dysregulation with adults, the family creates a paper chain (i.e., strips of paper are folded and taped to make a ring, followed by additional circular strips successively linking each link of the paper "chain" to the next) to depict the events that took place prior to an incident of the child's affect dysregulation. The link begins by identifying the incident of affect dysregulation (e.g., when the youth "lost control" or felt overwhelmed). The therapist then inquires about cognitions, behaviors, and conditions (i.e., vulnerabilities) that occurred immediately prior to the incident. If the child and parent report "nothing happened right before" the child became dysregulated, the clinician aids the family by prompting them to start from the night prior to the incident and then asks them about the young person's sleep patterns, eating patterns, illnesses, and stressors (i.e., these can be vulnerabilities that influence a child's or parent's ability to regulate affect). Each vulnerability is written or drawn on a link of the paper chain. If no vulnerabilities are described, the clinician prompts the family by asking them to describe their day from the moment they woke up. The clinician continues to help the family describe events that took place prior to the emotional dysregulation incident by asking, "What happened next?" and allowing the family to continue describing each event, including thoughts, behaviors, and events. A new link is added after every step in the sequence. If desired, different color strips of paper can be used to differentiate behaviors, cognitions, and vulnerability factors of both caregiver and child. After the pattern of cognitions, behaviors, and events has been depicted, the therapist and family engage in a discussion of the vulnerabilities and triggers to the incident. After this dialogue, the family develops a plan for alternate responses in future scenarios.

As additional tools for affect regulation, Paula (2009) proposes the use of physically arousing games that elevate children's physiological reactivity so that youth can more effectively identify somatic signs of distress and apply specific relaxation skills in a more naturalistic manner. In concluding this discussion of interventions for affect regulation, it should be mentioned that play and play therapy have long been noted to inherently possess a number of self-regulating benefits (Perry, 2006). When affect, cognitions, actions, and experiences are symbolically portrayed or expressed in play, one naturally relies on one's own ability to pace, tolerate, and enhance regulatory capacity via successful exposure to the material expressed. When children experience gratification from their play, this experience helps modulate arousal, restore equilibrium, and process cognitions, affect, and experiences.

RELEVANT INTERVENTION

In another intervention used to assist with affect regulation, children and caregivers are asked to create separate *coping boxes*, in which items are placed to facilitate the use of coping skills use in the event of dysregulation.

Typical coping boxes include several sensory-rich items (e.g., objects with soothing texture, items that have pleasant smells, pictures of favorite people or experiences, a small snack, music lyrics, CDs, bubbles, a stuffed animal, and short letters of encouragement written by the child to him- or herself, as well as by beloved friends and adults). When children become dysregulated, they are told to access their individualized coping boxes in order to facilitate the return to an equilibrated emotional state. As another intervention, coping menus can be developed based on the notion of a restaurant menu that offers a variety of food options. In this intervention, children create a list of coping options and write or draw them on the menu they decorate. Based upon the age and preferences of the child, the youth may be asked to identify coping behaviors (e.g., playing outside, getting exercise, having a play date), helpful cognitions (e.g., reminding oneself that the distressing emotion always passes, telling oneself that he or she can get through this), sensory experiences (e.g., activities involving sight, sound, taste, smell, or touch) and seeking social support (e.g., identifying whom and how the support will be obtained). Youth in middle childhood can typically hypothesize as to whether or not the selected strategies would be viable coping options in imagery or whether the selected strategies need to be experienced directly. If some of the strategies might be effective in imagery, the coping menu would then include both real and imagined coping options (e.g., thinking about being at the beach, or smelling a favorite food in imagery, as well as actually engaging in a selected activity or smelling a pleasant aroma in vivo). In both coping-based interventions, the coping menu or coping box should be readily accessible to the child, the caregiver creates his or her own coping menu or coping box, and each is asked to use and rate the effectiveness of the selected strategies as therapy homework assignments. During the following session, the therapist reviews the effectiveness of the selected strategies and helps the family members adjust their coping plans as needed.

As a further intervention conducted in session, mindfulness stations are provided during sessions to develop and to encourage family members to enhance their mindfulness capacity. In a typical forty-five-minute session, approximately fifteen mindfulness stations might be arranged. At each station, there are different mindfulness activities in which the child and/or caregiver can engage (e.g., smelling vanilla extract, touching shaving cream in a bowl, rubbing cotton balls between one's palms, raking sand in a miniature zen garden, tasting a piece of fruit, looking at a bowl of chocolate candy, listening to chimes, meditating, or balancing on one leg). The child—or family members if the intervention is conducted as a family session—selects an initial station, partakes in the sensory experience, shares his or her reaction to the activity, and then rotates to the next station after one to two minutes. By the end of the session, each patient or family member will have completed all fifteen stations, including some from each sensory channel (i.e., sight, sound, taste, smell, and touch). As mindfulness skills develop, some stations can include slightly averse or challenging experiences, such as balancing on one leg for longer periods of time, smelling strong spices, leaving one's eyes closed while leaning against a wall, or placing one's hand in cold water. Mindfulness exercises might become part of each session in order to facilitate mindfulness practice, and clinicians are encouraged to assign mindfulness exercises as homework as well.

CASE STUDY

To demonstrate how a child with complex trauma symptoms in a community mental health setting might be treated using some of these interventions, we now describe Joseph, a nine-year-old boy referred for treatment following his teacher's report that he was repeatedly found fondling a fourth-grade peer in the restroom. (Information has been altered to obscure the identity and protect the confidentiality of the child and family.) As he awaited his initial appointment, Joseph and his siblings argued with each other, knocked over chairs in the reception area, and frightened a younger child with their rambunctious behavior. During the initial assessment, Joseph was inattentive, easily distracted, and had difficulty concentrating. He was small for his age, and had multiple scratches on his face and limbs, which he said were accidents from playing with his brother. His hairline revealed several scars from events which he said he did not recall. Joseph had difficulty controlling his actions, frequently leaving his seat and grabbing materials from both his father and the therapist. Both during this and a subsequent collateral session with the father, the therapist learned that Joseph had lived with his father, twelve-year-old brother, and eight-year-old sister since Joseph's mother and father divorced when Joseph was three years of age. The father reported that the mother's substance abuse issues had left her incapacitated, that she had physically abused the boys "once or twice" when they were younger, that the children had witnessed domestic violence between their parents, and that she had only sporadic contact with the children now. The father conveyed his sense of overwhelm and detachment from his children and reported that the family's financial situation was precarious. They moved frequently from one home to another, and child care arrangements during the father's long working hours were chronically problematic. The family currently lived with two adult cousins in a small one-bedroom apartment.

When asked about the father's concerns for his son, he focused on Joseph's disruptive behaviors at home (e.g., Joseph did not follow directives, and was not completing homework assignments). Notably, the father did not spontaneously report concern related to the sexual behaviors reported at school. When asked, Joseph's father said that he was not very concerned about his son's sexual behaviors at school, and denied that Joseph had been exposed to inappropriate sexual material or sexually abused. When asked more about what might have prompted the bathroom behaviors to occur, the father said that his brother and the brother's girlfriend also lived in the small apartment and Joseph might have seen his uncle with his girlfriend once.

Whereas the father demonstrated less concern than expected, subsequent sessions with Joseph revealed many noteworthy signs and symptoms. Joseph's mood was labile, with a broad affective range (e.g., appearing happy when singing loudly, smiling when calm, irritable with his brother, and anxious when the topic of his behaviors at home and school were discussed). Joseph's level of distractibility fluctuated based on the topic of discussion. When asked directly about the sexual behavior at school, Joseph reported his brother "showed" him, but immediately after this disclosure Joseph crawled under the therapy room table, denied that anything had happened, and began to suck his thumb. "Don't tell him!" he implored as he sobbed.

After obtaining consents to communicate with child protective services and school personnel, the therapist learned that Joseph's older brother was also mandated to attend treatment because of additional allegations of sexually inappropriate behavior. Joseph's teacher said that she was overwhelmed and exasperated by Joseph's behavior. She described that the sexual behaviors in the restroom were only the "tip of the iceberg" with other concerns including persistent noncompliance, aggressive behaviors, poor academic performance, intrusion into her personal space and belongings, and frequent tearfulness related to relatively minor incidents (e.g., not being scheduled to perform a classroom duty during the week or disliking the food selection during lunch). The teacher further expressed her concern that Joseph was sometimes the target of bullying by his peers (i.e., particularly related to his tearful outbursts at school), and for his hygiene, saying that Joseph's clothes were often dirty and his he attended school with an unkempt appearance.

During one of Joseph's initial assessment sessions, Joseph looked around the room as if he were suddenly aware that his father was not with him. He began shrieking that he wanted his father. As the therapist responded reassuringly, Joseph bolted from the treatment room, kicked every office door on the way back to the waiting room, and attempted to kick and bite the receptionist who approached him to say that his father was in the restroom.

With Joseph's history of attachment issues, sexual behavior, safety concerns at home, and highly dysregulated behavior and affect, it was clear that Joseph and his family needed intervention focused on the first two domains identified by the NCTS workgroup. Based upon his symptoms and history of attachment issues and recurrent, interpersonal trauma exposure, Joseph's case was conceptualized using a complex trauma approach. The initial treatment goals were to assess and enhance safety and then target affect regulation. The father's lackadaisical approach to child welfare concerns, inadequate monitoring, Joseph's disclosure/recantation of sexual behavior with his older brother and subsequent intense concern about the disclosure being revealed to his brother, and his behaviors at home and school combined to raise the index of child maltreatment concern.

During the first few sessions, both Joseph and his father created safety contracts, engaged in psychoeducation about appropriate boundaries, and the family improved the child care arrangement so that there was increased monitoring (e.g., due to the father's long work hours, the children spent a significant amount of time outside of his car with multiple and sometimes unsuitable monitors). Each child was enrolled in individual therapy in addition to the family safety-based sessions, which was particularly important after several incidents of severe intersibling violence were revealed. Frequent crises interrupted the family's work on safety-related goals, but the therapist provided in home visits, telephone consultations, and live coaching as the father attempted to resolve the crises sufficiently to return to the focus on enforcing intrafamilial boundaries.

During collateral session, the therapist and father explored his own familial patterns of abuse and trauma exposure via the genogram activity, and subsequent to that, his attendance and motivation improved as he understood his passivity in the context of his own repeated victimization experiences and use of substances to cope with life stressors. Through interventions such as the jack-in-the-box technique, the spill the beans intervention, and the hidden object activity, as well as in sessions focusing on open communication about intrafamilial events, barriers to communication were exposed and addressed. The father revealed his fear that his children would be placed to live with their substance abusing mother if they revealed every incident to which they had been exposed during his custody. Eventually, the father began to understand the importance of enhancing both safety and communication, and he encouraged the children to speak openly, even about issues that had been "family secrets in the past." In fact, after Joseph's father's encouragement, Joseph asked "I can talk about *everything*?" a subtle acknowledgment that there was additional material to disclose.

With parental consent to speak about the events they experienced, the therapist was then able to reassess their environment and historical exposure to traumatic events. Although Joseph did not want to speak about the events that transpired at school or with his brother, he responded openly to safety stimulus cards with labels and nongraphic illustrations of typical safety related issues (e.g., someone hurt someone else, someone touched someone in a private area) that were used on a weekly basis to assess safety related issues in the family. Joseph's siblings and father were also asked about their experiences during the week using the cards, and eventually family sessions to discussed reported incidents (e.g., yelling at home, the children hitting each other, the boys being found clothed but in bed together) were held to further promote intrafamilial communication. Additional suspected child abuse reports were filed twice during these sessions, but the therapist maintained a supportive, calm, matter-of-fact approach to the mandated report and the therapeutic alliance was maintained. After several home visits, the family's living situation, schedule, and home environment were addressed and improved. The male relatives were asked to move, the boys were required to sleep in separate locations, child care arrangements were modified, and privacy boundaries were honored during toileting and dressing. With the therapist's assistance, the children were informed about reproduction, bodily changes, and appropriate ways in which sexual feelings could be expressed. Soon thereafter, during a session in which the therapist again reviewed the family's schedule in terms of all unsupervised contact the youth had with other adults, Joseph revealed being sexually abused by one of his male relatives, which then allowed the therapist and father to finally report the incident to child protective services and law enforcement personnel, speak directly to Joseph's siblings about their own sexual abuse, and refocus on establishing a safer home environment, after which other symptoms and issues could be addressed.

With enhanced communication, a parental protective response, and the source of the children's sexual behaviors better understood, the family increased their focus on self-regulation stage of treatment though an assessment of family boundaries and safety-related issues occurred at the beginning of every session. Joseph's emotional outbursts persisted at home and school, though they became somewhat less frequent and intense following the father's encouragement of open communication and protective response. To address Joseph's affect regulation deficits, Joseph made a coping box filled with items that he found soothing and helpful during his episodes of dysregulation at home.

During corresponding collateral sessions, the father was encouraged to enhance his own coping and affect regulation skills, but also to alter the patterns he had learned from his own upbringing so that he could recognize situations that required his intervention, modulate his own affective response, and respond more quickly and consistently to his children's incidents of escalating affect, arguments, or boundary encroachments. Both individual and collateral sessions typically included mindfulness activities. Joseph's "emotional outbursts" were chained every week using the paper chains technique described earlier. When the father failed to respond to sibling violence or used poor judgment with respect to his children's well-being or monitoring, the chain technique was used in individual, collateral, or family sessions. The family learned to notice vulnerable factors that may have contributed to one of the children's "outbursts" and identified specific triggers such as aggressive play, interpersonal physical play (i.e., rough housing), video game violence, and violent or sexual media content. With practice chaining their

past experiences and choices, they learned to use alternative behaviors, coping strategies, and choices and illustrated their alternative courses of action
with sparkling gold and silver paper strips, which they added to their chains.
With his affect better regulated, Joseph's school functioning improved and
he was less frequently the target of his classmates' criticism. As the family's
environment involved increased safety, monitoring, and protective parental
judgment, Joseph and his father engaged in a parent–child dyadic play therapy developed to repair attachment, trust, and mutual enjoyment as well as to
strengthen the caregiver's ability to manage his children's behaviors. Joseph's father was referred for his own therapy to address his own history of
abuse and his pattern of avoidant coping. After the dyadic treatment, Joseph
received trauma-focused therapy, where he engaged in a play-based narrative
and cognitive restructuring related to the events he experienced. Despite the
challenges they faced and child maltreatment incidents that occurred in his
family prior to and during the course of therapy, Joseph and his family
worked arduously to bring about a safer, healthier, and happier way of interacting with each other.

FINAL NOTE ABOUT ASSESSMENT

Clinicians know that accurate assessment is critical to diagnosis, treatment
selection, and case conceptualization. Yet, family members may not be moti-
vated, comfortable, forthcoming, or cognizant when they are asked to describe a child's maltreatment and other adverse events. Therapists are therefore encouraged to collect data at several phases of therapy, and to collect
more extensive data than may be typical, including information and/or
records from each parent/caregiver, medical providers, the child's school,
extended family members, child protective services, siblings, and child care
service providers. Home visits are also fruitful sources of information, with
attention paid to safety conditions, privacy considerations, availability of
food and access to dangerous substances, living space issues (i.e., including
presence of toys, photographs of the child, and the child's art or school
projects), and areas that children are not allowed to access. Family schedules
are always obtained for a twenty-four-hour period on each day of a typical
week in order to detect issues and challenges that caregivers might not otherwise reveal (e.g., meals, bathing and hygiene practices, adult supervision,
exposure to other children or adults, and sleep quality and quantity). Even
with complete and accurate information, children presenting with complex
posttraumatic symptoms are vulnerable to misdiagnosis, because complex
trauma affects multiple domains of children's development and it can be
difficult to detangle from other disorders (e.g., attentional, disruptive behavior, mood, and nontrauma-related anxiety disorders). Also, the majority of

traumatized children do not meet diagnostic criteria for PTSD (Cook et al., 2005), and a PTSD diagnosis may not sufficiently account for the multiplicity of complex trauma experiences (Van der Kolk, 2005). As Cook et al. (2005) note, several distinct diagnoses may capture a limited aspect of the traumatized child's impairment, though none currently accounts for all common aspects of complex trauma impairment.

FINAL NOTE ABOUT THERAPISTS' SELF-CARE

The work of treating childhood complex trauma requires a great deal from the therapist, who must simultaneously empathize with victimized children and bond with caregivers who may have significant deficits as parents. The therapist must both hold hope that parents can develop adequate protective capacities and also remain attentive to the reality that many caregivers may not yet be able protect—and in fact may endanger—their children. The therapist must tolerate the pain and suffering of children, while maintaining optimism and faith in each child's capacity to heal and grow. Therapists must examine the darkest sides of familial functioning during their work hours, and then reground themselves in the different contexts of their own homes and families. These are challenging endeavors, but masters of this work learn to devote themselves to pursuits of joy, renewal, reciprocity, and growth which comingle with the tragedy, suffering, and acceptance that is part of their work. Effective complex trauma therapists learn to accept and embrace the dualities of their work, transforming their memories of children's maltreatment disclosures into positive experiences shared or lessons learned.

CONCLUSION

Most children treated in community mental health settings for trauma-related issues have been exposed to more than one incident of trauma, and many have been exposed to multiple types of trauma. Yet, the literature on childhood trauma has historically emphasized youth who survive single or relatively short-term traumatic events, and the play therapy literature on complex trauma is sparse. In our child trauma clinic, we realized that fundamental child safety issues needed to be addressed in the vast majority of cases, and that most EBTs were limited in their effectiveness when overarching child safety concerns were not first targeted. Similarly, we realized that too many traumatized youth in middle childhood would eventually reappear in therapy as adolescents with intentional self-injurious behaviors and/or suicidal ideation, if we did not address both safety and affect regulation skills extensively. By addressing these issues during childhood, we discovered that families could be helped to change multigenerational patterns of trauma exposure, and that complex trauma symptoms manifested during one developmental era were not predestined to recur with greater severity at later times in development. The strategies described in this chapter were presented to link play therapy methods to best practice guidelines. We hope that this discussion contributes to play therapists' complex trauma practice and strengthens awareness of safety-based and affect-regulation-focused interventions until evidence-based, safety-focused, developmentally sensitive complex trauma treatments are more widely disseminated.

REFERENCES

Berk, M. S., Neece, C., & Combs-Ronto, L. (2013). Dialectical behavior therapy and suicidal behavior in adolescence: Linking developmental theory and practice *Professional Psychology: Research and Practice, 44*(4), 257–265.

Blaustein, M., & Kinniburgh, K. (2010). *Treating traumatic stress in children and adolescents: How to foster resilience through attachment, self-regulation, and competency.* New York, NY: Guilford Press.

Bratton, S. C., Ray, D., Rhine, T., & Jones, L. (2005). The efficacy of play therapy with children: A meta-analytic review of treatment outcomes. *Professional Psychology: Research and Practice, 36*, 376–390.

Briere, J. & Hodges, M. (2008, November). Do we need a child complex trauma diagnosis, or a way to diagnose ongoing attachment symptoms beyond age 5? In K. Nader & K. Gletcher (Chair), *Complex trauma in children and adolescents: Conceptualization and assessment.* Symposium conducted at the meeting of the International Society for Traumatic Stress Studies, Chicago, IL.

Briere, J., & Lanktree, C. (2008). Integrative treatment of complex trauma for adolescents (ITCT-A): A guide for the treatment of multiply-traumatized youth. Retrieved from http://www.johnbriere.com/Adol%20Trauma%20Tx%20Manual%20%20Final%208_25_08.pdf.

Cohen, J. A., Mannarino, A. P., & Deblinger, E. (2006). *Treating trauma and traumatic grief in children and adolescents.* New York, NY: Guilford Press.

Cook, A., Spinazzola, J., Ford, J., Lanktree, C., Blaustein, M., Cloitre, M., & Mallah, K. (2005). Complex trauma. *Psychiatric Annals, 35*(5), 5, 390–398. Retrieved from http://www.harriscountytx.gov/CmpDocuments/86/Annual%20Reports/Complex%20Trauma%20in%20Children%20and%20Adolescents.pdf.

DeRosa, R., Habib, M., Pelcovitz, D., Rathus, J., Sonnenklar, J., Ford, J., et al. (2006). Structured Psychotherapy for Adolescents Responding to Chronic Stress. Unpublished manual.

Eyberg, S. M., Funderburk, B. W., Hembree-Kigin, T. L., McNeil, C. B., Querido, J. G., & Hood, K. (2001). Parent-child interaction therapy with behavior problem children: One and two year maintenance of treatment effects in the family. *Child & Family Behavior Therapy, 23*, 1–20.

Ford, J. D. & Russo, E. (2006). Trauma-focused, present-centered, emotional self-regulation approach to integrated treatment for posttraumatic stress and addiction: Trauma Adaptive Recovery Group Education and Therapy (TARGET). *American Journal of Psychotherapy. 60*(4), 335–355.

Grasso, D., Greene, C., & Ford, J. D. (2013). Cumulative trauma in childhood. *Ford & Courtois, Eds,* 79–99. Retrieved from: http://www.traumacenter.org/initiatives/CumulativeTraumaChildhoodChapter.pdf.

Herman, J. L. (1992). Complex PTSD: A syndrome in survivors of prolonged and repeated trauma. *Journal of traumatic stress, 5*(3), 377–391. doi: 10.1002/jts.2490050305.

Hewitt, S. (1999). *Assessing allegations of sexual abuse in preschool children: Understanding small voices.* Thousand Oaks, CA: Sage.

Jernberg, A. (1979). *Theraplay: A new treatment for using structured play for problem children and their families*. Washington, DC: Jossey Bass.

Kessler, R. C. (2000). Posttraumatic stress disorder: The burden to the individual and to society. *Journal of Clinical Psychiatry, 61*(5), 4–12.

Kolko, D. J., & Swenson, C. C. (2002). *Assessing and treating physically abused children and their families: A cognitive behavioral approach*. Thousand Oaks, CA: Sage.

Landreth, G. L., & Bratton, S. C. (2006). *Child Parent Relationship Therapy (CPRT): A 10–session filial therapy model*. New York, NY: Brunner-Routledge.

Lanktree, C., & Briere J. (2008). *Integrative Treatment of Complex Trauma for Children (ITCT-C): A Guide for the Treatment of Multiply Traumatized Children Aged Eight to Twelve Years*. National Child Traumatic Stress Network (NCTSN). Retrieved from http:// www.johnbriere.com/Adol%20Trauma%20Tx%20Manual%20%20Final%208_25_08.pdf.

Lieberman, A. F. & Van Horn, P. (2008). *Psychotherapy with infants and young children: Repairing the effects of stress and trauma on early attachment*. New York, NY: Guilford Press.

Linehan, M. M. (1993). Cognitive-behavioral treatment of borderline personality disorder. New York, NY: Guilford Press.

Miller, A. L., & Linehan, M.M., & Rathus, J. L. (2006). *Dialectical Behavioral Therapy with suicidal adolescents*. New York, NY. Guilford Press.

Myrick, A. C., & Green, E. J. (2014). Establishing safety and stabilization in traumatized youth: Clinical implications for play therapists. *International Journal of Play Therapy, 23*(2), 100–113. doi: 10.1037/a0036397.

Munns, E. (2000). *Theraplay: Innovations in attachment enhancing play therapy*. New York, NY: Jason Aronson.

Paula, S. T. (2009). Therapy techniques for affect regulation. In A. A. Drewes (Ed.) *Effectively blending play therapy and cognitive behavioral therapy: A convergent approach* (pp. 353–372). New York, NY: Wiley & Sons.

Perry, B. (2006). Applying principles of neurodevelopment to clinical work with maltreated and traumatized children: The neurosequential model of therapeutics. In N. Webb (Ed.) *Working with traumatized youth* (pp. 27–52). New York, NY: Guilford Press.

Saxe, G. N., MacDonald, H. Z., & Ellis, B. H. (2007). Psychosocial approaches for children with PTSD. In M. J. Friedman, T. Martin, & P. A. Resick (Eds.) *Handbook of PTSD: Science and practice* (359–375). New York, NY.

Shelby, J. Ellingsen, R. & Schaefer, C. (in press). Play therapy research: Issues for twenty-first century progress. In C. Schaefer, K. O'Conner, & L. Braverman (Eds.) *Handbook of Play Therapy, 2nd Edition*. New York, NY: John Wiley & Sons.

Shelby, J. & Maltby, L. (in press). Child maltreatment: Safety-Based clinical strategies for play therapists. In D. A. Crenshaw & A. Stewart (Eds.) *Play Therapy: A comprehensive guide to theory and practice*. New York, NY: Guilford Press.

Spinazzola, J., Ford, J., Van der Kolk, B., Blaustein, M., Brymer, M., Gardner, L., M., Silva, S., et al. (2003, November). *Complex trauma in the national child traumatic stress network*. Paper presented at the 19th Annual Meeting of the International Society for Traumatic Stress Studies, Chicago, IL.

Terr, L. C. (1991). Childhood traumas: An outline and overview. *American Journal of Psychiatry, 148*, 10–20.

Turner, H. A., Finkelhor, D., & Ormrod, R. (2010). Poly-victimization in a national sample of children and youth. *American Journal of Preventive Medicine, 38*(3), 323–330. doi: http:// dx.doi.org/10.1016/j.amepre.2009.11.012.

Van der Kolk, B. A. (2005). Developmental trauma disorder. *Psychiatric Annals, 35*(5), 401–408. Retrieved from: http://byronclinic.com.au/workshop/Developmental_Trauma.pdf

Van der Kolk, B. A., Roth, S., Pelcovitz, D., Sunday, S., & Spinazzola, J. (2005). Disorders of extreme stress: The empirical foundation of a complex adaptation to trauma. *Journal of Traumatic Stress, 18*(5), 389–399. doi: 10.1002/jts.20047.

Van der Kolk, B. A., et al. (2009). Proposal to include a developmental trauma disorder diagnosis for children and adolescents in DSM-V. Retrieved from http://traumacenter.org/announcements/DTD_papers_Oct_09.pdf.

Vickerman, A. K., Margolin, G. (2007). Posttraumatic stress in children and adolescents exposed to family violence: I. Overview and issues. *Professional Psychology: Research and Practice, 38*(6), 613–619.

Chapter Four

Healing Young Children Affected by Sexual Abuse

The Therapeutic Touchstone

Eileen Prendiville

This chapter focuses on the use of a specific technique, the *therapeutic touchstone* (Prendiville, 2014b), in the early stages of psychotherapeutic interventions for young children affected by sexual abuse. The therapeutic touchstone is a play- and story-based intervention used to assist a child in experiencing the therapist as genuine and the experience as psychologically safe. In directly addressing the child's need for safety—a *deficiency need* in Maslow's Hierarchy of Needs model—the stage is set for the child to benefit from the acceptance offered by the child psychotherapist. The touchstone story, which is a synopsis of significant events in the child's life, uses the child's language, that of play and imagining, in deference to the child's developmental stage, and provides psychological distance to facilitate children in engaging and identifying with the content of their own story. Providing this material in a structured and contained way, with a clear beginning, middle, and end, and in the company of supportive allies, clinicians address some of the confusion common among children who have experienced sexual abuse and other difficult potentially traumatic events.

Given that one of the main benefits of using the therapeutic touchstone story is the speedy establishment of the therapeutic relationship and the child's experience of the therapist as trustworthy, the story addresses one of the main needs of the abused child: providing an experience of safety in this new aspect of their life. Finkelhor and Browne's Traumagenic Dynamics Model (1985, 1988) suggested that one of the specific trauma-causing factors of sexual abuse is the betrayal of trust. This can contribute to distorting the child's worldview and may lead to mistrust and create an impaired ability to judge the trustworthiness of others. This leads to an intense need to regain trust and security (Finkelhor & Browne, 1985, p. 392); therefore it is critical that therapists demonstrate their trustworthiness to the child, and their main caretakers, as clearly and as early as possible within the psychotherapy process. Letting the child know what we know about them, and how we found it out, provides for openness, honesty and clarity and serves to reassure, relieve tension, establish a context for the therapy, and removes a burden from children (James, 1989; Lacher, Nichols, Nichols, & May, 2012) as we share both our knowledge of their situation and our unconditional acceptance of them. The touchstone is a directive narrative-based technique, used in the first joint session with the child or adolescent and their supportive ally(s) to address the child's need for clarity and honesty. It sets the stage for either the child- or therapist-led work and introduces a systemic approach to the work from the beginning. This is important when working with psychosocial issues that impact the whole family and for which the child will need extensive familial support. Additionally, the family will likewise benefit from being therapeutically *held* and supported.

RESEARCH SUPPORT

Play therapy is a developmentally appropriate intervention for traumatized children (Baggerly, Ray, & Bratton 2010; Bratton & Ray, 2000; Bratton, Ray, Rhide, & Jones, 2005; Drewes, 2009; Dugan, Snow, & Crowe, 2010; Gil, 2006). Ramussen and Cunningham (1995) made a clear case for using a multimodal approach with children who experience sexual abuse. They recommended an initial assessment strategy, including a focus on the family system, followed by an integrative strategy that blends both nondirective play therapy and focused techniques including art therapy, bibliotherapy, use of metaphors, and cognitive behavioral therapy. They suggested that focused techniques are necessary to address symptoms of posttraumatic stress disorder, cognitive misattributions, and traumagenic dynamics of abuse. Shelby and Felix (2005) proposed a similar integration of nondirective and directive approaches of play therapy, and also emphasized the critical role of parental involvement in the treatment of traumatized children. The emphasis on parental involvement is central to the trauma-focused cognitive behavioral approach (Cohen, Mannarino & Deblinger, 2006); and the necessity to integrate play when using a CBT approach with child clients is becoming more recognized (Briggs, Runyon, & Deblinger, E., 2011; Drewes, 2009, 2012).

Most child therapists now use an integrated and/or blended approach (Drewes, 2011; Drewes, Bratton, & Schaefer, 2011; Gil, 2010) so as to ensure that they remain attentive and responsive to the emerging needs of the particular child rather than simply implementing a single model. The "one size fits all" approach is not likely to be successful in working with a range of clients of varying ages, developmental stages, and different backgrounds including those who have experienced developmental trauma (Van der Kolk, 2005). Critical judgment and reflective practice undergirded by a strong theoretical framework will support clinical decision making and mitigate against the rigid application of interventions. Gil (2010) highlighted the need for the therapist to maintain a careful balance between directive and nondirective work. She recognized children's need to direct their own healing but noted that the therapist may need to provide active assistance to help them confront material that could be uncomfortable but is best not avoided.

Davis (1989) provided an extensive collection of therapeutic stories to benefit children who have experienced sexual, and other, abuse and neglect. Useful guidance on writing such stories is provided by Sunderland (2000). The benefits of using narrative approaches in play therapy is likewise well recorded (Taylor de Faoite, 2011, 2014), and the systemic use of this approach with families is described by Freeman, Epston, and Lobovits (1997). Le Vay (2011) explores and describes a co-constructive narrative approach in play therapy interventions with children who sexually harm others. He discussed the benefits of symbols and metaphors being used in play narratives to provide "a degree of externalization so that the overwhelming or intolerable feelings are projected onto objects and into stories and dramatic enactments" (p. 173). This protects the child's coping strategies and allows the child to engage in a way that does not overwhelm them or trigger defensiveness or negative emotions. Such considerations are of importance when working with children who have been exposed to and had direct experience of situations that might well have aroused feelings of shame, blame, disgust, and terror. Storytelling approaches (a) support healing, integration, and the development of coherent narratives that can organize both memory and perceptions and allow for the reinterpretation of experiences (Bruner, 1987; Lacher et al., 2012) and (b) can link and reorganize many areas of the brain (Cozolino, 2002). Narratives are effective in heaing the pain of trauma, shifting the child's internal working model, and in assisting parents and carers in understanding and gaining empathy for their child (Lacher et al., 2012, pp. 113–117). Everyday language is not enough for therapists working with hurt children (Sunderland, 2000): we must access the language of play and imagining so as to protect our must vulnerable clients and work safely and effectively. It is not enough for us to learn to listen to and understand children's language of play: we must learn to speak it too when we have important information to communicate. This is the essence of the therapeutic touchstone.

OVERVIEW OF VULNERABLE POPULATION

Child sexual abuse is a common problem that can be experienced by children of all ages. It can occur within or outside families in all social classes, and the offender may be a stranger or a trusted member of the family or community. It may be a one-time event or may be ongoing for a number of years. It may involve direct physical contact or exposing the child to sexually explicit material. The perpetrator may be of any age. Of primary importance is the awareness that the children who may experience sexual abuse are not different from the rest of the population. Any child may be assaulted by a stranger or groomed by a perpetrator. The child who is most at risk of sexual abuse is the one whose primary or secondary caregiver is a pedophile. The nonabusing family members whose children experience sexual abuse are not necessarily neglectful or complicit in the abuse of their child. In cases where the offender is known and trusted by adult caregivers it is likely that they too will be groomed in order to facilitate the offender in gaining and maintaining access to the child. Consider these examples (all details have been altered to protect client confidentiality):

- Mary was four years old when she disclosed that her father had sexually abused her. She disclosed when her mother asked her what she was doing when she was demonstrating oral–genital contact between two dolls as part of her play. She was not aware of the significance of what she was saying when she described the activities involved.
- Peter was sixteen years old when it was discovered that the parish priest had been arrested for the sexual abuse of a number of alter boys. Peter had been an alter boy for four years, nine to thirteen years old, and Fr. Brown was a regular visitor to his family home since Peter was eight years old. Fr. Brown regularly brought gifts for Peter and had encouraged his parents, who were very protective of their children, to allow him to serve at Sunday Mass. One of the boys who had disclosed abuse has stated that he also saw Peter being abused.
- Jane had been married to John for ten years and has been impressed with how much time he spent caring for their three children. She believed that his parenting skills were naturally superior to hers. She was in love when they married. After the wedding, Jane lost contact with friends as John seemed to be jealous and insisted that it was not appropriate for her to socialize outside the home now that she was a married woman. John regularly derides and criticizes her in front of their children, encourages her son to insult and swear at her, tells her she was stupid, and encouraged her to see herself as incompetent as a person and as a parent. Jane did not have contact with her family of origin as such contact led to many arguments between herself and John: he insisted that they were interfering with

his family. Jane discovered her husband was engaging in sexual activity with her seven-year-old child. She did not know what to do and believed that she had nobody to discuss this with. She phoned the child protection services but did not give identifying information. She did not believe she would be capable of managing on her own with three children.

• John and Sarah, ages six and seven years old, were at a friend's birthday party. John became upset when he did not win a game, and Sarah decided to bring him home—a journey of two hundred yards. They left without telling any adults of their intention. As they made their way home a car driven by a man pulled up alongside them, and a female passenger pulled them into the back seat.

Each of the children described above has experienced at least one event that is potentially traumatic for them. Each of their families will also be impacted by the events described: rather than only being a family problem, child abuse causes problems for families.

INTEGRATIVE PLAY THERAPY TREATMENT PLANNING AND PROTOCOL

Careful treatment planning is needed to respond to the individual needs of children who are known to have experienced sexual abuse. Gathering extensive information and considering this from an informed perspective that takes account of relevant theoretical models and complex dynamics will assist the therapist to conceptualize the likely needs of each child. Even a single incident of abuse can incorporate many traumatic moments; ongoing sexual abuse can be even more traumatizing. Both will be confusing for the child who is experiencing events that are developmentally inappropriate, emotionally overwhelming, and beyond their comprehension. Extremely traumatic events are experienced on a sensory and somatic level, the limbic system is activated, and the language center (Broca's area) shuts down. There is neurobiological evidence that such memories are stored in the somatic and visual areas of the brain (Van der Kolk, 1996). This contributes to the invasive and repetitive nature of traumatic memories (i.e., in play, dreams, and flashbacks) as this primitive level of processing does not facilitate the building of coherent narratives. "Instead we are left with a more primitive sensory and somatic level of processing that does not facilitate us in being able to coherently understand and transfer the experience to long term memory" (Prendiville, 2014a, p. 88). There is no way the child can fit their experiences into a coherent narrative and make sense of them. Additionally, children tend toward egocentrism and may misappropriate feelings of blame, guilt, and shame rather than attributing blame to the perpetrator. Children find a way to interpret what is happening to them as being somewhat in their own interest or being their own responsibility. To attribute that blame to someone else would mean affirming to themselves that they have no control over what is happening—a very scary acknowledgment, especially given the fragmented nature of their awareness. If a person can believe that they are somehow responsible for an event that they experience they can imagine that they potentially have the power to stop it being repeated. When abuse is ongoing children often adapt by taking on an inappropriate role—sometimes a *paren-tified* or *adultified* role that involves holding themselves responsible for the care of and emotions of the adults who surround them. This can include continuing to be available for abusive contact.

This elaborate process is an outgrowth of the grooming process (McAlinden, 2012) which may be designed to frighten or to entice the child: it is a staged process that includes gaining access to the child (perhaps including befriending if child is previously unknown), preparing them for abuse, and securing secrecy. It may be based on gaining cooperation by meeting some of the child's needs, instilling intense fear or by making the child feel special, and manipulating the child to ensure they remain entangled in the sexualized relationship. The child may develop a damaging bond with the offender due to the level of powerlessness experienced. In some cases there is little need for grooming due to a preexisting relationship between the offender and the child in which the child is already dependent. The more dependent on the offender that the child (or the target of the groomer—regardless of their age) is, the more helpless, hopeless, and entrapped they will be. The child may also be groomed in ways that isolate them from others, exploit their vulner-ability, lead them to believe that nonabusive adults are unreliable, or to expect catastrophic consequences (to self, pets, loved ones, etc.) should they disclose. The grooming process might well include progressively invasive comments, touches, and activities that are designed to exploit the child's curiosity and confuse the child about

- the appropriateness or otherwise of the interaction;
- the level of awareness parents/caregivers have of this contact;
- caregiver approval of this contact;
- the "invincibility" of the offender;
- responsibility, and blame/shame attributable to the child; and
- the power that the offender has over the child and his/her family.

Prior to grooming the child, many offenders engage in a grooming process of the child's caregiver/s who would otherwise be more equipped to ensure the ongoing safety, protection, and well-being of the child. Nonabusing family members are often groomed to trust or fear the offender, to see themselves as incompetent, reduce self-confidence and self-esteem, and/or to see the child as precocious, having an overactive imagination, or as a liar.

RELEVANT INTERVENTION

When planning psychotherapeutic interventions for children, and associated services for other family members following discovery or disclosure of child sexual abuse, the mindful therapist will pay particular attention to ensuring that their interventions serve to empower both the child and their caretakers. Ideally, the nonabusive parent/s will regain (or develop) the capacity to fully support, protect, and empathize with their child and to become an active participant in their healing. This will necessitate taking a supportive, educative, nonjudgmental, and empathetic stance. The first priority will be to secure protection, which must always come before therapy, for the child. Ideally the adult caregivers will be actively involved in this task so that they feel empowered and develop confidence in their ability to take appropriate action on behalf of their child. This can be a difficult time for the parent who may also be dealing with feelings of shock, betrayal, fear, uncertainty, powerlessness, and may well be grieving the loss of a relationship that contributed to their definition of self (e.g., as a partner or as a parent). Just as we support adults who mourn the loss of a loved one following bereavement (including being patient with them when they express denial), we must be open to supporting the parent who struggles with new knowledge that changes their world immeasurably. In common with the children, adult family members will also be subject to mistaken beliefs in relation to the whole area of child sexual abuse. As part of the grooming process, the offender may even have attempted to deliberately distort perceptions and thoughts.

A second priority in cases of child sexual abuse should be to ensure that the child is aware of the measures taken to secure their protection, and to ensure that this protection will be maintained. Without this knowledge, the child will not benefit emotionally by the changes that ensue, and the changes may in fact increase the child's anxiety as they struggle to restore predictability. The unknown is frightening: fear of the unknown can push us back into familiar dangerous situations. The therapeutic touchstone story, when used with families when sexual abuse has occurred, provides a defining opportunity to reiterate both the steps taken and the commitment of the supportive ally to continue to keep the child safe. In addition, it provides an opportunity to address the betrayal experienced by giving the therapist the opportunity to demonstrate transparency, clarity, and honesty. The script of the therapeutic touchstone story may further address the dynamics of the grooming process, the behavior of the offender, the impact on the child, the responses to disclosure or discovery of the abuse, and the presenting problems. Before exploring the actual writing of such complex stories, let us explore briefly the steps involves in writing simpler stories—that is, those that address less complex issues and that do not have such a strong psychoeducational component. The general rationale for and the steps involved in writing and telling these stories is described in detail elsewhere (Prendiville, 2014b). The simplest stories are written for children with emotional/behavioral issues that did not arise in response to known difficult life events.

For children struggling with adjustment issues, points 2 and 3 in box 4.1 are expanded so that the story begins with events that occurred before the difficult life event, and a brief description of the event is included *after* emphasizing positive events, attachments, and supportive adults. Age-appropriate language is used to describe the difficult event.

Box 4.1. Therapeutic Touchstone Story for Children with Emotional/Behavioral Issues

1. Give the story a title.
2. The beginning of the story is set at a stage before the presenting problems emerged.
3. Show the emergence of emotional or behavioral difficulties (including presenting problems) and the response to these. Emphasize the presence of any secure attachments or supportive adults and do not ignore positive life experiences.
4. Refer to current presence of supportive ally.
5. Include the referral, intake sessions, and information that was made available to you.
6. Include references to the child's strengths and attractive qualities.
7. The story ends in the present tense—with the child attending the appointment and their story being told.

For children with traumatic and complex histories, additional steps are included as listed in box 4.2 below. Given the need to keep the duration of the story three to six minutes, clinicians are advised to engage the child fully by using small world play to (a) provide additional psychological distance and allow for both externalization and miniaturization, and (b) to ensure that the child does not become overaroused or anxious, the story script will of necessity be carefully written to achieve the right balance between including only the most important events using developmentally appropriate language.

Here is a sample story for a four-year-old whose beloved dog has gone missing. Can you identify the various steps as listed above? Remember it is not a rigid formula: some flexibility is desirable to facilitate personalizing the story for the specific child and situation and assist them in identifying with and traveling calmly on the same journey as the main character in the story. This trip incorporates safe starting and ending points but also holds the difficult experience in the middle so that the telling of the story and the accompanying activation of mirror neurons facilitates a transformational experience (Levy, 2008).

Box 4.2. Therapeutic Touchstone Story for Children with Complex Histories

1. Give the story a title.
2. The beginning of the story is set at a stage before any traumatic events occurred.
3. Emphasize the presence of any secure attachments or supportive adults and do not ignore positive life experiences.
4. Describe the difficult life event/s in child-friendly language.
5. If grooming was involved include this.
6. Emphasize the child's coping.
7. Include psycho-educational component if appropriate, especially addressing cognitive distortions.
8. It may be appropriate to incorporate some elements of trauma debriefing into the story (for example sensory elements, emotional context, fears).
9. Refer to any difficulties that ensued (including presenting problems).
10. Address any feelings of guilt or shame (normalizing and reframing).
11. Refer to parental responses and address any deficiencies.
12. Refer to current presence of supportive ally.
13. Include the referral, intake sessions, and information that was made available to you.
14. Include references to the child's strengths and attractive qualities.
15. The story ends in the present tense—with the child attending the appointment and their story being told.

Reproduced with permission from Prendiville and Howard (2014, p. 20).

Remembering Scamp

Once upon a time, in a land very close to here, there was a little girl called Mary who lived a very happy life with her Mummy and Daddy. She was loved so very much, and she had a lovely house, her own bedroom, lots of toys, and two pets, a doggie called Scamp and a goldfish called Goldie. Scamp had been a part of Mary's life since he was a puppy and she was just one year old. She loved him very, very much and played with him every single day. He loved her too—I think she was his favorite person in the whole world. Goldie was pretty new, Mary just got him on her fourth birthday and she made up his name all by herself. She had a big celebration that day and everyone was so excited to see her blow out the candles on her bunny rabbit-shaped cake. It was a great day. Mary got so many hugs and kisses, cards and presents, and her cousins and aunts and uncles came to her party. What fun everyone had playing in the garden and in the house.

Mary's house was on a busy road and everybody knew to keep the gate closed so that Mary and her friends, and Scamp, would stay safe inside the garden. But one day, just a few days after Mary's birthday, a terrible thing happened. Scamp got out of the garden! Everybody was worried when he did not come home by dinnertime. Daddy went out in the car searching for him. Mummy and Mary made posters with his picture on them. They wrote MISS-ING in big letters and put Mummy's phone number on them. They hoped that someone would find Scamp and phone Mummy so that they could bring him back home. But sadly, that did not happen. Mary cried when Daddy read her a bedtime story and tucked her into bed that night. She really missed Scamp. Days passed and still Scamp did not come home. Mary got sadder and sadder. She started to get pains in her tummy, didn't want to eat her dinner, and she worried a lot! She wasn't sad all the time though, sometimes she still played and had fun, especially on her swing, having snuggle time with her Mummy, and when Daddy read her bedtime stories. But, the hurting feelings were not too far away and whenever she could not find something—her book, her cardigan, her favorite toy (even if it was right where she left it!), Mary began to cry . . . and shout . . . and punch . . . and stamp her feet . . . and generally get very, very upset. Mummy would help her find whatever was missing but then Mary would think of something else that might be lost and it would all start over again. Mummy and Daddy did their very best to help Mary feel better— sometimes it felt like their hearts would burst with all the love they felt for Mary and they really did not like to see her hurting so much.

After a while Mummy and Daddy tried not to talk about Scamp as they were worried that that would make Mary even sadder. He had been missing for a very long time by now. Mary did not talk about him either. But this was not a good plan as it didn't help anyone! So Mummy and Daddy decided to go to see a lady called Eileen who plays with children to help after sad things happen. They told Eileen all about Mary and the very sad day when Scamp went away. They talked about how much everyone missed him. They told Eileen that Scamp was a beautiful black dog, with a white spot on his tail. They told lots of stories about how much Scamp loved Mary and how he would sleep outside Mary's bedroom door at night, about how Mary would put ribbons on his hair sometimes, and a very funny story about the hot day when Scamp got into the paddling pool in the garden with Mary! They also told about the day Scamp got lost and how they never found him. Eileen thought is would be a good idea for Mummy and Daddy to help Mary to make a Memory Box about Scamp and they agreed. A Memory Box is a very special box that gets filled with treasures and pictures that remind us of a loved one who has gone away. It keeps all the memories safe and everyone can look at the treasures and talk about Scamp whenever they want to. Eileen also explained that everyone who loves Scamp always holds a special place in his or her heart for him; nobody can ever take this away and it cannot get lost.

It was also decided that Mary would come to the special playroom where she can be the boss of playing and Eileen will be the boss of keeping us safe. Playing like this can help children sort out the hurting feeling that they get when they miss a loved one, especially one they did not have a chance to say goodbye to. Mummy was delighted to hear that all Mary would need to do would be to play! It is one of the things that Mary is especially good at and she loves dressing up and making up exciting stories! Eileen has lots of toys for playing with—houses, and cars, animals and puppets, art materials and dressing up clothes. Actually—maybe we could go and have a look at the playroom now?

The props used in telling this story might include doll characters for family members, a toy dog, a photograph of Scamp, maybe a gate, and a copy of the poster referred to in the story. Think about the voice tone, facial expressions, gestures, and sound effects you might use in telling the story so as to create a picture and engage the child on a sensory and somatic level and "create a meta-message that has the potential to bypass cognitive defenses" (Lacher et al., 2012, p. 59) and engage both right and left sides of the brain simultaneously to support neural integration. Additional guidance on gathering important information, formulating story content to address relevant dynamics, patterns, events, and to support integration, the telling of the story itself, plus reflections on the use of the technique and understanding how and why it works, is available elsewhere (Prendiville, 2014b).

Touchstone Stories for Children with Complex Histories

When a child has experienced complex traumatic experiences we need to be particularly aware that the touchstone story will have emotion-laden content and the therapist will strike a careful balance between not giving enough versus giving too much detail in relation to the difficult life events. It remains important, however, to bring up the traumatic material early (James, 1989), and safely within the context of the touchstone story. There are many additional considerations in writing such stories; see box 4.2 for a list of potential topics to include. The initial touchstone story will address what the therapist considers to be the most significant, and immediately relevant, areas so as to provide a short (remember the six minute rule!), coherent, structured narrative that serves to reduce anxiety and build trust. The list below describes the possible ingredients—not a strict recipe! It is not necessary to go into details of each aspect. Limit the amount of potentially distressing content and provide suitable synopsis expressions such as "it happened again and again" or "it went on for a very long time" rather than describing each incident. The therapeutic touchstone provides an organizing framework that should assist the child and family in making sense of confusing events and in laying foundations for experiencing control over the level of negative arousal linked to these experiences. It also serves to facilitate the early appearance of play that is directly linked to the child's unresolved issues, and to elicit the therapeutic power of abreactive play (Prendiville, 2014a).

The earlier examples have given suggestions on the start and end of the story. These remain the same for more situations where sexual abuse has occurred. The differences will be held in the middle of the story where abuse specific dynamics will be addressed.

Grooming

When gathering information about what is known of the methods used by the offender to secure secrecy, gain trust, secure uninterrupted access, and manipulate the child and family, this may be included in the story in simple form. This will be helpful for all family members to begin to understand the grooming methods (McAlinden, 2012) used to entangle them. When writing stories for children who have been groomed, I sometimes add a line that says something like "Sometimes people who hurt children say things that are not true, and (name the offender) might have done that. The not true things might be to trick children into keeping secrets or to make them get mixed up thinking. (Child's name) can check out anything that they are not sure is true or not."

Child's Response

Despite that fact that children will have done their very best at the time of trauma, they are likely to be self-critical in this regard. Well-meaning adults, in efforts to be helpful ("You should have just hidden in the wardrobe."), or in asking inappropriate questions (e.g., "Did you tell her to stop?"), may compound this self-doubt. Poorly worded personal safety programs might even have led him to infer that he should have been able to protect himself better. Telling the touchstone story gives us the opportunity to reframe what we know of the child's coping as a strength "and Johnny's body knew exactly the right thing to do' followed by whatever he actually did (as long as you have reliable information in this regard), for example, 'run away as fast as he could,' or 'stay as still and as quiet as he possibly could' or 'just close his eyes and pretend to himself that the bad stuff wasn't happening again'" (Prendiville, 2014b, p. 14).

Abuse Dynamics, Mistaken Beliefs, and Negative Worldview

Children who experience sexual abuse experientially learn many unpleasant realities and untruths about the world. The offender may also deliberately confuse them about what is normal, appropriate, and permissible in adult–child relationships. The child's learning, which may impact on behavior that they learn to display and underpin and negatively impact their developing worldview, could include some of the following:

• that sexual activity between adults and children is ok,
• that getting what you need is contingent upon giving sexual pleasure,
• that it is ok for adults to hurt children,
• that their feelings do not count,
• that someone other than the offender is responsible for the abuse, and
• that when adults show affection they might be looking for sex.

The touchstone story is an ideal vehicle for holding and presenting more helpful and accurate information about children's right to safety, adults responsibilities to keep children safe, and the therapist's own worldview.

> Some of the expressions I have used in touchstone stories are references to how the most important "rules of the world" are about keeping children safe and that we know someone broke these rules if a child gets hurt by someone touching them on a private part of the body and causes them to have mixed up, muddled feelings. Children who act out sexually can be described as having a "touching problem." Feelings of guilt and shame are addressed directly as many children will need particular assistance in overcoming these difficult emotions. (Prendiville, 2014b, p. 12)

Emphasis on Sensory and Somatic

Traumatic memories can be disjointed, disorganized, incomplete, intrusive, and disturbing. Until processed satisfactorily they are unable to be transferred to past memory. In addition, memories may be primarily experienced on a somatic level without an accompanying narrative to help the child recognize or respond to their own physiological cues. In some circumstances, it can be useful to include references to the sensory elements that are known about the events that the child experienced while also presenting the facts in a logical sequenced manner. These can be in relation to any sensations the child is likely to have experienced, anything seen, heard, smelled, touched, or tasted (e.g., a noise of an ambulance coming to the scene, someone calling their name, rainfall, smell of alcohol, bright lights, sticky blood) as well as to the physiological sensations (e.g., heart pounding, hands cold and clammy, breath held) that might have accompanied an affective state. Naming emotions will be appropriate at times—sometimes these will be phrased in terms of, "Sometimes children get really, really frightened (so sad, worried, angry) when things like this happen." In relation to ongoing coping it can be useful to describe, how a child's heart might be "beating really fast, going boom, boom, boom, on the inside," how their "tummy might be all wobbly," how they might be "hardly able to breath with the big fright they are getting," but they still manage "to look all calm on the outside and even keep a big smile on their face" (Prendiville, 2014b, p. 12).

A Second Chance at Responding Appropriately to Disclosure

The healing process for abused children begins when they receive an appropriate response to their disclosure and when this is combined with the provision of safety. The information processing of trauma model (Hartman & Burgess, 1988) identifies the disclosure phase as being directly related to how the child will be impacted by the trauma. Therefore, as part of the intake process with children who have experienced interpersonal trauma, the clinician should explore the way in which the abuse surfaced and the responses that the child received. If it emerges that the abuse was discovered rather than disclosed, or if the disclosure was not handled sensitively, then the clinician should try to facilitate a more appropriate response on the basis that it is better to have this late than never. The clinician should work with the child's nonoffending caretakers to prepare them to revisit the disclosure and to ensure that the child hears some important messages in relation to the parents being sorry that the abuse occurred but being glad that they know about it so that they can keep the child safe now. It is important that the response to the disclosure does not engender any additional feelings of guilt or shame for the child. Corrective responses can come later if the initial response was lacking:

> *Even though Mummy loved her little boy, Johnny, very much she was not able to stop him getting hurt. She thought that Pat knew how to keep Johnny safe. She didn't know that Pat was hurting him. When Johnny told her what had happened she got such a fright that at first she though it might not be true and she asked Johnny if he was making up a story. She even got a bit cross and Johnny started crying because he thought he was in trouble for telling. But then Mummy realized that Johnny was telling her the truth. She was so sorry that he had been hurt, she even cried, but she was so proud of him for telling. She knew that he had done exactly the right thing by telling her. She thought to herself, "I am not going to let Pat hurt my little boy any more" and she made sure that Pat was not allowed into her house again. She forgot to tell Johnny this and he did not know, until now, that that is why Pat will never be coming back into his house again.*

By including something like this in the story the therapist can further facilitate the child's parent(s) in transmitting more helpful responses to any disclosure that was not appropriately responded to in the past. When telling the story, and acting it out with miniature toys, this would be one of the times that the therapist might look directly at the child and parent and make a comment that will enhance the child's experience of safety. Maybe something like: "That is what you told me Mummy isn't it? I remember you were upset that you hadn't told Johnny that you believed him straight away and you told me that you were really glad that he was brave enough to tell you."

CASE STUDY

Tony was a wanted baby by his parents and a beloved child (all details have been altered to protect client confidentiality). When he was six months old, his mom, Sarah, returned to work. His parents were delighted that they had the ideal solution to their child caretaking needs as their next-door neighbor, Patricia, cared for a few children in her home. Most of the time, Tony separated easily and went into Patricia's welcoming arms. During the summer when Tony was three years old he began to cry bitterly almost every morning when dropped off in daycare. However, Patricia said he settled quickly; and he generally seemed to be happy enough when his parents returned. His parents figured it was just a phase and that he would grow out of it. They explained to him that they had to go to work and they would be back in the afternoon. He did seem to settle after a few weeks and the separations got easier as time went on. However, Tony remained (until engaged in therapy) an anxious child, easily distressed, prone to dysregulated behaviors, and disturbed sleeping patterns. When Tony was four, one of the older children being cared for in Patricia's house disclosed sexual abuse by Patricia's eighteen-year-old son Dennis. An investigation ensued and Dennis admitted that he had abused all three children being cared for in his home. Each child's parents were notified and the daycare facility was closed down. Tony's parents were devastated and felt hugely guilty that they had been unable to ensure their son's safety and protection. Sarah was pregnant at this time; and feeling unable to trust any other childcare service providers, she took early maternity leave and became a stay-at-home mom. The authorities did not offer any intervention to Tony and suggested that time would heal; and that now that he was safe and would soon forget. His parents hoped that was true. Time passed; and when Tony was six years old, it was discovered that he was engaging in sexually inappropriate behavior with his eighteen-month-old sister and with a seven-year-old cousin who was developmentally delayed. Tony called this "doing sexing" and "the sex game." Tony's father, David, was furious. He shouted at Tony, sent him to his room, told him he was disgusted at him and suggested that he be grounded "for life." Sarah was also extremely distressed. She cried extensively and told Tony she was disappointed in him. At a time of extreme crisis, David and Sarah sought help from a qualified therapist.

In the initial session both parents were allotted time to share their experiences, their feelings, and their concerns for their children and niece. I (the author of this chapter) was the therapist, and I provided an open space for them to tell their story in a free-flowing manner. Given their distress, the story was quite disjointed. Strong feelings were expressed. I responded with empathetic and normalizing comments during the initial "spilling." Gradually I began to pull the threads together. I told them what I had heard, attempting to put it into sequence, ask a few clarifying questions, and confirmed that I had the correct story. It was clear that, despite their inappropriate responses to the news of Tony's sexual behavior problem, these were concerned and dedicated parents who were committed to protecting and supporting both their children. They simply did not know the right thing to do. They needed education and support.

As the session progressed I moved into a psychoeducational approach, answered questions, and helped both parents understand more of the dynamics of their son's experiences and his abuse reactive behavior. They began to see his behavior as an expression of his continued confusion and need for therapeutic intervention and particular supports. An initial plan was made to manage Tony's sexual behavior problem. I also prepared them for the first session that they would attend with Tony in which the touchstone story would be told. I was clear that the touchstone story would be written to facilitate both parents and Tony to move forward.

The touchstone story might address the following key features: (a) Tony is loved; (b) his parents always wanted the very best for him; (c) they were delighted Patricia could help him because they thought that he would be safe and well cared for by her; (d) nobody knew that Dennis would break the rules of the world with him or any other child; (e) nobody knew when this was happening; and (f) when it was discovered Sarah and David did exactly the right thing. They did everything they could to keep Tony safe. They love him very, very much. They forgot to tell him that sex games are not meant for children. When children play sex games, or someone else does sex things to them, they get hurt inside. Tony made a mistake in playing the sexing game with his cousin and his sister. Everybody had forgotten to tell him that this was not allowed and would make others mixed up just like he had been when Dennis did the sex stuff with him. Sarah and David are sorry for what they said and did (describe this) when they found out about the sex games. They got a shock and were worried. Tony is not in trouble, but it is important that the grown ups get to know all about the game so that they can help Tony not to do it again. When Sarah and David came to see the therapist a plan was made. They figured out that the sex games never happened when there were adults in the room so they thought it would help Tony not to play the game again if they made sure to always have a grown up in the room any time that Tony was with another child. We are also going to figure out other ways for Tony to get help when he wants to do it. Readers may be interested to know that the very first thing that Tony said when he entered the playroom was, "Do you have Transformers here?" and during his final session (six months later) he invited his parents to the room, having rearranged its contents, and announced, "I made big changes in this room! Now there is more room to play."

CONCLUSION

The therapeutic touchstone may be adapted to suit the individual needs of any child affected by sexual trauma and their family. It is structured like a psychological feedback *sandwich* with a gentle lead in and supportive ending and with the difficult experiences held securely in the middle. Developmentally appropriate props and child-friendly language are used and the story is told when the child is in the company of, and supported by, their protective ally. When used in this way it should kick-start the therapy process safely, provide immediate relief from anxiety, and begin the process of transforming intrusive memories. Further touchstone stories can be told at various stages in the therapy process. Writing touchstone stories for children who have experienced sexual abuse may be a challenge initially, but the psychological rewards can be significant and the therapy process will be rich. Play therapists will soon have a rich store of phrases and stories to draw upon. Enjoy your journey into this new world!

REFERENCES

Baggerly, J., Ray, D., & Bratton, S. (2010). *Child-Centered Play Therapy Research: The evidence base for effective practice.* Hoboken, NJ: Wiley.

Bratton, S., & Ray, D. (2000). What the research shows about play therapy. *International Journal of Play Therapy, 9*(2), 47–88.

Bratton, S., Ray, D., Rhide, T., & Jones, L. (2005). The efficacy of play therapy with children: A meta-analytic review of treatment outcomes. *Professional Psychology: Research and Practice, 36*(3), 378–390.

Briggs, K. M., Runyon, M. K., & Deblinger, E. (2011). The use of play in trauma-focused cognitive-behavioral therapy. In S. W. Russ & L. N. Niec (Eds.), *Play in clinical practice: Evidence based approaches* (pp. 168–200). New York, NY: Guilford Press.

Bruner, J. (1987). Life as narrative. *Social Research, 4*(1), 11–32.

Cohen, J. A., Mannarino, A. P., & Deblinger, E. (2006). *Treating trauma and traumatic grief in children and adolescents.* New York, NY: Guilford Press.

Cozolino, L. J. (2002). *The neuroscience of psychotherapy: Building and rebuilding the human brain.* New York, NY: W.W. Norton & Co.

Davis, N. (1989). *Therapeutic stories to heal abused children*. New York: Institute for Rational Living.

Drewes, A. A. (2009). *Blending play therapy with cognitive behavioral therapy: Evidence-based and other effective treatments and techniques*. Hoboken, NJ: Wiley.

Drewes, A. A. (2011). Integrative play therapy. In C. E. Schaefer (Ed.), *Foundations of play therapy* (2nd edn., pp. 349–364). Hoboken, NJ: Wiley.

Drewes, A. A. (2012). Play Applications and Skills Components. In J. A. Cohen, A. P. Mannarino & E. Deblinger (Eds.), *Trauma Focused CBT for Children and Adolescents: Treatment Applications*. New York, NY: Guilford Press.

Drewes, A. A., Bratton, S. C., & Schaefer, C. E. (2011). *Integrative play therapy*. Hoboken, NJ: Wiley.

Dugan, E., Snow, M., & Crowe, C. (2010). Working with children affected by Hurricane Katrina: Two case studies in play therapy. *Child & Adolescent Psychiatry, 15*(1), 52–55.

Finkelhor, D., & Browne, A. (1985). The traumatic impact of child sexual abuse: A conceptualization. *American Journal of Orthopsychiatry*, 55(4), 387–400.

Finkelhor, D., & Browne, A. (1988). Assessing the long-term impact of child sexual abuse: A review and conceptualisation. In L. E. Walker (Ed.), *Handbook on sexual abuse of children* (pp. 55–71). New York: Springer Publishing Co.

Freeman, J., Epston, D., & Lobovits, D. (1997). *Playful Approaches to Serious Problems: Narrative therapy with children and their families*. New York, NY: Norton & Co.

Gil, E. (2006). *Helping abused and traumatized children: Integrating directive and nondirective approaches*. New York, NY: Guilford Press.

Gil, E. (2010). *Working with children to heal interpersonal trauma*. New York, NY: Guilford Press.

Hartman, C. R. & Burgess, A. W. (1988). Information processing of trauma: Case application of a model. *Journal of Interpersonal Violence, 3*(4), 443–457.

James, B. (1989). *Treating traumatized children: New insights and creative interventions*. Lexington, MA: Lexington Books/DC Heath & Co.

Lacher, D. B., Nichols, T., Nichols, M., & May, J. C. (2012). *Connecting with kids through stories: Using narratives to facilitate attachment in adopted children*. London, England: Jessica Kingsley.

Le Vay, D. (2011). Journey into the Interior: Narrative play therapy with young people who sexually harm. In A. Taylor de Faoite (Ed.) *Narrative Play Therapy: Theory and practice*. (pp. 151–168). London, England: Jessica Kingsley.

Levy, A. J. (2008). The therapeutic action of play in the psychodynamic treatment of children: A critical analysis. *Clinical Social Work Journal, 36*, 281–291.

McAlinden, A. (2012). *'Grooming' and the Sexual Abuse of Children: Institutional, Internet, and Familial Dimensions*. Oxford, UK: Oxford University Press.

Prendiville, E. (2014a). Abreaction. In C. E. Schaefer & A. A. Drewes (Eds.) *The therapeutic powers of play: 20 Core Agents of Change* (2nd edn., pp. 83–102). NJ: Wiley & Sons.

Prendiville, E. (2014b). The Therapeutic Touchstone. In E. Prendiville & J. Howard (Eds.) *Play Therapy Today: Contemporary Practice for Individuals, Groups, and Parents* (pp. 7–28). London, England: Routledge.

Prendiville, E., & Howard, J. (2014). *Play Therapy Today: Contemporary Practice for Individuals, Groups, and Parents*. London, England: Routledge.

Ramussen, L. A., & Cunningham, C. (1995). Focused play therapy and non-directive play therapy: Can they be integrated? *Journal of Child Sexual Abuse, 4* (1), 1–20.

Shelby, J. S. & Felix, E. (2005). Posttraumatic Play Therapy: An integrated model of directive and non-directive approaches. In L. Reddy, T. Files-Hall, and C. Schaefer (Eds.), *Empirically based play therapy* (pp. 79–103). Washington, DC: APA Press.

Sunderland, M. (2000). *Using storytelling as a therapeutic tool with children*. London, England: Speechmark.

Taylor de Faoite, A. (2011) *Narrative Play Therapy: Theory and practice*. London, England: Jessica Kingsley.

Taylor de Faoite, A. (2014) Indirect Teaching. In C. E. Schaefer & A. A. Drewes (Eds.) *The therapeutic powers of play: 20 Core Agents of Change* (2nd edn., pp. 51–67). NJ: Wiley & Sons.

Van der Kolk, B. A. (1996). The body keeps the score: Approaches to the psychobiology of posttraumatic stress disorder. In B. Van der Kolk, A. Mc Farlane, & L. Weisaeth (Eds.), *Traumatic stress: The effects of overwhelming experience on mind, body and society* (pp. 214–241). New York, NY: Guilford Press.

Van der Kolk, B. A. (2005). Developmental trauma disorder: toward a rational diagnosis for children with complex trauma histories. *Psychiatric Annals, 35*, 401–408.

Chapter Five

Animal Assisted Play Therapy to Empower Vulnerable Children

Risë VanFleet and Tracie Faa-Thompson

Animal Assisted Play Therapy (AAPT) is a relative newcomer to the array of treatment modalities used with children, although elements of it have been employed by clinicians for many years. Defined as "the integrated involvement of animals in the context of play therapy, in which appropriately trained therapists and animals engage with child, family, & adult clients primarily in play interventions" (VanFleet, 2013, p. 6), AAPT's uniqueness lies in its full integration of play therapy and animal assisted therapy, separating it from other forms of animal assisted therapy (Chandler, 2012; Fine, 2010). AAPT is "aimed at improving the client's psychosocial health, while simultaneously ensuring the animal's well-being and voluntary engagement in the process" (VanFleet, 2013, p. 6). Thus, play therapists and the animals they involve in their work must have many competencies that go beyond a simple working knowledge of either play therapy or animal assisted therapy.

Nonhuman animals (i.e., "animals") are involved in both nondirective and directive play sessions with clients of any age as a means of expressing feelings, developing relationships, and resolving psychosocial problems (VanFleet, 2008; VanFleet & Faa-Thompson, 2010, 2014). Canines and equines have been used most frequently, and are therefore the focus this chapter, but other species have been included in AAPT by some practitioners; cats, birds, rabbits, pot-bellied pigs, cows, and even tortoises have participated in the play therapy process. Dogs can be included in either nondirective or directive play therapy sessions, while horses and other species are more commonly used in more directive play therapy interventions.

AAPT's relationship-oriented approach requires humane treatment of the animals at all times while ensuring attention to the child's therapeutic needs.

Many features of the therapist–animal relationship provide a model for children's relationships. Mutual respect, acceptance, and safety are key components. The therapist and animal have a healthy relationship based on positive training, time spent together, and avoidance of any coercive or force-based equipment or interactions. It is important that the animal enjoy the experience, not merely tolerate it. For example, if a play therapy dog is stressed or tired and walks away showing lack of interest in participating further in a session, the therapist allows this to happen. Not all animals are suitable for this work; careful selection is important, followed by socialization to ensure that the animal feels comfortable with the play therapy environment and the clients. Teaching animals to have appropriate behaviors around children requires the exclusive use of positive training methods, and that involves an in-depth knowledge of the species, the individual animals, and how learning theory applies to that species. Offering quality play therapy while ensuring animal welfare at all times requires a unique ability to split one's attention between child and animal without losing sight of either mandate. Furthermore, it is part of the therapeutic process to help children recognize and work through any feelings that the animals' behaviors might bring up.

In AAPT, the therapist provides an atmosphere of emotional safety that is developmentally attuned and that provides opportunities for clients to work on a wide range of difficulties. Specifically, the therapist offers empathic acceptance of naturally occurring play by both the child and animal; encourages playful interactions between the child and the animal; suggests specific playful tasks and activities; facilitates the session using a playful tone of voice and style; models playful behaviors with the child and animal; and gently processes the child's reactions and experiences (VanFleet, 2013). The therapist's directedness ranges from relatively little to a great deal. In interventions on the lower end of this directedness continuum, play sessions might resemble nondirective play therapy, except that the therapist selects the initial activity and then moves into a rather nondirective stance, reflecting the child's feelings, participating when invited, and setting limits when needed. On the higher end of the continuum, the therapist provides significant structure, suggesting activities and assisting in a way that will lead to a desired outcome. These are usually activities that have more specific behaviors, such as clicker training a dog or horse to learn a particular behavior. In all forms of AAPT, the therapist must be prepared to work empathically and flexibly.

This chapter provides a description of AAPT and how it is used with nondirective and directive interventions for individuals, groups, and families affected by single-event and interpersonal traumas. Two case studies illustrate how AAPT using horses and dogs can assist with healing for traumatized children and their families.

RESEARCH SUPPORT

AAPT is a synthesis of two forms of therapy that have received empirical support. Play therapy has been shown to be an effective treatment (Bratton, Ray, Rhine, & Jones, 2005; Reddy, Files-Hall, & Schaefer, 2005; Topham, Wampler, Titus, & Rolling, 2011; VanFleet, Ryan, & Smith, 2005), and animal assisted therapy has received some empirical support, although more controlled research is needed (Bowers & MacDonald, 2001; Chandler, 2012; Fine, 2010; Parish-Plass, 2013). A meta-analysis of forty-nine studies showed moderate effect sizes for animal assisted therapy in treating issues such as behavior problems, anxiety, and various symptoms that are associated with autism spectrum disorders, and moderately high effect sizes when dogs were included in therapy sessions (Nimer & Lundahl, 2007). In another study, researchers compared a twelve-week group equine-assisted counseling program to an empirically validated classroom-based counseling program for students with serious behavior issues, learning difficulties, and social adjustment problems (Trotter, Chandler, Goodwin-Bond, & Casey, 2008). While both treatments yielded statistically significant improvements, the equine-assisted counseling program participants demonstrated greater improvements than the classroom program participants.

Other lines of research point to the potential benefits of AAPT; for example, the importance of animals to children has been demonstrated in developmental psychology (Melson, 2001; Melson & Fine, 2010). Children from many cultures are attracted to animals and seek their company. They draw them, tell stories about them, and dream about them. AAPT capitalizes on this breadth and depth of interest. Recent attention to the role of oxytocin in the human–animal bond (Olmert, 2009) may eventually yield insight into the value of animals in play therapy as a source of emotional connectedness and safety (Olmert, 2014, personal communication).

Anecdotal data and case studies that suggest the value of AAPT is growing rapidly. In one study, Thompson (2009) used participants as their own controls in a study of the impact of dogs on children's anxiety. She found significant positive impact of the presence of a dog in nondirective play therapy, including more easily established rapport, improved mood, ability to engage in thematic play, and decreases in aggression and behavioral disruptions. In another study, VanFleet (2008) conducted a pilot investigation wherein eleven children participated in AAPT and ten children received play therapy without animals. The children completed sandtrays at the end of treatment to illustrate their favorite parts of the experience. All of the children receiving AAPT selected a dog for the "liked best" sandtray, while only 20 percent of the play therapy-only children did. This, too, provides preliminary data and a possible route to exploring children's perceptions of the process.

Several studies are currently underway to look at different aspects of the AAPT process; however, no well-designed controlled study currently exists. Adequate pools of play therapists that are fully trained in AAPT are needed before such studies can be conducted. The establishment of the AAPT certification process (International Institute for AAPT Studies, 2014) is a step in establishing sufficient proficiency for stronger studies to be conducted. The AAPT certification program is stringent and requires mental health and play therapy credentials, online and live AAPT training programs, and supervised practice. For more information, please visit http://play-therapy.com/playful-pooch/.

OVERVIEW OF VULNERABLE POPULATION

Since Lenore Terr's (1990) groundbreaking book, *Too Scared to Cry*, mental health professionals have developed a much clearer understanding of the profound effects of traumatic experiences on children. Prior to this, children's trauma reactions tended to be discounted or minimized, and it was common to redirect children's comments or play about trauma to other more "pleasant" topics. Now the serious and potentially long-lasting impact of trauma on children is well documented (Gil, 2010; La Greca, Silverman, Vernberg, & Roberts, 2002; Perry & Szalavitz, 2010; VanFleet & Sniscak, 2003; VanFleet, 2006, in press; Webb, 2007). Indeed, single-event traumas such as natural disasters, school violence, house fires, and more complex forms of trauma, such as maltreatment, neglect, and domestic violence impact children, often in myriad ways.

Webb (2007) provided a comprehensive review of factors that influence child reactions to trauma as well the forms that trauma-related distress can take. The National Child Traumatic Stress Network (www.nctsn.org) provides substantial resources for understanding child trauma as well. It is important to keep in mind that children vary greatly in the circumstances that traumatize them, their levels of resilience and adaptability, and the forms their symptoms take. In general, children may experience feelings of helplessness and hopelessness, poor emotional regulation, somatic complaints, distortions in their self-perceptions and sense of identity, anxiety and fear reactions, inability to trust others, attachment and relationship disruptions, academic problems, poor behavior regulation and oppositional/conduct disorders, avoidant behaviors, night terrors and dissociative episodes, cognitive distortions, separation anxiety, aggression and victimization of others, and overwhelming guilt and shame (e.g., Briere & Spinazzola, 2005; Gil, 2010; Perry & Szalavitz, 2010; van der Kolk, Roth, Pelcovitz, Sunday, & Spinazzola, 2005; Webb, 2007).

While children are affected profoundly by trauma, so are their parents and siblings. Families are *always* affected by trauma whether it befalls all of them or a single family member. Figley (1989) has described four primary ways that trauma impacts families. *Simultaneous effects* occur when all family members are directly affected by a trauma. Some examples might include natural disasters, home invasions, and some motor vehicle accidents. *Vicarious effects* occur when the trauma directly affects a family member who is out of direct contact with the rest of the family; violence at school and parental deployment to war zones would be included. *Chiasmal effects* occur when one family member's trauma reactions are transferred to other members in the form of caregiver distress or intergenerational traumatization. Finally, *intrafamilial effects* occur when the source of the trauma lies within the family itself as in cases of interfamilial abuse, domestic violence, or divorce.

Nondirective play therapy, directive interventions, and integrated therapies, among others, have been valuable in the treatment of different forms of child trauma (e.g., Gil, 2010; Shelby, 2000; VanFleet, 2014; VanFleet, Lilly, & Kaduson, 1999; VanFleet & Sniscak, 2003; VanFleet, Sywulak, & Sniscak, 2010; Webb, 2007). AAPT has also been used successfully with this clinical population. Because AAPT is a process- and relationship-oriented intervention, it can be applied flexibly to meet the needs of children with a wide range of traumatic experiences and symptoms.

INTEGRATIVE PLAY THERAPY TREATMENT PLANNING AND PROTOCOL

Given the many potential needs of traumatized children, multimodal treatment is often warranted. AAPT can easily be provided in conjunction with any other form of psychotherapy. Usually, AAPT forms one part of the treatment plan with sessions ranging twenty to thirty minutes of the therapy hour. Occasionally, group or family AAPT interventions involving dogs or horses may take longer. Some AAPT services begin in the early stages of therapy and continue throughout the course of treatment, while other AAPT interventions only occur for time-limited periods within the larger therapeutic process. In the initial stages of therapy, animals can provide "social lubricant effects"; that is, they seem to help children feel more relaxed in the therapeutic environment and with the therapist, and permit faster engagement with the process. Just as play therapy creates emotional safety so children can deal with difficult emotional material through distance and symbolism, animals create a further sense of safety. It is common for children to express delight when offered the opportunity to work with animals as part of their therapy.

The theoretical models used within AAPT depend on the form of play therapy being conducted with the animals. For example, if a therapist conducts nondirective AAPT in a playroom with a dog, the theoretical framework would be humanistic, just as with child-centered play therapy (Van-Fleet et al., 2010). If the therapist asks a family to complete a task with the horses that requires communication, teamwork, and problem solving, the operative theories might be family systems and cognitive–behavioral play therapy.

Early Stages of AAPT

The early stages of AAPT involve orienting the children or families to treatment and preparing them for sessions to come. Children learn how to meet a dog safely and several basic body language and cues to use during their sessions. When horses are involved, the children are introduced to the horses through the use of observations, and then gradually meet them and interact with them. Essential safety considerations are covered, but these are kept to a minimum, with limits being set *only* when needed. Excessive focus on safety factors can increase client anxiety. The therapist makes final decisions about what forms of AAPT (i.e., nondirective, directive, group, or family) will be most useful to start with the child.

Nondirective AAPT

Nondirective AAPT is most applicable to the involvement of canine partners, or other animals that can safely be included in the playroom. In nondirective AAPT, the therapist conducts the session similarly as would be done without the animal. The child initially has a choice about bringing the dog into the playroom; and once in the playroom, the child can decide when to include the dog in the play and when not to. When the child is playing alone, the therapist reflects the behaviors and feelings to the child as usual, but also reflects through the dog: "Kirrie, Chloe is cooking supper. She's very busy. Oh, she said she's making supper for you! She's really pleased to do that!" If the child seems uninterested in the dog's involvement, the therapist can ask the dog to retire to a designated corner of the room that has a dog bed, water, and possibly a bone to chew.

When the child asks the dog to play a particular role, the therapist helps the dog to perform that role, giving hand signals or short verbal cues for specific behaviors. At times, children will ask for a behavior the dog doesn't know, and the therapist simply pretends that the dog is doing it: "Kirrie, Chloe wants you to be the dragon and to roar with fire at the bad guys. Speak Kirrie! Speak! Those bad guys look like they're shaking in their boots!" In this case, the "Speak" cue is known by the dog, resulting in barks rather than a roar, but the child's basic desire for the imaginary play is fulfilled when the therapist captures the essence of "making the bad guys pay."

At any time that the child's behavior is potentially and imminently unsafe, the therapist sets a limit, just as would be done if the dog were not there: "Chloe, you wish Kirrie would put the bad guys in her mouth for real, but one thing you may not do here is touch her mouth or teeth with your hands. You can do just about anything else." If the child persists, the therapist would move to a warning, "Chloe, remember I said that you may not touch Kirrie's mouth and teeth. If you try that again, we will have to leave the special playroom for today." If the child complains about the limit but no longer performs the unsafe behavior, the therapist returns to empathic listening to the child's feelings, "You're really mad that you couldn't get Kirrie to eat them for real. You want me to know that you wouldn't get hurt. It's hard when you can't do things that you want to do."

Directive AAPT

In directive AAPT, the therapist provides more initial structure, which can vary from light directedness to very specific activities for the child or family to perform. The key difference between nondirective and directive AAPT is that in directive AAPT, the therapist makes the decision about what activity to perform, what props or toys to use, and so on. The therapist introduces the activity, permits the child, group, or family to engage in it, and then facilitates it during the session and/or afterward. Empathic listening is often used during these interventions, too, but the therapist is not obligated to let the child lead the way. Usually, directive AAPT interventions are selected to accomplish specific goals, increase awareness of certain feelings or dynamics, provide a unique experience for client reflection and insight, and build new coping or other skills. Some examples of directive AAPT activities are teaching a new trick to a dog, negotiating an obstacle course with a horse, giving advice to a dog for a problem similar to one of the child's, or brushing a horse at the end of a session. Many examples are included in VanFleet (2008).

AAPT for Traumatized Children

Most of the needs of children who have experienced trauma can be met, at least partially, through the use of AAPT. Because nondirective AAPT is both process- and relationship-oriented, it can address many of the needs of traumatized children. This includes the emotional, behavioral, and interpersonal/ attachment issues that arise. It offers endless opportunities for children to feel safe to express all feelings, tell one's story about the trauma, and develop mastery over the traumatic experiences. The presence of the animal can enhance the feeling of safety while providing additional options for the use of touch and interpersonal interaction in the service of these goals. More directive forms of AAPT can be used to target specific problem areas or needs.

Ability to Trust

When children have had experiences that compromise their ability to trust the adults in their lives, it can take some time for therapists to build rapport. Because animals are of such interest to children, and may be perceived as "safer" emotionally, the use of AAPT can help the child engage in the therapeutic process more readily. As the child interacts with the animal, the therapist shows empathy and attunement to the feelings being expressed. Both by association and the impact of the therapist's empathy and playfulness, the child begins to trust the therapist. Later that trust can be transferred to other worthy adults in the child's life, such as parents or other caregivers.

Helplessness and Adaptation

The vulnerabilities that children feel during and after a traumatic event or abuse result in feelings of helplessness and hopelessness. One way to restore a sense of control over their lives is to provide children with experiences where they can develop competencies and see that they can handle things, even simple things. The way out of helplessness is to do something and see that it works.

In AAPT, children can develop self-efficacy, competence, and confidence in a number of ways. They can teach a dog new behaviors or tricks. This involves selecting a trick the dog doesn't know from several options that the therapist considers suitable for that particular dog, then using positive reinforcement-based dog training methods, such as lure-reward or clicker training, to teach the dog. This might take place across several sessions. It is helpful because the child can see with his own eyes that the dog has learned something completely from him. He has also developed new skills of his own in the process. It can add to the child's development of self-efficacy for the therapist to arrange a demonstration of the new trick for the parents or caregivers, so that they, too, can see the child's capabilities. Similarly, a child who is asked to catch and halter a horse and then lead it through an obstacle course using only a ribbon instead of a rope may think the task sounds impossible at first. When she finally succeeds through trial and error, empathy, and creativity, she can see how persistence with tasks and trying new things lead to success.

These types of interventions counteract the sense of helplessness and build a sense of adaptability and mastery. Specific activities can be selected that are likely to serve as metaphors for resilience. The animals have minds of their own and sometimes add their own obstacles, but often children are better able to use patience and perseverance because of their interests in interacting with the animals.

Night Terrors and Avoidance

Children suffering with posttrauma symptoms sometimes need helping learning more effective coping strategies. If a child dislikes going to bed for fear of having nightmares or imagining bad things happening in the dark, a simple activity in which the child directs the dog to turn a tap light on and off can build confidence, mastery, and help overcome the fears. For this intervention, the play therapy dog typically is taught to turn the light on and off prior to working with the child, although a child could assist with the training of this, too. Simple paw targeting with sufficient pressure to turn the light on and off is taught with treats given as reinforcers. A verbal cue is assigned, and the child then asks the dog to perform the behavior, turning the light on and off. Gradually, the child can dim the lights in the room until he is able to tolerate increasingly lower light conditions. The entire interaction is done in a light-hearted manner. The final stage involves the dog "giving" the tap light to the child for use at home.

Sometimes it can be easier to face stressful situations when the child has a friend by his side. With the therapist's help, the child can play games or scenarios in which the child interacts with the dog and shares "tips" about how to handle the situation. For example, a child with separation anxiety can help a dog who "feels uncomfortable being left alone" by telling the dog what to think about or do in an imaginary situation that includes the dog being alone. Next, they practice with the child giving instructions to the dog. It is important that this is enacted as imaginary play rather than as a more serious behavioral rehearsal to retain emotional safety in the intervention. The therapist facilitates lightly by commenting on the dog's feelings, encouraging the child to give advice, and pointing out how well the child's ideas are working for the dog during the role-play. Another way a child can work on this issue is by helping a therapy horse or dog who is missing an eye or is blind. The focus of intervention is on some playful task, such as leading the animal into a different room or pasture, and providing encouragement with each treat given. At the end, the therapist asks how the child felt about the activity, empathically listens to those reactions, and comments how the child seemed to know just how to help the animal who was "in the dark."

Attachment, Empathy, and Victimization

Children who have been maltreated often have attachment problems and difficulties with interpersonal relationships as part of the trauma landscape. Before these children can be expected to demonstrate empathy or caring for others, however, they need to experience what it feels like to be cared *for*. Sociable therapy animals show interest in the children, become excited when greeting them, and readily accept appropriate touch. The therapist can help a child learn how to touch animals in ways that are safe and enjoyable for the animals, and can point out times when the animal seeks out touch from the child. The give-and-take interactions provide many opportunities for a mutually respectful relationship to emerge, and the therapist can also reinforce the "cared for" component by commenting on signs that the animal finds the child interesting and enjoyable. Finally, targeting games, in which the animal makes a physical connection with part of the child's body, such as a palm or shoulder, can enhance these skills. Hide-and-seek games where the child hides and the dog becomes a "search and rescue" dog can help children feel valuable. This is useful for children who have been separated from their families during a natural disaster as well as for those who have been neglected or rejected by their parents in dysfunctional family situations. Many metaphors about attachment and relationship typically emerge during AAPT sessions, and the therapist can reflect them when they do.

Much of the emphasis in AAPT is on the relationship. The therapist helps the child develop healthy, mutual, and fun relationships. When the dog shows various emotional reactions, positive or somewhat stressed, the therapist might cue the child to look at the animal and wonder how the animal is feeling If the child has difficulty identifying animal emotions, the therapist might provide more information, such as, "When you were waving your arms just now, I noticed that Buster (horse) trotted away from you. What do you suppose was going on for Buster?" If the child still has difficulty, the therapist can provide specific information to help the child learn more about emotions, "Do you see how Kirrie is licking her lips and turning her head away? And she just took a step away from you? That means she is uncomfortable with something going on here. She's feeling a little nervous." In most cases, children will respond appropriately, or therapists can set a limit if they do not. It is common when a child begins attending to the animal's feelings to do so spontaneously after a short period of time. In these moments, the therapist can comment, "I saw how you caught yourself waving your arms again around Buster. And Buster stayed right there with you. That's a terrific way to keep Buster's feelings in mind so he will still want to play with you!"

Other caregiving activities that provide opportunities to reinforce empathic behaviors are offered through AAPT. In the authors' experiences, most children engage eagerly in such activities. Children can take animals for short walks, if privacy can be assured, or they can feed and water them. They provide treats when training them, can groom the horses at the end of the sessions, and can learn how to massage the animal for relaxation.

Many children who have histories of being injured themselves are cruel to animals or other children, and parents and teachers sometimes describe them as "lacking empathy." AAPT offers a more direct route to intervene in those behaviors than other treatment modalities. While the therapist certainly sets limits if the animal is threatened by the child in any way, it rarely goes that far. As AAPT provides numerous playful interactions coupled with attentiveness to healthy interactions and focus on the feelings of all parties, children begin to see the animals as individuals. They find it harder and harder to depersonalize them. The therapist creates a climate in which children can have true relationships with another being, receive care and attention *from* that animal, and provide care and attention *to* that animal. In every case where the authors have provided AAPT to children who have histories of hurting animals, their caregivers and/or teachers have reported a cease in cruel behaviors after only a few AAPT sessions. It appears that this learning transfers to other animals that reside with the families. This has not been researched to date, but the clinical findings are compelling.

Anxiety and Fear

One of the primary advantages of involving animals in therapy is that they live mostly in the here and now. Most human anxiety comes from dwelling on the past and worrying about the future. While part of any traumatized child's therapy needs to provide ways to process the past and create a better future, there is also value in living in the present. One perceptive teen, Tina, recognized this for herself, reporting during one session that she began thinking "What would Kirrie do?" when she found herself worrying excessively about a social situation at school. Tina knew that Kirrie had been relinquished to a shelter at a young age by her previous owners, and Tina and her therapist had discussed how unfair that seemed. They also observed how Kirrie had blossomed when put in situations that suited her, and how wonderful it felt to be accepted for oneself. When the school situation arose, Tina remembered that Kirrie was always herself and that she focused on enjoying every minute. This helped Tina move past the unpleasant group in the cafeteria and find someone else to join for lunch.

Self-Regulation

Very often, the AAPT elements of connection, attunement, and playful interaction with the animals within a safe, accepting context created by the therapist helps strengthen self-regulation without more specific intervention. The play activities help calm children, allowing them to lower their defenses and learn to appreciate and accept themselves. Sometimes children must learn to be quieter around animals, or simply to be present with them. Group or family AAPT helps clients learn to communicate and work together more effectively. This can help families look at their own difficulties with less defensiveness, and help them try new behaviors with each other in a safe environment.

More specific self-regulation activities can also be introduced, however. Games that alternate playful arousal with quiet periods, such as a version of the children's game, "Red Light, Green Light," played with a dog or horse in tow. There are some dog training games wherein the child helps the dog do something energetic followed by something slow paced. These activities can be done with individual children or in small groups. The therapist acts in a directive manner with a playful tone during these interventions and cues the children when to move from arousal to quieter behaviors. More examples of activities and targeted symptoms can be found in VanFleet (2008) and Van-Fleet and Faa-Thompson (2010, 2014).

RELEVANT INTERVENTION

The single AAPT intervention described in detail here is called the "No! Game." This activity is designed to encourage children to reveal things they really dislike and provide an outlet for anxieties underlying oppositional behavior. The power of this intervention typically comes from having permission and encouragement to say things the child dislikes doing, and as well as from the laughter involved.

A single prop, a No! button, is a red button with "No!" written on it. Each time the button is pushed, a man's voice says "no" in a different manner. Before engaging in the activity with the child, the therapist trains the dog to press the button with a paw. Once the behavior is established, the cue word of "Answer!" is added so the dog will push the button whenever he or she hears the word "answer." The therapist shows the child the button and explains, "This is a special button that Kirrie will push when you say the word 'Answer!' (During the explanation, the correct intonation of the command is demonstrated.) What you can do is think of some things you really don't like to do, and then, one at a time, you ask Kirrie if she likes those things. After that, you tell her to 'Answer!' Can you think of some things to ask her about? Great, let's start!"

Children often think of things such as (a) Do you like doing your homework? (b) Do you want to do your chores? (c) Do you like bullies? (d) Do you like getting in trouble all the time? (e) Do you want to go to bed early every night? If needed, the therapist can assist the child in coming up with questions that represent things that the child doesn't like. The therapist facilitates during the game, laughing along with the child and commenting about Kirrie's responses, "Ha! Kirrie doesn't like doing chores either!" or "Kirrie really doesn't like those bullies!" In this way, the therapist shows empathic understanding of the things the child dislikes. During this game, children often bring up topics that they rarely have an opportunity to acknowledge openly. They also find it quite funny and their oppositional demeanor changes rather quickly. Children begin to feel that they are not alone with their feelings of frustration or unhappiness. The dog shares them, and the therapist accepts them.

The No! Game can be play with an entire family, with some preparation of the parents to be sure they understand the purpose and process. Parents' fears that the activity will increase oppositional behaviors may need to be addressed. It is important in families or groups to ensure everyone knows that they may not criticize other family members or peers during the game. Often, the No! Game provides release and relief to the whole family, allowing each member to express things they do not like and to put those things in perspective.

CASE STUDIES

Identifying information in the following cases has been disguised to preserve the confidentiality of the individuals.

Case 1: Domestic Violence

A mother, Reba, and her seven-year-old son, Danny, came for equine-assisted play therapy. The boy's father was in prison for domestic violence, which Danny had witnessed on many occasions. Danny was reluctant to go to school and had problems with attention and communication with adults and peers. Reba was frustrated by a number of Danny's behaviors, including his inability to follow her instructions. Danny and Reba were referred to one of the authors (Faa-Thompson) by a domestic violence intervention team for six sessions of two hours each.

Danny was interested in the horses, and he and his mother were cooperative during their first two sessions. They engaged in observations of the horses, an activity with the horses, and brushing the horses at the end. All had gone smoothly and Danny had been able to maintain his attention on the horses and the activities. In their third session, I asked Reba and Danny to make an obstacle course for the horses. I also asked them to place pictures of cartoon hand grenades, bombs, and dynamite within the obstacle course for an activity called "Landmines." I explained that if anyone stepped on a bomb, grenade, or dynamite, they would have to start over. Either Reba or Danny would be blindfolded and would hold the end of the horse's rope. The other, nonblindfolded person's job was to direct the blindfolded person and the horse safely through the obstacle course. Danny and his mother decided that she would be the director this time, and Danny could be the director during the next session. This was interesting as one of Reba's complaints about Danny was that he never listened to her and didn't take instruction well. His teachers had said the same thing.

They selected a pony and then got close enough to put on a halter. Danny put on the blindfold. Almost immediately, Reba began directing Danny toward the first obstacle by pointing in the direction he was to go. I wondered aloud how pointing might work since Danny was blindfolded. Reba burst out laughing and started again, giving Danny long and elaborate directions. At times, she gave directions from her own point of view rather than Danny's which resulted in his going the wrong way. Danny began walking with the pony but soon stopped in confusion. Reba once again gave lengthy and complicated instructions, and Danny followed them exactly. Before long, Danny and the pony were walking around in small circles; they had not yet reached the first obstacle. Reba and Danny both laughed together as he demonstrated that he could follow instructions precisely. The pony, who had a reputation for stopping unexpectedly and refusing to move, followed the blindfolded Danny with a slack rope and without question.

The session went on with Reba giving confusing directions and Danny following them. Despite being "blown up" a few times in the obstacle course, they completed the activity successfully. As they discussed their experience, Reba realized how unclear her directions actually were, and connected the activity with the listening problems at home. She realized that the problems might be more related to her own vagueness rather than Danny's inability to listen.

In the fourth session, it was Danny's turn to direct his blindfolded mother. They chose the same pony. Danny was extremely clear with his instructions and at times, he physically held Reba's elbow to guide her. As Reba was unused to relying on Danny, she seemed unsure about following his directions despite their clarity. Her uncertainty carried down the lead rein to the pony, who stopped many times during the activity and was reluctant to follow Reba. Danny found this highly amusing, yet still wanted to help his mother succeed. Despite the numerous stops, the threesome negotiated the landmines course more quickly than in the previous session and without being "blown up" at all!

At the end of these two sessions, Reba understood just how clear Danny's communications were, and who had to make the biggest changes. Danny and Reba continued to make progress in other areas as well. Pleased with their treatment, Reba sent a text message about Equine Assisted Play Therapy to her social worker to be read at a national seminar on domestic violence. She sent a copy to me as well. The last line read, "Thank you for the opportunity for me and Danny to do Equine Assisted Play Therapy. Thank you for giving me my son back."

Case Study 2: Natural Disaster, Loss, Attachment, Kinship Care

Kiki was eight years old when a tornado struck her town. She had been living with her grandparents on their farm for approximately two years prior to the tornado while both of her parents were incarcerated for drug-related offenses. During the storm, Kiki's grandparents were both killed by a large piece of metal that landed on them. Kiki survived by hiding behind a concrete wall that remained standing. Immediately after this traumatic event, Kiki showed no overt signs of serious trauma symptoms, and it was during this period that she went to live with her aunt and uncle, Margie and Mike, in another state. Her initial adjustment was smooth, but six months later, Kiki's behavior deteriorated. She became hypervigilant of the weather, startled easily by unexpected sounds, frightened by nightmares, and withdrawn at school. She also developed separation anxiety, crying and grabbing her aunt's leg each morning as Margie left for work. After witnessing these symptoms for three months, Margie and Mike sought treatment for Kiki with one of the authors (VanFleet).

Kiki's early treatment included individual, child-centered play therapy without animals and Filial Therapy (VanFleet, 2014), which involves training caregivers to conduct play sessions with their children in the home. These two treatment modalities allowed Kiki to work through many of her trauma fears, and deepen her relationship with Margie and Mike. Her anxious attachment had begun to a shift to a more secure one, and her separation anxiety was considerably reduced. She was still uncomfortable when Margie left in the mornings, or at any time when Margie left home without her. AAPT was introduced to continue building Kiki's confidence and security while providing her with skills for dealing with Margie's absence.

Kiki learned how to greet and interact safely with Kirrie, the play therapy dog. At the time, Kirrie still barked if left in the playroom by herself, and the therapist thought it might provide an opportunity to work on Kiki's separation anxiety further. The first two AAPT sessions were filled with Kiki learning Kirrie's cues, asking Kirrie to perform various behaviors, playing ball with Kirrie, and playing hide and seek with Kirrie. Kiki was delighted when she hid and Kirrie found her every time, laughing heartily. As the game progressed, Kiki confided in the therapist that Kirrie reminded her of the search and rescue dogs she had seen after the tornado who were looking for people. She had never mentioned this to anyone before but clearly, she had drawn a connection. After Kirrie had found Kiki several times, the therapist suggested reversing roles so that Kiki would close her eyes while the therapist helped Kirrie hide somewhere in the playroom. The therapist thought this might help Kiki tolerate being alone while taking some active steps to resolve feelings of isolation. Kirrie "hid" behind the kitchen set, in the puppet theater, and in a chair turned toward the wall. Again, Kiki was happy to play this game and find her.

During the next session with the dog still present, the therapist told Kiki, "Kirrie has this problem that I hope you can give her some good advice about. Kirrie really likes to be with people most of the time, and if she has to stay in a room by herself, she gets a little lonely and uncomfortable. Then she starts to bark. Can you give Kirrie any advice about how she might get more comfortable staying in the room?" All of this information about Kirrie was true, although exaggerated slightly. Kiki provided several ideas, including (a) advising the therapist to leave Kirrie alone only for very short periods; (b) encouraging Kirrie to find something to distract her; and (c) suggesting that Kirrie keep one of the therapist's sweaters nearby so that she knew the therapist would come back for it. Interestingly, these were all strategies that had been tried with her. The therapist responding by saying, "Kirrie, are you listening to this? Kiki is giving us some very good ideas so you will feel more comfortable!" Kiki also suggested that it might help Kirrie to have the television turned on and to make sure there would be some adult she trusted in the house that she could go talk to if she became uncomfortable. Again the therapist commented on her ideas, "I think Kiki has some great ideas for you, Kirrie. You will have to think which your favorite TV show is so we can put that on! Don't you think that Kiki is helping a lot? She really seems to know her stuff!"

After this, the therapist directed a game to help Kirrie become more comfortable being on her own without barking. In the game, they used Kiki's suggestion to leave Kirrie alone only for very short periods of time. After Kiki asked Kirrie for a "down-stay" several times and gave her some treats, Kiki gave the cue for a down-stay one more time, and she and the therapist left the room. The therapist kept her hand on the door knob in the hallway. With an exaggerated facial expression and a whispered voice, said, "Let's count to three! 1–2–3!" They went back into the room, and Kiki gave Kirrie some treats for staying quiet. Using the same approach, they went back out of the room several times, increasing the time Kirrie was alone each time. The therapist carefully managed the time to ensure Kirrie's ability to stay quiet when left alone. At the end of the session, they were able to count to thirty without any barking from Kirrie, and the therapist praised Kiki for helping Kirrie so much. She grinned and told her aunt all about it at the end of the session.

At the next session, Margie mentioned privately to the therapist that she had heard Kiki counting aloud to herself a couple times when they left her bedroom at night. Kiki and the therapist continued the game to help Kirrie feel more and more comfortable being alone. At the end of the session, Kiki gave Kirrie some words of advice before going home: "You can do it, Kirrie! You don't have to worry about anything!" The family continued to engage in home FT play sessions, and Kiki worked with Kirrie every other week on some of her remaining problem areas. Her separation anxiety was almost completely gone after just the second session with Kirrie. Kiki continued to do well in therapy, and her improved adjustment was apparent to Margie, Mike, and her teacher at school. Margie called two years later to refer a friend, and told the therapist that Kiki was doing very well and that they were still having parent–child play sessions on a regular basis.

CONCLUSION

AAPT is an integrative approach that combines play therapy and engaging interactions with live animals. While more research is needed, AAPT has demonstrated clinical effectiveness with traumatized children. Because children often are fascinated by animals, their presence in play therapy can provide motivation, emotional safety, and sufficient therapeutic distance for children to work on a wide range of trauma- and attachment-related problems. Furthermore, the flexibility of AAPT permits its use in nondirective and directive play therapy and can be used with individuals, groups, and families to achieve therapeutic goals. Most importantly, having a friendly and nonthreatening animal as part of the therapeutic process allows the therapist to emphasize the building of healthy relationships that children can learn from and apply to other relationships. Sometimes, the presence of a properly trained play therapy animal can help children learn to trust again, an important milestone after traumatic experiences have shaken that essential ability.

REFERENCES

Bowers, M. J., & MacDonald, P. M. (2001). The effectiveness of equine-facilitated psychotherapy with at-risk adolescents. *Journal of Psychology and the Behavioral Sciences, 15*, 62–76.

Bratton, S. C., Ray, D., Rhine, T., & Jones, L. (2005). The efficacy of play therapy with children: A meta-analytic review of treatment outcomes. *Professional Psychology Research and Practice, 36*(4), 376–390.

Briere, J., & Spinazzola, J. (2005). Phenomenology and psychological assessment of complex posttraumatic states. *Journal of Traumatic Stress, 18*(5), 401–412.

Chandler, C. K. (2012). *Animal assisted therapy in counseling* (2nd ed.). New York: Routledge.

Figley, C. R. (1989). *Helping traumatized families.* San Francisco: Jossey-Bass.

Fine, A. H. (Ed.). (2010). *Handbook on animal-assisted therapy: Theoretical foundations and guidelines for practice* (3rd ed.). New York: Elsevier.

Gil, E. (2010). *Working with children to heal interpersonal trauma: The power of play.* New York: Guilford.

International Institute for AAPT Studies. (2014). *Certification in Animal Assisted Play Therapy.* Boiling Springs, PA: Play Therapy Press.

La Greca, A. M., Silverman, W. K., Vernberg, E. M., & Roberts, M. C. (Eds.). (2002). *Helping children cope with disasters and terrorism.* Washington, DC: American Psychological Association.

Melson, G. F. (2001). *Why the wild things are: Animals in the lives of children.* Cambridge, MA: Harvard University Press.

Melson, G. F., & Fine, A. H. (2010). Animals in the lives of children (pp. 223–245). In A. H. Fine (Ed.), *Handbook on animal-assisted therapy: Theoretical foundations and guidelines for practice.* New York, NY: Elsevier.

Nimer, J., & Lundahl, B. (2007). Animal-assisted therapy: A meta-analysis. *Anthrozoos, 20*(3), 225–238.

Olmert, M. D. (2009). *Made for each other: The biology of the human-animal bond.* Cambridge, MA: Da Capo Press.

Parish-Plass, N. (Ed.). (2013). *Animal-assisted psychotherapy: Theory, issues, and practice.* West Lafayette, IN: Purdue University Press.

Perry, B. D., & Szalavitz, M. (2010). *Born for love: Why empathy is essential—and endangered.* New York: William Morrow.

Reddy, L, Files-Hall, T., & Schaefer, C. E. (Eds.). (2005). *Empirically based play interventions for children.* Washington, DC: American Psychological Association.

Shelby, J. S. (2000). Brief therapy with traumatized children: A developmental perspective. In H. G. Kaduson and C. E. Schaefer (Eds.), *Short-term play therapy for children* (pp. 69–104). New York: Guilford.

Terr, L. (1990). *Too scared to cry: How trauma affects children . . . and ultimately us all.* New York: Basic Books.

Thompson, M. (2009). Animal-assisted play therapy: Canines as co-therapists. In G. R. Walz, J. C. Bleuer, & R. K. Yep (Eds.), *Compelling counseling interventions: VISTAS 2000* (pp. 199–209). Alexandria, VA: American Counseling Association.

Topham, G. L., Wampler, K. S., Titus, G., & Rolling, E. (2011). Predicting parent and child outcomes of a filial therapy program. *International Journal of Play Therapy, 20*(2), 79–93.

Trotter, K. S., Chandler, C. K., Goodwin-Bond, D., & Casey, J. (2008). A comparative study of the efficacy of group equine assisted counseling with at-risk children and adolescents. *Journal of Creativity in Mental Health, 3*(3), 254–284.

van der Kolk, B. A., Roth, S., Pelcovitz, D., Sunday, S., & Spinazzola, J. (2005). Disorders of extreme stress: The empirical foundation for a complex adaptation to trauma. *Journal of Traumatic Stress, 18*(5), 389–399.

VanFleet, R. (2006). Short-term play therapy for adoptive families: Facilitating adjustment and attachment with Filial Therapy. In H. G. Kaduson & C. E. Schaefer (Eds.), *Short-term play therapy for children* (2nd ed.) (pp. 145–168). New York: Guilford Press.

VanFleet, R. (2008). *Play therapy with kids & canines: Benefits for children's developmental and psychosocial health.* Sarasota, FL: Professional Resource Press.

VanFleet, R. (2013). *Animal Assisted Play Therapy: Theory, research, and practice training manual.* Boiling Springs, PA: International Institute for Animal Assisted Play Therapy Studies.

VanFleet, R. (2014). *Filial Therapy: Strengthening parent-child relationships through play* (3rd ed.). Sarasota, FL: Professional Resource Press.

VanFleet, R. (in press). Short-term play therapy for adoptive families: Facilitating adjustment and attachment with Filial Therapy. In H. G. Kaduson & C. E. Schaefer (Eds.), *Short-term play therapy for children* (3rd ed.). New York, NY: Guilford Press.

VanFleet, R., & Faa-Thompson, T. (2010). The case for using animal assisted play therapy. *British Journal of Play Therapy, 6*, 4–18.

VanFleet, R., & Faa-Thompson, T. (2014). Including animals in play therapy with young children and families. In M. R. Jalongo (Ed.), Teaching compassion: Humane education in early childhood (pp. 89–107). New York: Springer.

VanFleet, R., Lilly, J. P., & Kaduson, H. (1999). Play therapy for children exposed to violence: Individual, family, and community interventions. *International Journal of Play Therapy, 8*(1), 27–42.

VanFleet, R., Ryan, S. D., & Smith, S. K. (2005). Filial Therapy: A critical review. In L. Reddy, T. Files-Hall, and C. E. Schaefer (Eds.), *Empirically-based play interventions for children* (pp. 241–264). Washington, DC: American Psychological Association.

VanFleet, R., & Sniscak, C. C. (2003). Filial Therapy for children exposed to traumatic events (pp. 113–137). In R. VanFleet & L. Guerney (Eds.), *Casebook of Filial Therapy* (pp. 113–137). Boiling Springs, PA: Play Therapy Press.

VanFleet, R., Sywulak, A. E., & Sniscak, C. C. (2010). *Child-centered play therapy*. New York: Guilford.

Webb, N. B. (Ed.). (2007). *Play therapy with children in crisis: Individual, group and family treatment* (3rd ed.). New York: Guilford.

Chapter Six

Disaster Response Play Therapy with Vulnerable Children

Jennifer N. Baggerly and Marshia Allen-Auguston

Natural disasters are destructive, overwhelming physical phenomena with catastrophic consequences for children, families, and communities (Rosenfeld, Caye, Ayalon, & Lahad, 2005). The millions of children and families who experience natural disasters every year are threatened by potential loss of human life, injury, and destruction of property. In 2012, a total of 357 natural disasters (e.g., earthquakes, tornadoes, floods, wildfires, and epidemics) across the globe caused 124.5 million victims, 9,655 deaths, and $157 billion U.S. dollars in damage (Guha-Sapir, Vos, Below, & Ponserre, 2013). Four types of natural disasters that children and families may experience include (a) geophysical such as earthquakes, landslides, and tsunamis; (b) hydrological such as avalanches and floods; (c) climatological such as hurricanes, tornados, drought, wildfires, freezes; and (d) biological such as disease epidemics, insects, and animal plagues (Centre for Research on the Epidemiology of Disasters, 2005). Unfortunately, natural disasters are increasing due to climate changes (Guha-Sapir et al., 2013).

Children are the most physically and psychologically vulnerable population in natural disasters due to their physical and cognitive limitations as well as their lack of experience, social power, and resources (Belfer, 2006; La Greca et al., 2013). Yet, their mental health needs are frequently overlooked. To address this concern, the National Commission on Children and Disasters (2010) stated "Children under the age of 18 comprise nearly 25 percent of the U.S. population, or 74 million Americans. Given the significant number of children in our nation, the Commission recommends that the unique needs of children must be more thoroughly integrated into planning and made a clear and distinct priority in all disaster management activities" (p. 5).

Mental health professionals have an ethical and professional duty to be prepared to provide services to children with disaster-related psychological problems (APA, 2008; CACREP, 2009; NASW, 2003). The National Commission on Children and Disasters (2010) encourages mental health professionals who work with children to receive disaster mental health training:

> The Commission continues to recommend that professionals and others who work with children receive basic training in a range of disaster mental and behavioral health issues, to include psychological first aid, cognitive-behavioral interventions, social support interventions, and bereavement counseling and support. (p. 36)

The purpose of this chapter is to prepare mental health professionals to provide evidence-informed, developmentally appropriate mental health interventions for the unique pediatric population of children who experienced a natural disaster. Specifically, the chapter will provide (a) research support on disaster mental health interventions with children; (b) an overview of the vulnerable population of children who survived a natural disaster; (c) the integrative play therapy treatment planning and protocol of Disaster Response Play Therapy; (d) relevant interventions; and (e) a case study of children recovering from a natural disaster.

RESEARCH SUPPORT

Research on treatment interventions with children following natural disasters is limited because the chaotic nature of disasters makes it difficult to conduct randomized treatment control group design (Fox et al., 2012). The National Commission on Children and Disasters (2010) stated "Although research has repeatedly documented the adverse impact of trauma and loss on children, little research exists evaluating the effectiveness of services and interventions to address these impacts" (p. 34). Some of the few disaster mental health children's treatment research studies that do exist show the effectiveness of group and individual interventions based in cognitive behavior therapy (CBT) while other studies show the effectiveness of child centered play therapy (CCPT).

Both individual and group CBT treatment interventions were found to be effective with children after disasters. Two years after Hurricane Iniki, children receiving individual and group CBT psychosocial interventions from school-based counselors had significant decreases in trauma symptoms, compared to those of control groups (Chemtob, Nakashima, & Hamada, 2002). Three to six months after the 2010 Chilean earthquake, second grade at-risk children received school-based group CBT gamelike activities (e.g., using a mandala to calm down, drawing pictures of painful emotions, role-playing a difficult situation to increase self-efficacy, self-esteem, self-control, social skills, conflict resolution, and empathy) (Garfin et al., 2014). Results showed that treatment group children had significantly less earthquake-related worry and PTS than the control group.

Four months after Hurricane Katrina, second- through sixth-grade children who were randomly assigned to individual or group CBT-based interventions showed significant decreases in PTSD symptoms, depression, and traumatic grief symptoms (Salloum & Overstreet, 2008). Fifteen months after Hurricane Katrina, fourth- through eighth-grade children received ten group and one to three individual school-based Cognitive-Behavioral Intervention for Trauma in Schools (CBITS) sessions or twelve individual (option of conjoint parent) clinic-based Trauma-Focused Cognitive-Behavioral Therapy sessions (Jaycox et al., 2010). "Both CBITS and TF-CBT incorporate cognitive-behavioral skills, including psychoeducation, relaxation skills, affective modulation skills, cognitive coping skills, trauma narrative, in vivo mastery of trauma reminders, and enhancing safety" (Jaycox et al., 2010, p. 227). Results revealed statistically and clinically significant improvement of PTSD for children in both treatment groups and statistically significant improvement in depression for the CBITS group.

Child centered play therapy (CCPT) was shown to be effective with children after disasters as well (Shen, 2010; Schottelkorb, Doumas, & Garcia, 2012). CCPT is "a dynamic interpersonal relationship between a child and a therapist trained in play therapy procedures who provides selected play materials and facilitates the development of a safe relationship for the child to fully express and explore self (feelings, thoughts, experiences, and behaviors) through the child's natural medium of communication, play" (Landreth, 2012, p. 14). CCPT is a developmentally appropriate intervention because it uses play, children's natural language, as the therapeutic element of change (Landreth, 2012).

In a randomized control study, Shen (2010) demonstrated CCPT was effective with elementary school-aged Taiwanese children who experienced an earthquake. After receiving CCPT, treatment group children showed significant decreases in their anxiety and suicide risk in comparison to the control group. Schottelkorb, Doumas, and Garcia (2012) also demonstrated effectiveness of CCPT with refugee children who experienced man-made disaster of armed conflict. Children showed significant decreases in posttraumatic stress symptoms in both the CCPT and Trauma-Focused CBT (TF-CBT) groups. Schottelkorb et al.'s finding was important because it showed that CCPT was as effective in decreasing trauma symptoms as evidence-based TF-CBT.

OVERVIEW OF VULNERABLE POPULATION

The research studies described previously are intended to help resolve common disaster-related symptoms in children. After a natural disaster, children's symptoms range from none at all to temporary (i.e., less than a month) to chronic (i.e., more than a month). Typically, children will experience only temporary symptoms that endure for several days to several weeks (Brymer et al., 2006; La Greca, 2008). These potential symptoms can be categorized into six domains of neurophysiological, physical, cognitive, emotional, behavioral, and spiritual (Baggerly, 2010). Neurophysiological symptoms include continuous looping of the fight or flight response and/or the freeze and surrender response (La Greca, 2008). Physical symptoms include headaches, stomachaches, decreased appetite, sleeplessness, bedwetting, or fatigue (Brymer et al., 2006; La Greca, 2008; Vijayakumar, Kannan, & Daniel, 2006). Cognitive symptoms entail persistent negative cognitions such as "the world is ruined," difficulty concentrating, indecisiveness, poor judgments, and diminished academic performance (La Greca, 2008). Emotional symptoms include fear, anxiety, anger, depression, dysphoria, and moodiness (La Greca, 2008). Behavioral symptoms tend to be social withdrawal, clinginess, hypervigilance, bedwetting, belligerence, aggressiveness, school refusal, and traumatic play reenactment (Brymer et al., 2006; La Greca, 2008, Terr, 1990). Spiritual symptoms include negative beliefs about God, abandoned spiritual rituals such as prayer, and refusal to attend religious ceremonies.

Some children may have severe and ongoing symptoms such as depression, anxiety, and Post Traumatic Stress Disorder (PTSD) for months and years after a disaster (Kronenberg et al., 2010). For example, 55 percent of school aged children experienced moderate to very severe symptoms three months after Hurricane Andrew and 34 percent continued to show symptoms ten months post-disaster (La Greca et al., 2013). Similarly, one year after Hurricane Katrina, 61 percent of elementary school children living in high impact areas screened positive for elevated PTSD symptoms (Jaycox et al., 2010). Two years after Hurricane Katrina, 31 percent of parents surveyed reported their children had clinically diagnosed depression, anxiety, or behavior disorders and 18 percent reported notable decreases in academic achievement (Abramson, Stehling-Ariza, Garfield, & Redlener, 2008). Sixteen to eighteen months after the 2010 earthquake in Haiti, 42 percent of children experienced high levels of PTSD symptoms (Derivois, Mérisier, Cénat, & Castelot, 2014).

Demographics that predict higher susceptibility to PTSD include younger age, female gender, and racial ethnic minority (La Greca et al., 2013). Younger children exposed to a wildfire had a higher prevalence of PTSD than older children (McDermott, Lee, Judd, & Gibbon, 2005). Female students exposed to Hurricane Katrina in grades four through twelve reported higher symptoms of trauma and depression in comparison to their male peers (Kronenberg, Hansel, Brennan, Lawrence, Osofsky & Osofsky, 2010). Ethnic minorities, particularly Latinos and non-Hispanic blacks, had worse PTSD-related symptoms than whites (Norris & Alegría, 2008). Other predictors of higher PTSD symptoms after natural disasters include close exposure to traumatic event, high stress after the disaster, limited social support, and negative coping strategies (e.g., blame and anger) (La Greca et al., 2013).

INTEGRATIVE PLAY THERAPY TREATMENT PLANNING AND PROTOCOL

Children's mental health interventions after a natural disaster are needed to prevent and treat severe and ongoing symptoms (Kronenberg et al., 2010; National Commission on Children and Disasters, 2010). Since CBT-based interventions and CCPT have been shown to be effective with children after disasters and since play is a developmentally appropriate approach with children, Baggerly (2006, 2010, 2012; Sweeney, Baggerly, & Ray, 2014) integrated these two approaches to develop Disaster Response Play Therapy (DRPT). Rooted in the literature reviewed above, DRPT is an evidence-informed, manualized treatment protocol for children who experience disaster-related symptoms. The goal of DRPT is to increase positive coping and decrease disaster related symptoms in children ages three to ten years old. DRPT is delivered during the short-term recovery phase of a disaster after Psychological First Aid has already been provided. It is delivered by trained play therapists (i.e., Master degree in Counseling, Social Work, or Psychology with at least a graduate level course in play therapy) who are supervised by a Registered Play Therapist with the Association for Play Therapy.

The DPRT protocol incorporates the NCTSN (n.d.) fourteen core components of children's trauma interventions as detailed in table 6.1. For easy recall, Baggerly (2012) consolidated the fourteen core components into Judith Herman's three phases of trauma recovery, specifically (1) establish safety via assessment, play-based psychoeducation, and effective coping skills, (2) restorative retelling of the trauma narrative via play therapy, sandtray therapy, and expressive arts, and (3) connection with others via Theraplay, thank you cards, helper coupons, and parent consultation (see figure 6.1).

DPRT is intended to be delivered in a group format with individual sessions for sandtray therapy. It is optimal to deliver DPRT through one-hour sessions over a series of days and weeks to allow children and parents time to integrate the therapeutic experiences. If DPRT is delivered over a series of days and weeks, then the format is thirty minutes of CCPT followed by twenty minutes of psychoeducation and parent consultation (Baggerly,

Table 6.1. DRPT Protocol Activities for Addressing Core Components of Children's Trauma Interventions

Core Components of Children's Trauma Interventions	DRPT Protocol Activities
1. Risk screening and triage	PT conducts parent and child interview including assessment prior to treatment.
2. Systematic assessment, case conceptualization, & treatment planning	PT reviews assessment information, determines if symptoms appear typical or atypical, conceptualizes child according to CCPT, and tailors individual treatment plan for child.
3. Psychoeducation	Storybook, puppet show, and expressive arts to teach coping strategies.
4. Addressing children & families' traumatic stress reactions/experiences	Puppet show to normalize typical symptoms and address children and families' traumatic stress reactions/ experiences.
5. Trauma narration and organization	CCPT, sandtray therapy, and expressive arts to facilitate trauma narration and organization.
6. Enhancing emotional regulation and anxiety management skills	Game-based grounding and containment activities. Expressive arts to enhance emotional regulation and anxiety management skills.
7. Facilitating adaptive coping and maintaining adaptive routines	Parent consultation and resources to encourage adaptive coping and routines.
8. Parenting skills and behavior management	Parent consultation to encourage reflection of feelings, therapeutic limit setting, and behavior management.
9. Promoting adaptive developmental progression	Parent resources to educate ways to promote developmental progression.
10. Addressing grief and loss	CCPT and expressive arts to address grief and loss.
11. Promoting safety skills	Storybook and puppet show to promote safety skills.
12. Relapse prevention	Parent resource to prevent relapse and resources if it occurs.
13. Evaluation of treatment response and effectiveness	Post-assessment and follow-up evaluation.
14. Engagement/addressing barriers to service-seeking	Resources to local child advocates.

Source. National Child Traumatic Stress Network (2013).

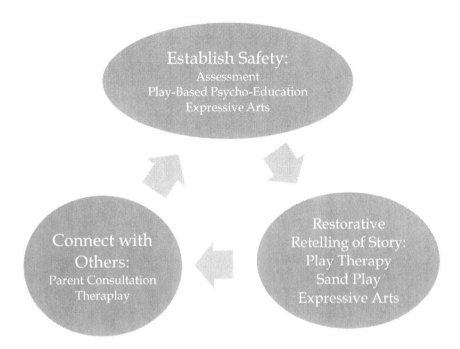

Figure 6.1.   Catagories of Treatment Protocol

2012). However, DPRT can be delivered in one day if a disaster response team has limited time in an area. For example, in response to the 2013 Moore, Oklahoma tornados, our DPRT team adhered to the schedule in table 6.2 for treatment protocol and team development activities. Flexibility with this one-day schedule is essential to meet individual and group needs.

DRPT teams should only go to a disaster area when invited by a government or nongovernment agency (NGO) such as the county Emergency Operations Center, World Vision, Jewish Family Service, and so on. The agency's logistics team will arrange a location such as a school or church and will ask their local contacts to invite children to attend DRPT. Despite preplanning by local logistics teams, the number of children who attend DRPT can fluctuate greatly. No matter how many children arrive, they should be divided into groups based on a two-year age span (e.g., three- to five-year-old; six- to eight-year-old; and nine- to ten-year-old children together) with two to four children per group (Sweeney et al., 2014). The maximum number of children served will be limited by the number of therapists available. If there are five therapists with four children in each group, then the maximum number of children for DRPT will be twenty. Each therapist should be assigned to be

Table 6.2.   DPRT Schedule for Treatment Protocol and Team Development Activities

Time	Activity
8:00 am	Team Group Check In: Greet, focus, and motivate
8:30 am	Therapists set up toys and materials
9:00 am	Parent & child check in: Informed consents, name tags, and brief "where were you during disaster: Was there physical damage to property or persons? What are current concerns regarding your child?"
9:15 am	Large group activities for children while parent completes pre-assessments: Introduction Name Games and Grounding and Stabilization games
9:45 am	Large group CBT Psycho-Education: Accurate information about disaster, dispel myths, and normalize symptoms via puppet shows
10:30 am	Snack & Free Play Break into Small Groups
10:45 am	Coping Skills via Expressive Arts (Mandalas, Shield of Strength, Garbage or Treasure)
11:45 am	Lunch
12:30 pm	Retelling story via Group CCPT
1:30 pm	Relay Races
1:45 pm	Restorative Retelling Story via Sandtray Therapy and Expressive Arts (Chapman Art Therapy, Life Doesn't Frighten Me at All, and Transform a Memory)
3:00 pm	Snack & Free Play
3:15 pm	Reconnecting with others: Group Theraplay and Helping Others via Cards and Helper Coupons
4:00 pm	Parent consultation, referrals, and resources
4:15 pm	Children Depart & Therapist Pack Up
4:45 pm	Team After Action Review: Evaluate strengths and areas for improvement
5:00 pm	Therapist Self Care: Exercise, meditate, read, and rest
6:30 pm	Team dinner

| 7:30 pm | Group Debrief and Supervision: Salient thoughts, feelings, and learnings; Q & A; Recommendations |
| 8:00 pm | Adjourn |

with the same children all day to tailor individual treatment plans and lead them through the activities as detailed below.

RELEVANT INTERVENTIONS

Parent and Child Check In

Establishing safety with children begins with a parent or legal guardian providing informed consent, answering brief screening questions (described in table 6.1), and completing a preassessment such as *Child's Reaction to Traumatic Events Scales–Revised* (Jones, Fletcher, & Ribbe, 2002). This information enables therapists to develop an accurate case conceptualization for individual treatment planning.

Large Group Activities

Physical and emotional safety begins by assembling all children in a child-friendly, safe space to play large group introduction games. For example, the Theraplay Institute (2005) developed a name game in which a child says "My name is ___" with a silly voice or gesture and the group imitates it three times. This game-based introduction activity helps children realize they are allowed to have fun during the day.

Grounding and containment gamelike activities are delivered to the large group of children to decrease hyperarousal and increase physiological and emotional regulation. With soap bubbles, children learn to blow slowly, which emphasizes deep breathing. In butterfly breathing, children place their hands behind their head and gently move their arms back and forth like a butterfly to promote breathing from the diaphragm and decrease their heart rate (Baggerly, 2006). In butterfly hugs, children cross their arms over their chest and gently pat their arms in a bilateral stimulation to self soothe (Baggerly, 2006). In the 3–2–1 game, children identify three things they see above their heads, three things they hear, three things they can touch followed by two and one of each (Baggerly, 2006). This 3–2–1 game helps them focus on the here and now rather than obsessing about the past or worrying about the future. In *Tense like a Tinman and Relax like a Ragdoll*, children learn progressive muscle relaxation by tensing different muscle groups for five seconds and then relaxing (Baggerly, 2006). In the *Delightful Detective* game, children are prompted to detect evidence that they are safe now and interview people on how to develop safety plans and emergency kits (Felix, Bond, & Shelby, 2006). This activity helps children develop discernment to reassure their sense of safety, thereby managing any anxiety they may have. By singing familiar children's songs with revised lyrics that emphasize safety, children learn positive cognitions while promoting physiological regulation. For example, the following words can be sung to the tune of *Twinkle, Twinkle, Little Star* (Baggerly, 2007):

> I am safe and I am strong.
> Take a breath (pause to breathe) . . . and sing this song
> I'm growing stronger every day.
> I know that I'll be O.K.
> I am safe and I am strong.
> Take a breath (pause to breathe) . . . and sing this song.

While singing, children enjoy doing sign language or hand gestures to reinforce key words of safe, strong, and breath.

CBT Psychoeducation

Accurate information about disasters, dispelling common myths, and normalizing typical symptoms can be accomplished through reading a children's storybook such as *A Terrible Thing Happened* (Holmes, 2000) or *Brave Bart* (Shephard, 1998). Therapists can also put on a puppet show in which a smaller puppet acts scared and asks common questions while a larger puppet acts wise and answers the questions:

Lamb: "The tornado blew away my food. I wonder if the Big Bad Wolf caused the tornado."

Owl: "You were scared and unsure of why that storm happened. Tornados are not caused by wolves. They are caused when warm air rises into cold air. The air spins so fast that a funnel develops. It is no bodies' fault. It is just part of nature."

Lamb: "I was so scared of the tornado that every time I try to eat, I get a stomachache."

Owl: "You and lots of other animals were scared. Many animals have a stomachache or wet the bed or refuse to go outside. Usually these things only happen for a short time. You can tell your parent or teacher when it happens. I can also show you ways to calm your body down."

Therapists should develop puppet dialogue to address the concerns parents reported about their children. However, the puppet show should not embarrass children by unwittingly revealing too much specific information.

Coping Skills via Expressive Arts

In order to help children increase effective coping skills, a variety of expressive arts activities are provided. For the mandala activity, calming music is played, lights are dimmed, and children are given a mandala to color (Green, 2014). This meditative activity accesses archetypal energy to calm children's rattled psyche and gives them a visceral experience of physiological and emotional regulation.

For the *Shield of Strength* activity, children are given a plain white paper plate cut into the shape of a shield or crest (Baggerly, 2007). Then they are asked to identify and draw onto the plate one coping strategy to strengthen each of the following five areas: (1) thoughts are calmed by drawing happy memories, writing happy thoughts, thinking of a plan, asking questions, etc.; (2) bodies are calmed by taking deep breaths, exercising, relaxing, eating healthy, drinking water, etc.; (3) emotions are calmed by talking about feelings, laughing, swaying when crying; (4) behavior is helped by playing, cuddling with a safe person, dancing, and helping others; and (5) spiritual is strengthened by praying, singing, reading or listening to scriptures, attending religious gatherings, and so on. The Shield of Strength activity is intended to respect and reinforce coping activities common to children's culture and family.

In the *Garbage or Treasure* activity, children sort out wasteful (garbage) thoughts and actions from valuable (treasure) thoughts and actions (Felix et al., 2006). Children are given a tissue box to decorate as a garbage can and a treasure chest. Then children sort through prewritten statements on pieces of paper (e.g., "The tornado was my fault"; "It is OK to be sad"; "My family and I will never have any fun again"; "I can help by cooperating") and decide if the statement goes in the garbage can or the treasure box. Children are encouraged to write their own thoughts and actions for others to guess if they are garbage or treasure. The therapist helps process these thoughts and actions to facilitate accurate positive cognitions.

Restorative Retelling of the Trauma Narrative

After safety has been established through the activities above, most children will have the needed physiological and emotional regulation and coping strategies to tolerate gradual exposure of their trauma narrative. A restorative retelling of the trauma narrative is facilitated through CCPT, sandtray therapy, and expressive arts. These processes can be conceptualized as systematic desensitization in which children relax through the inherent fun of play while gradually approaching disaster related experiences in the safe presence of an attentive therapist who provides therapeutic responses. CCPT, sandtray, and expressive arts help children reach an emotional understanding of the disaster, resolve internal conflicts, and satisfy needs.

Group CCPT with two to four children is provided in a warm, inviting play area with carefully selected aggressive-release, nurturing, and expressive toys (Landreth, 2012; Sweeney et al., 2014). If needed, therapists can set up a makeshift playroom in a school or church preschool classroom. The therapist observes Axline's (1947) eight basic principles (e.g., establishing a warm, friendly relationship; accepting the child exactly as is; establishing permissiveness; respecting feelings; yielding to child's ability to problem solve, allowing the child to lead; respecting the gradual process; and only establishing limits as needed). Therapists implement standard CCPT procedures of (a) allowing the child to lead the play (e.g., "In here you can play with all the toys in most of the way that you want"); (b) tracking play behavior without asking questions (e.g., "The ambulance drove to the house"); (c) reflecting verbal content without asking questions (e.g., "You had to move to a shelter"); (d) reflecting feelings (e.g., "The baby doll is scared and sad that no one is there" or "You are angry that the tornado took your toy"); (e) returning responsibility (e.g., "That is something you can try"); (f) encouraging (e.g., "You are working hard on that"); (g) building self-esteem (e.g., "You know a lot about hospitals"); (h) setting therapeutic limits by acknowledging the feeling, communicating the limit, and targeting an alternative (e.g., "I know you are angry but people are not for hitting. You can choose to hit the bop bag"); (i) facilitating understanding by stating play themes (e.g., "You are powerful and in control"); and (j) enlarging the meaning by connecting the play to other experiences and accurate cognitions (e.g., "You know what it is like to have your home be destroyed. It was no ones' fault. Sometimes disasters happen"). This restorative retelling of the trauma narrative through CCPT gives children a gross motor, kinesthetic, energy-releasing opportunity to reenact, discharge, and master experiences.

Individual sandtray therapy is provided by displaying hundreds of miniatures in an organized fashion and providing a twenty- by thirty-inch tray with clean white sand in a quiet room (Homeyer & Sweeney, 2010). In order to facilitate a restorative retelling of the disaster narrative, the therapist invites the child to use the miniatures to make a picture in the sand about what happened when he or she was in the disaster. "There are lots of miniature toys here. I would like you to use the miniatures to make a picture in the sand about what happened when you were in the disaster. You have twenty minutes so you can take your time to choose which miniatures you want to use to make your picture. I will be sitting here quietly. When you are finished, tell me and then we can look at it together." After the child finishes the sand picture, the therapist observes the tray quietly for a minute or two to honor the sacredness of it (Green, 2014). Then the therapist states "would you like to tell me about your picture?" If the child is open to discussing it, the therapist can state "tell me about this one or section." Further processing can be facilitated with "if you were going to give this a title, what would it be"; "are you or anyone you know in here"; "what is this one thinking and feeling"; "what happens next"; "what would you add or change to make the picture have a happier ending"; and "what did you learn about yourself by doing this." As part of closure, the therapist affirms the child by pointing out strengths and signs of resilience. Typically, the therapist returns the miniatures to the shelf after escorting the child out of the area. This restorative retelling of the trauma narrative via sandtray gives the child a powerful macro perspective or bird's eye view that facilitates a sense of control and mastery.

Three group expressive arts activities are used to facilitate the restorative retelling of the trauma narrative. In the first activity, the therapist facilitates the Chapman (2014) art therapy treatment intervention by giving each child about ten pieces of white eight- by eleven-inch paper. On the first piece of paper, the therapist asks each child to scribble as much as possible. Then the paper is placed face down. On the next paper, the therapist asks the child to draw a picture of where he/she was and what happened to him/her when the disaster hit. Then the paper is placed face down on top of the other without processing the picture. On the next paper, the child draws who came to help and how they were helped (e.g., the rescue effort). The paper is placed face down on top of the others. On the next paper, the child draws what happened next and places the paper face down. On the last paper, the child draws how they will cope in the future and places the paper face down. After the drawings are complete, the therapist turns over each paper and says "please tell me about this" until all papers have been processed. The therapist affirms each child's strength and resilience.

In the second activity, the therapist reads Maya Angelou's illustrated poem of *Life Doesn't Frighten Me At All*. Then the therapist asks children to identify an image, theme, or character that was salient (e.g., stood out) to them (Green, 2014). After discussing the images, each child is asked to draw a horizontal line down the middle of a large piece of paper and then draw a large circle on both sides of the line. In the first circle, the child draws a scene of something he or she fears. The therapist says "tell me about it and your thoughts about it?" In the second circle, the child draws a picture of how they would conquer the fear followed by the therapist asking them "how did you conquer the fear."

In the *Transform a Memory* activity (Green, 2014), the therapist asks each child to draw or mold out of clay one memory from the disaster. After the child is finished, the therapist says "Tell me about it." Then then the therapist asks the child to transform the image into something helpful or meaningful. Again, the therapist says "tell me about it" and affirms the child's strengths and resilience. These three expressive arts activities help the restorative retelling of the trauma narrative by allowing each child to explicitly tell their trauma story from start to future, resolve "worst moments," and transform lingering fearful images.

Reconnecting With Others

Group Theraplay (Theraplay Institute, 2005) activities are facilitated so children can have a positive, fun ending while connecting with others. The Theraplay Institute (2005) recommends several group activities for (a) structure such as clapping pattern imitation, (b) engagement such as holding hands while singing row, row, row your boat, (c) nurture such as placing lotion on each other's hands, and (d) challenge such as leading a blindfolded person through an obstacle course.

In order to help children focus on others, therapists guide them in making thank you cards for their parents, teachers, firefighters, police officers, and construction workers. They are also guided in making *helper coupons* (e.g., "This coupon is good for fifteen minutes of cleaning or cooperating") to give to parents, trusted neighbors, and teachers. These activities help children develop altruism.

Parent consultation, referrals, and resources are provided when parents come to retrieve children. Therapists who were assigned to specific children inform parents of their child's strengths, resilience, and accomplishments throughout the day. If therapists have concerns or see a need for ongoing therapy, referrals collected by the NGO logistics team are provided. Each parent receives disaster resource material including *After the Storm* (La Greca, Sevin, & Sevin, 2005) and *Parenting in a Challenging World* (NCTSN, 2005). Finally, each child is asked to demonstrate a coping skill they learned for their parent. This parent consultation process fosters hope for the parent and child for a bright future.

CASE STUDY

In order to demonstrate parts of the detailed process above, a case study will be provided. All details have been altered to protect client confidentiality. Four weeks after the 2013 tornados destroyed two elementary schools and hundreds of family homes in Moore, Oklahoma, the first author was contacted by a NGO, World Vision, to lead a DRPT team to the most impacted area. The World Vision logistics team invited children, ages three to ten, to a church to receive DRPT from 9 am to 4 pm.

Nick (pseudonym) was a six-year-old Caucasian boy who was in his garage storm shelter with his mother and older brother during the tornado. His father was out of town. Nick's home was destroyed and his family was forced to move to another town with only the clothes on their back. According to Nick's mother, his current disaster-related symptoms were hyperactivity, aggressiveness, and sleeplessness. Katelyn (pseudonym) was a seven-year-old Caucasian girl who was ducking in the hall with her teacher and classmates at a local elementary school during the tornado. Unfortunately, two teachers and three classmates were killed during the tornado. Katelyn's family home sustained some damage but the family remained in the home while it was being repaired. Katelyn's mother reported her disaster-related symptoms were separation anxiety, hypervigilance, and stomachaches.

Nick and Katelyn both participated fully in the psychoeducational activities. Both held common misperceptions that they could have done something different to protect home and other people. This misperception was addressed during the puppet show by the Wise Owl who said "even the strongest people in the world could not have stopped the tornado and even the smartest people in the world could not have known exactly where the tornado would go to get away from it." During Group CCPT, Nick and Katelyn began playing "run to the shelters" (see table 6.3).

During sandtray therapy, both Nick and Katelyn made separate sandtrays with buildings, cars, and people upside down but rescue cars in the middle on the wreckage. When asked if they would like to add something to make it have a happier ending, Nick added a large muscular male figure he called dad (his father was out of town during the tornado) and Katelyn added an angel to take the teachers and children to heaven.

During the transform a memory activity, Nick used the clay to make a tornado and then transformed it into an Iron Man superhero mask. This transformation seemed to indicate Nick's desire to be strong and protective but acceptance of himself as a boy with limited powers. Katelyn drew the school with a roof caved in and then transformed it by adding a large wooded cross to keep the roof up. This transformation reflected Katelyn's strong religious faith that helped her accept an ability to face the future despite potential danger.

During the parent consultation, both children gave their parents the helper coupons and showed them how to do the butterfly hug and play the Theraplay row, row, row your boat activity. Parents were provided with referrals and resources. The parents and children left DRPT with a sense of confidence and hope to live in a challenging world.

CONCLUSION

Of the millions of children who will experience a natural disaster this year, many of them will have temporary physiological, cognitive, emotional, behavioral, and spiritual symptoms. Unfortunately, some children will experience severe ongoing symptoms that disrupt their development. Children's

Table 6.3.   "Run to the Shelters" Transcript

Transcript	Analysis
K: "Oh no. Hear that. The sirens are sounding again. Run to the shelters."	Play re-enactment is common. She may be experiencing intrusive memories that make it seem like the disaster is reoccurring constantly.
N: "Wait, let's take food and water and the dog."	Signs of resilience in knowing what to do.
PT: "Katelyn, you sound scared but know to run to shelter. Nick, you are trying to be calm and know what to take to the shelter."	Reflection of feeling. Building self-esteem by giving them credit for what they know.
N: "I'll go out to check to see if it is gone."	Child attempts to establish power and mastery. This need many be the basis for his aggressiveness.
K: "No, it is not safe to ever go out again. Come back and duck!"	Statement reflects child's fear and perhaps misperception that the world is no longer safe. This belief may be the basis of her separation anxiety.
N: "Don't worry, I have my army hat and gun."	Another attempt at power and mastery over something more powerful than him.
PT: "Katelyn, you are worried and think it will never be safe. Nick, you are brave and think that gun may protect you from something big and scary. It's important to figure out when it is safe and how to stay safe."	Reflection of feeling and content. Facilitating understanding with balanced thought to help both children learn discernment.
K: "Let me know when it is safe."	Begins to accurately symbolize the fact that the world can be safe again.
N: "Let me check around this corner. All clear. You can come out now."	Begins to accurately symbolize that he needs to carefully look for signs of safety.
PT: "Together, you are helping each other learn how to be safe."	Linking children and encouraging interdependence.

Key: K = Katelyn; N = Nick; PT = play therapist.

mental health practitioners can fulfill their ethical and professional duty to provide disaster relief services by integrating CBT and CCPT.

Disaster Response Play Therapy is an evidence-informed, integrative, manualized treatment protocol for children who have disaster-related symptoms (Baggerly, 2006, 2010, 2012; Sweeney, Baggerly, & Ray, 2014). The goal of DRPT is to increase positive coping and decrease disaster related symptoms in children ages three to ten years old. DRPT incorporates NCTSN's fourteen core competencies in three phases of establishing safety, restorative retelling of the trauma story, and connecting with others. Establishing safety begins with parent and child check-in followed by large group and small group activities. Large group activities include name games, grounding and stabilization games, and CBT psychoeducation to provide accurate information about disaster, dispel myths, and normalize symptoms via puppet shows. Small group activities focus on developing coping skills via expressive arts activities of mandalas, Shield of Strength, and Garbage or Treasure.

A restorative retelling of the trauma narrative is facilitated through small group CCPT, individual sandtray therapy, and small group expressive arts activities of Chapman Art Therapy, Life Doesn't Frighten Me at All, and Transform a Memory. Reconnecting with others is promoted through Group Theraplay activities and art activities to create thank you cards and helper coupons. Parent consultation, referrals, and resources ensure ongoing monitoring and help. DPRT can facilitate healing and confidence for children to live in a challenging world.

REFERENCES

Abramson, D., Stehling-Ariza, T., Garfield, R., & Redlener, I. (2008). Prevalence and predictors of mental health distress post-Katrina: Findings from the Gulf Coast Child and Family Health Study. *Disaster Medicine and Public Health Preparedness, 2*(2), 77–86.

American Psychological Association (APA) (2008). *Disaster Response Network Member Guidelines*. APA Online. http://www.apa.org/practice/drnguide.html.

Axline, V. (1947). *Play therapy*. New York: Ballantine Books.

Baggerly, J. (2006). *Disaster Mental Health and Crisis Stabilization for Children*. (Video). Framingham, MA: Microtraining Associates and Alexander Street Press.

Baggerly, J. (2007). International interventions and challenges following the crisis of natural disasters. In N. Boyd Webb's (Ed.) *Play Therapy with Children in Crisis, 3rd ed* (pp. 345–367). New York: Guilford Publications.

Baggerly, J. (2010). Ring around the rosie: Play therapy for traumatized children. In J. Webber's *Terrorism, trauma, and tragedies: A counselor's guide to preparing and responding. Second edition* (pp. 127–130). Alexandria, VA: American Counseling Association.

Baggerly, J. (2012). *Trauma Informed Child Centered Play Therapy*. (Video). Framingham, MA: Microtraining Associates and Alexander Street Press.

Belfer, M. L. (2006). Caring for children and adolescents in the aftermath of natural disasters. *International Review of Psychiatry, 18*, 523–528.

Brymer, M., Layne, C., Jacobs, A., Pynoos, R., Ruzek, J., Steinberg, A., et al. (2006). *Psychological First Aid Field Operations Guide (2nd Edition)*. Los Angeles, CA: National Child Traumatic Stress Network and National Center for PTSD. [Available at: http://www.nctsn.org/content/psychological-first-aid and http://www.ptsd.va.gov/professional/manuals/psych-first-aid.asp].

Council of Accredited Counseling and Related Educational Programs (2009). *CACREP 2009 Standards*. Arlington, VA: Author.

Centre for Research on the Epidemiology of Disasters (CRED). (2005). *EM-DAT: The International Disaster Database*. Retrieved from www.em-dat.net/index.htm.

Chapman, L. (2014). *Neurobiologically informed trauma therapy with children and adolescents: Understanding mechanisms of change*. New York: Norton & Company.

Chemtob, C. M., Nakashima, J. P., & Hamada, R. S. (2002). Psychosocial intervention for postdisaster trauma symptoms in elementary school children: A controlled community field study. *Archives of Pediatrics and Adolescent Medicine, 156*(3), 211–216.

Council on Accreditation of Counseling Related Educational Programs (2009). *2009 Standards*. Author: Alexandria, VA.

Derivois, D., Mérisier, G., Cénat, J., & Castelot, V. (2014). Symptoms of posttraumatic stress disorder and social support among children and adolescents after the 2010 Haitian earthquake. *Journal of Loss and Trauma, 19*(3), 202–212. doi:10.1080/15325024.2013.789759.

Felix, E., Bond, D., & Shelby, J. (2006). Coping with Disaster: Psychosocial Interventions for Children in International Disaster Relief. In C. E. Schaefer, H. Kaduson (Eds.), *Contemporary play therapy: Theory, research, and practice* (pp. 307–328). New York, NY: Guilford Press.

Fox, J. H., Burkle, F. M., Bass, J., Pia, F. A., Epstein, J. L., & Markenson, D. (2012). The effectiveness of Psychological First Aid as a disaster intervention tool: Research analysis of peer-reviewed literature from 1990–2010. *Disaster Medicine and Public Health Preparedness, 6*(3), 247–252.

Garfin, D., Silver, R., Gil-Rivas, V., Guzmán, J., Murphy, J., Cova, F., . . . Guzmán, M. (2014). Children's Reactions to the 2010 Chilean Earthquake: The Role of Trauma Exposure, Family Context, and School-Based Mental Health Programming. *Psychological Trauma: Theory, Research, Practice, And Policy*. Advanced online publication. doi:10.1037/a0036584.

Green, E. J. (2014). *Handbook of Jungian play therapy with children and adolescents*. Baltimore, MD: Johns Hopkins University Press.

Guha-Sapir, D., Vos, F., Below, R., & Ponserre, S. (2013). *Annual Disaster Statistical Review 2012: The Numbers and Trends. Brussels: CRED*. Retrieved from http://www.cred.be/sites/default/files/ADSR_2012.pdf.

Holmes, M. (2000). *A Terrible Thing Happened—A Story for children who witnessed violence or trauma*. Washington, DC: Magination Press.

Homeyer, L. & Sweeney, D. (2010). *Sandtray therapy: A practical manual*. New York: Routledge.

Jaycox, L. H., Cohen, J. A., Mannarino, A. P., Walker, D. W., Langley, A. K., Gegenheimer, K. L., . . . Schonlau, M. (2010). Children's mental health care following Hurricane Katrina: A field trial of trauma-focused psychotherapies. *Journal of Traumatic Stress, 23*(2), 223–231.

Jones, R. T., Fletcher, K., & Ribbe D. R. (2002). *Child's Reaction to Traumatic Events Scale-Revised (CRTES-R): A self-report traumatic stress measure*. Available from the author, Dept. of Psychology, Stress and Coping Lab, 4102 Derring Hall, Virginia Tech University, Blacksburg, VA 24060.

Kronenberg, M. E., Hansel, T., Brennan, A. M., Osofsky, H. J., Osofsky, J. D., & Lawrason, B. (2010). Children of Katrina: Lessons Learned about Postdisaster Symptoms and Recovery Patterns. *Child Development, 81*(4), 1241–1259.

La Greca, A. (2008). Interventions for posttraumatic stress in children and adolescents following natural disasters and acts of terrorism. In R. C. Steele, T. D. Elkin, & M. C. Roberts (Eds.) *Handbook of evidence-based therapies for children and adolescents: Bridging science and practice* (pp. 121–141). New York, NY: Springer Science.

La Greca, A. M., Lai, B. S., Llabre, M. M., Silverman, W. K., Vernberg, E. M., & Prinstein, M. J. (2013). Children's postdisaster trajectories of PTS symptoms: Predicting chronic distress. *Child & Youth Care Forum, 42*(4), 351–369. doi:10.1007/s10566–013–9206–1.

La Greca, A. M., Sevin, S. W., & Sevin, E. L. (2005). *After the storm: A guide to help children cope with the psychological effects of a hurricane*. Coral Gables, FL: 7–Dippity.

Landreth, G. L. (2012). *Play therapy: The art of relationship* (3rd ed.). New York, NY: Routledge/Taylor & Francis Group.

McDermott, B. M., Lee, E. M., Judd, M., & Gibbon, P. (2005). Posttraumatic stress disorder and general psychopathology in children and adolescents following a wildfire disaster. *Canadian Journal of Psychiatry, 50*(3), 137–143.

National Association of Social Workers (NASW) (2003). Disasters. Social work speaks: *National Association of Social Workers policy statements, 2003–2006* (6th ed., p. 83). Washington, DC: NASW Press.

National Child Traumatic Stress Network (2005). *Parenting in a challenging world.* Available at http://www.nctsn.org/resources/audiences/parents-caregivers/parenting-in-a-challenging-world.

National Child Traumatic Stress Network (n.d.). *Core components of interventions.* Available at http://www.nctsnet.org/resources/topics/treatments-that-work/promising-practices#q3.

National Commission on Children and Disasters (2010). *Report to the President and Congress. AHRQ Publication No. 10–M037.* Rockville, MD: Agency for Healthcare Research and Quality.

Norris, F. H. & Alegría, M. (2008). Promoting disaster recovery in ethnic-minority individuals and communities. In A. J. Marsella, J. L. Johnson, P. Watson, & J. Gryczynski (Eds.) *Ethnocultural Perspectives on Disaster and Trauma Foundations, Issues, and Applications* (pp. 15–35). New York: Springer.

Rosenfeld, L. B., Caye, J. S., Ayalon, O., & Lahad, M. (2005). *When their world falls apart: Helping families and children manage the effects of disasters.* Washington, DC: NASW Press.

Salloum, A. & Overstreet, S. (2008). Evaluation of individual and group grief and trauma interventions for children post disaster. *Journal of Clinical Child and Adolescent Psychology, 37*(3), 495–507. doi: 10.1080/15374410802148194.

Schottelkorb, A. A., Doumas, D. M., & Garcia, R. (2012). Treatment for childhood refugee trauma: A randomized, controlled trial. *International Journal of Play Therapy, 21*(2), 57–73. doi:10.1037/a0027430.

Shen, Y. (2010). Effects of postearthquake group play therapy with Chinese children. In J. N. Baggerly, D. C. Ray, S. C. Bratton (Eds.), *Child-centered play therapy research: The evidence base for effective practice* (pp. 85–103). Hoboken, NJ: John Wiley & Sons Inc.

Shephard, C. (1998). *Brave Bart—A story for traumatized and grieving children.* Clinton Township, MI: Trauma and Loss in Children.

Sweeney, D. S., Baggerly, J. N., & Ray, D. C. (2014). *Group play therapy: A dynamic approach.* New York, NY: Routledge.

Terr, L. (1990). *Too scared to cry: Psychic trauma in childhood.* New York, NY: Harper & Row Publishers.

Theraplay Institute (2005). *Theraplay Group Activities: 85 Fun Theraplay Activities for Groups of Children (Or Even Teens and Adults!).* Chicago: Author.

Vijayakumar, L., Kannan, G. K., & Daniel, S. J. (2006). *Mental health status in children exposed to tsunami. International Review of Psychiatry, 18,* 507–513.

Chapter Seven

Holistic Mental Health Care and Play Therapy for Hospitalized, Chronically Ill Children

Judith A. Parson

Play therapists work in a variety of settings, including private homes, schools, hospitals, and community-based public and private clinics. Families sometimes require assistance to ensure continuity in the therapeutic process, a particularly relevant issue for children who require frequent hospitalizations and experience interrupted schooling because of chronic illnesses. Children diagnosed with chronic diseases or illnesses often endure concurrent mental health and psychosocial problems associated with their illnesses, repeated hospitalizations, and invasive medical procedures. The complex interactions between the biological and psychosocial have the potential to greatly impact development. A conceptual framework is useful in guiding play therapists to meet holistic mental health treatment needs, particularly as children endure frequent hospital visits and changes in their daily routines. Bioecological systems theory (Bronfenbrenner, 2005) is a framework that can be used to guide research and practice in the context of a holistic worldview.

Children with chronic or life-limiting illnesses may benefit from directive and nondirective play therapies encompassed within a holistic mental health care model that considers physiology, psychology, sociology, environment, and culture. This chapter demonstrates how a *mobile* version of play therapy can assist children in integrating their experiences, memories, social systems, and mental health needs without interruption when hospitalizations must occur. A case study involving a child diagnosed with cystic fibrosis illustrates how such integration may facilitate holistic mental health care for children across different institutional settings.

RESEARCH SUPPORT

Holistic mental health care considers all aspects of the child's inner and outer worlds, including past experiences. Memory structures in the brain, such as the *amygdala*, store data during infancy and early childhood. Located within the medial temporal lobe, the amygdala is involved in emotional memory throughout life and is a key structure in the neuroscience of social relationships (Cozolino, 2006; Tottenham, Shapiro, Telzer, & Humphreys, 2012). The amygdala's primary role is to rapidly process and express emotions, especially anger and fear (Siegel & Payne Bryson, 2012). Every emotionally meaningful experience, whether it is a joyful or a painful memory, has a lasting impact on the developing nervous system, whether or not it is able to be recalled later. This process influences our emerging personality, emotionality and relating style (Grille, 2005) and is particularly important when considering the effects of hospitalization and medical interventions on children.

Invasive medical procedures are potential sources of trauma that inevitably become stored as emotional memories for children. Levine and Kline (2007) posited that medical procedures are

> the most potentially traumatizing to people of all ages due to the feelings of helplessness that come from being held down, at the mercy of strangers, and in a sterile room when you are in unprecedented pain. . . . Having to remain still while you are hurting and being hurt is the epitome of the terror of immobility! It is the prescription for trauma! (p. 199)

Many individuals who repeatedly experience this type of trauma learn to adapt to the painful procedures. *Habituation* involves becoming accustomed to a procedure and showing less reaction over time. Research shows that young children do not habituate to stressful invasive procedures as adolescents and adults do (von Baeyer, Marche, Rocha, & Salmon, 2004). Children who are traumatized during their first invasive medical procedure often find successive procedures more difficult (Harris, 1994, Weisman et al., 1998, cited in, McGrath, Irving, & Rawson-Huff, 2000). Rather than habituating, these children may become *sensitized* to the experiences, wherein there is increased reaction to pain over time and/or a reduced threshold to pain, due to severe, poorly understood pain and limited resources to cope (von Baeyer et al., 2004).

Children's procedural anxiety, fear, and distress is well documented (Nabors et al., 2013); specifically, the role of long-term recall in procedural trauma (D'Antonio, 1984; Salmon, Price & Pereira 2002) and use of medical play have been extensively discussed. Medical play is typically used to demystify medical procedures for children, and additional information is used and efficacy is available (see Dahlquist, Pendley, Landthrip, Jones, & Steuber, 2002; Moore & Russ, 2006; Nabors et al., 2013; Parson, 2009; Rollins, Bolig, & Mahan, 2005; Russell & Smart, 2007; Vessey, Carlson, & McGill, 1994; Zahr, 1998). Health care professionals must be aware of strategies to minimize or prevent procedural trauma, pain, anxiety, and fear. Moreover, they must understand the emotional consequences of procedural trauma. While it is easy to understand that health care professionals may focus on the immediate medical needs of the child, there is a risk that they may unintentionally overlook traumatic aspects of the child's experience (Parson, 2008; Shopper, 1995). It is important to ensure that children's medical procedural experiences are ones that they can integrate into their memories in the least traumatic ways.

Fortunately, an increasing range of disciplines offer play therapy to sick children. These include medical doctors, social workers, occupational therapists, early childhood educators, music and art therapists, pediatric nurses, and volunteers (Parson, 2008). Child life specialists, hospital play specialists, and educational play therapists are also employed in some pediatric hospitals (Rollins et al., 2005; Thompson, 2009); however, they are not available in all health care settings and are rarely available twenty-four hours per day.

Play therapy can assist the child in understanding and interpreting hospital-specific language, sights, and sounds (Haiat, Bar-Mor, & Shochat, 2003) within a child-friendly space with toys, activities, and a qualified therapist to facilitate and reflect play expressions. The hospital setting is a complex social system where pain and suffering are mixed with joy and healing. For children, the atmosphere may feel sad, scary, exciting, or very busy. It may look like a place full of strange faces and even stranger machines, smells, and noises. Some of the early promoters of play for children in hospital settings stated that play should be considered just as important as the medical treatment the child receives (Butler, Chapman & Stuible, 1975). Since this time, many play therapy strategies have emerged for children requiring hospitalization (Artilheiro, Chacon, & De Amorim Almeida, 2011; Baratee, Dabirian, Yoldashkhan, Zaree, & Rasouli, 2011; Hall, Kaduson and Schaefer 2002; Nabors et al., 2013) and to assist children as they work through trauma associated with medical procedures (Favara-Scacco, Smirne, Schiliro & Di Cataldo 2001; Nabors et al., 2013; Powers, 1999). These include post-procedural play and debriefing, integrative creative art and play therapy, medical play, or dramatic role-play where the role is reversed and the child provides the medical interventions to a soft fabric or silicon doll.

OVERVIEW OF VULNERABLE POPULATION

Children with cystic fibrosis (CF) may be marginalized because of the need for complex healthcare needs and ever-changing treatment plans. CF is one of the most severe, life-shortening, genetic diseases; and it affects one in every 2,500 births (Cystic Fibrosis Foundation, 2005; Moon, 2004; Shields et al., 2013). It is an autosomal recessive genetic illness, meaning that both parents must be carriers of the gene for their child to have any symptoms; one in twenty-five people are carriers (Cystic Fibrosis Australia, 2005; Moon, 2004; Roehrer et al., 2013). In the United States, approximately 1,000 new cases of CF are diagnosed each year, and three quarters are diagnosed before the age of two (Cystic Fibrosis Foundation, 2014). In previous decades, infants and young children with CF died, but today, more than half of people with CF are eighteen years or older with an average life expectancy of more than thirty years. Affected newborns are projected to live well beyond forty years (Cystic Fibrosis Foundation, 2014; Doull, 2001; Kianifar, Bakhshoodeh, Hebrani, & Behdani, 2013).

CF is a multisystem disorder that affects exocrine gland functioning. In CF, the glands in the respiratory and gastrointestinal systems produce thick, sticky secretions instead of thin, slippery secretions and the secretions may block ducts and passageways, leading to respiratory and digestive absorption problems (Cunningham & Taussig, 2005). Respiratory symptoms include wheezing, shortness of breath, and persistent coughing with phlegm production (Cystic Fibrosis Foundation, 2005). Although health management focuses on optimizing nutritional status and preventing lung infection and inflammation (Doull, 2001), persistent chest infections, which can lead to airway obstruction, require aggressive treatment with chemotherapy (Robinson & Roberton, 1998). Chemotherapy focuses on eliminating and preventing colonization of bacterial organisms, particularly *Pseudomonas aeruginosa,* the most common bacterial pathogen to cause respiratory infection in those with CF (Remmington, Jahnke & Harkensee 2007). Its prevalence in CF patients has led to changes in hospitalization practices aimed at minimizing cross infection (Robinson, 2001), which may mean isolating children in the acute paediatric ward (Wing Lung Alvin, 2013). Additionally, when a child is not responding to a first-line, oral antibiotic treatment at home, they often need a "tune up," which refers to a ten- to fourteen-day hospitalization involving physiotherapy, additional vitamin supplements, a high calorie diet, pancreatic enzymes, and a series of oral, inhaled, and intravenous (IV) antibiotics (Cystic Fibrosis Foundation, 2014; Robinson, 2004).

The administration of IV antibiotics to treat pulmonary exacerbations is the most common reason CF children are hospitalized (Remmington et al., 2007; Tolomeo & Mackey, 2003). In these situations, children with CF require additional care to assist with physical pain and possible psychosocial trauma associated with invasive medical treatment. Children can suffer from anxiety and stress when they enter the hospital environment (Gariepy & Howe, 2003; O'Connor-von, 2000; Parson, 2004, 2009; Whelan, 1997), or receive an injection (Cohen et al., 2001; Hosseinpour & Memarzadeh, 2010; Parson, 2009). The literature shows that the negative effects of hospitalization in children include regression, separation anxiety, sleep anxiety, eating disturbance, and serious aggression (O'Connor-von, 2000). Nurses report that children express procedural distress through crying, shaking, screaming, hostility, lack of cooperation, aggression, withdrawal, anger, vomiting, and incontinence (Parson, 2008).

INTEGRATIVE PLAY THERAPY TREATMENT PLANNING AND PROTOCOL

Play therapy emerges from the humanist perspective; healing occurs when the child plays in the presence of an empathic, sensitive, and accepting adult. The role of the play therapist is to reflect the child's actions and feelings and to participate in the play if invited by the child (Axline, 1969; Landreth, 2012). This method of working with the child is based on the belief that play is the child's natural medium to expression (Landreth). When children are provided with emotional and physical spaces to play out feelings and problems, they experience relief similar to adults' relief after being involved in traditional talk therapies (West, 1996). The therapeutic powers of play provide a means of communication without words and spoken language and enables therapeutic change (Schaefer & Drewes, 2014).

Since the biological, psychological and social well-being of the child contributes to the healing process, it is essential to identify the elements in the environment that support reducing stress in children. The *bioecological theory* of human development is an evolving theoretical system for researching human development over time (Bronfenbrenner, 2005). There are multiple interactions that influence the developing individual; these include the microsystem, mesosystem, exosystem, macrosystem, and chronosystem (Bronfenbrenner 1994). These are often seen as a set of concentric circles nested within each other (see figure 7.1; Bronfenbrenner). The *microsystem* is the innermost level, which contains the developing child and his/her face-to-face interactions with immediate surroundings. The second level, the *mesosystem*, refers to the connections and interactions between the microsystems, such as home and school, which directly influence the child's development. The *exosystem* is concerned with social settings affecting the child's life and development indirectly, through formal organizations. For example, a child may live in a single family home which is influenced by the parent, who is influenced by his/her workplace. The *macrosystem* is the societal

level; although it is not a tangible place, this level involves social construc-
tions regarding the rules, laws, values, and customs of a particular culture
that may impact the child's development. Finally, the *chronosystem* involves
change over time in both the child and the environment.

The bioecological model contains relevance to children with life-limiting
or chronic illnesses. *All* levels of the model impact a child who is affected by
hospitalizations, invasive medical procedures, and abrupt movement between
multiple environments, both directly and indirectly. A mobile play therapy

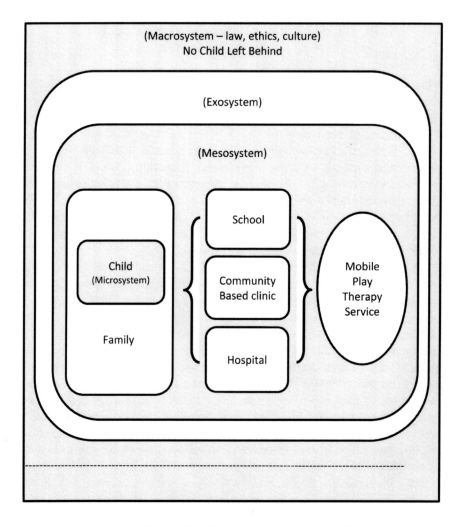

**Figure 7.1.   Integrating Mobile Play Therapy Practice Within a Holistic Bioeco-
logical Systems Framework Adapted from Bronfenbrenner (1994).**

service ensures minimal interruptions to the microsystem and mesosystem, while taking the exosystem and macrosystem into account. Referrals for play therapy begin with a formal assessment to obtain a comprehensive understanding of the child as situated within these systems. Assessment includes developmental history, including physical, emotional and mental health, behavior, identity, self-esteem, preferred learning styles, ability to provide self-care, and relationships. The therapist may observe the child in interactions with parents, teachers, siblings, and/or peers. These interactions assist the therapist in understanding attachment styles and relational behaviors, all occurring under the greater bioecological "umbrella."

The mobile play therapy service accommodates the various needs of children requiring specialized medical treatment and concurrent play therapy. Play mediums include general play therapy toys such as expressive and creative art supplies, puppets, and dolls. Specific medical play toys include doctor, nurse, and patient figures, hospital beds, chairs, tables, and ambulances. The play therapist incorporates "real" medical equipment such as medical dress-up costumes, stethoscopes, masks, tongue depressors, syringes, medicine cups, bandages, medical tape, gauze, cotton wool balls, IV tubing, and medicine bottles. Finally, a soft doll is included so that needling procedures may be demonstrated and/or practiced (Parson, 2009). Children use the toys and expressive materials to reenact their interpretations of experiences and/or to express fears and anxieties about anticipated procedures.

The requirements for a suitable space for play therapy are simple: a small, fairly empty and undisturbed room where the child can be assured there will be no one listening and no interruptions. In a hospital, the child's bed may be considered a safe environment and will sometimes be the only place to hold a play therapy session; curtains should be drawn to provide privacy in the case of open wards. The therapist informs hospital or school personnel about the importance of respecting the privacy of the child. A "do not disturb" sign may also be placed on the door or curtain during sessions.

Play therapists may be directive or nondirective in their approach; directive play therapists will select specific toys to demonstrate a medical procedure or familiarize the child with equipment prior to a procedure. Nondirective play therapists permit the child to choose what to play with during sessions and in what capacity. Therapists often use both approaches depending on the needs of the child and the treatment plan. Most important is that children have the opportunity to act out their anxieties and fears through the play (Webb, 2011) and to optimize healthy coping strategies.

Following therapy sessions, parents, teachers, and hospital staff are encouraged to respect the child's privacy and resist asking how a session has gone. Therapists may need to explain that children sometimes feel pressured when asked to comment on something they may not understand themselves. Furthermore, adults are taught not to place value on the child's actions during session (i.e., "Were you good?"). The child must feel free to express all feelings in an uncensored way; none are "good" or "bad." In the event that the child *chooses* to mention something about the session, parents and teachers are asked to listen and show an interest without making any suggestions or providing advice. While respecting the child's privacy, the play therapist maintains open communication with other adults by holding consistent multidisciplinary team meetings, consulting with parents, and encouraging feedback from teachers and hospital personnel.

RELEVANT INTERVENTION

Biofeedback

Innovative technology and biofeedback helps children through painful and stressful medical procedures. Biofeedback emphasizes the mind-body connection and allows children to become aware of and modify their physiological reactions to stress and fear (Olness, 2008). In biofeedback, the therapist's role is to train the child to control his/her physiological states through diaphragmatic breathing. Once children learn to recognize their body's reactions to pain and stress and begin to control reactions, treatment gains are immediate and provide reinforcement. The results are particularly beneficial for chronically ill children whose bodies may frequently fail them. Biofeedback not only assists children in experiencing feelings of control, but it also encourages them to develop more positive relationships with their bodies (Yetwin, 2011).

BrightHearts is a biofeedback iPad application that is used for children at the hospital. The device combines innovative creative arts with biofeedback. Using controlled breath and pulse rates, the child is able to control the images presented on the iPad, with more colors and images becoming available as the child experiences greater physiological relaxation. Research is underway to further validate this method of biofeedback for children in hospital settings (Khut, 2011).

The Magic Glove Technique

Although technology can be an exciting addition to preprocedural preparation, guided imagery, requiring no materials at all, can also be used with beneficial effects. In the *magic glove technique*, the child's imagination creates a "magic glove" to help reduce the pain associated with needling procedures (Kuttner, 1989). First, the child chooses the color, texture and images for the glove; then, the therapist puts the magic glove "on" by firmly gliding his/her fingers along the child's fingers, making sure the glove "fits." Once it is "on," the therapist locks the sensation in place by gently squeezing the arm where the glove "ends." The therapist suggests that the child's hand and arm with the glove are becoming heavy and relaxed and that the hand does not feel any pain because the glove is protecting it. This suggestion is repeated a number of times and then tested; for example, the therapist may gently press a sharpened pencil into a child's fingertip. The "magic glove" remains on throughout the procedure. Once finished, the therapist assists the child in taking the glove "off" so that the hand can once again feel typical sensations. This technique is easily taught to parents and children and readily available for future invasive procedures.

CASE STUDY

All details regarding the following case have been altered to protect the identity of the client. Eliza, a seven-year-old Caucasian girl diagnosed with CF, was referred to play therapy because her teacher noticed her becoming more withdrawn from her classmates and falling behind in her academic work. Eliza occasionally missed classes when she was required to go into the hospital for routine "tune-ups." Her teacher provided educational activities for Eliza to complete while hospitalized; however, over the winter, Eliza needed additional hospitalization and treatment for a prolonged chest infection. She returned to school approximately six weeks prior to the referral.

After a comprehensive review of Eliza's microsystem and mesosystem, an appropriate space was identified away from the classroom and play therapy began. The play therapist supplied the mobile toy kit described earlier in this chapter with an additional range of medical toys, and Eliza was informed that she was free to choose how she wanted to play with the toys. During the first couple of sessions, Eliza avoided the medical toys and focused on exploratory and relational play themes. Relationship building between Eliza and the therapist was enhanced by playing games, drawing together, and creating stories. In her fifth session, Eliza brought the theme of "power and control" into her play. She role-played being the "teacher" and wrote instructions on the board for the therapist (i.e., "pupil") to follow. She identified a range of activities that she wanted the pupil to complete in a particular order. The therapist reflected feeling helpless because she could not keep up with her school work; Eliza agreed readily that school was stressful.

After another three weeks passed, Eliza went to the hospital for another "tune-up." Her family asked the therapist for help with Eliza's fear of needles. Reportedly, Eliza responded to needling procedures by crying, screaming, kicking, and punching. She had endured repeated IV catheter insertions alone; her parents could no longer bear the emotional anguish involved with witnessing their child's suffering and elected to wait outside. She had been traumatized by multiple invasive procedures and developed correlated feelings of abandonment and powerlessness. The therapist discussed a number of strategies with Eliza and her family to assist with Eliza's fears. The treatment plan included guided imagery, relaxation techniques, and hypnosis. These interventions have been used effectively to support children undergoing medical and dental procedures and injections (Kuttner, 2009; Weigold, 2011). Procedural preparation play and distraction techniques were also integrated.

Eliza's description of a happy time with her family on the beach informed a guided imagery exercise. She recalled playing and running, feeling the sand, selecting rocks and shells, building sandcastles, and swimming in the ocean. Using this imagery, Eliza and her therapist constructed a story that could be retold again and again, beginning with the waves of the ocean. With every incoming wave, Eliza was instructed to breathe in and tense specific muscles. With the outgoing wave, she learned to exhale and relax her muscles. The story engaged her creative mind to build a sandcastle and to imagine the sensations. Eliza rehearsed the guided imagery regularly; and over time, she reported that it helped her relax prior to procedures.

Distraction techniques were devised and used during procedures. These techniques, which engaged Eliza and refocused her attention, included a large *I-spy* book where she could look for items in busy scenes, and a physiologic pain blocker called a *Buzzy* (http://www.buzzy4shots.com). The *Buzzy* is a bee-shaped ice pack that vibrates to provide different sensations and reduce the perception of pain. Current research demonstrates it is effective in relieving pain during blood collection (Baxter, Cohen, & Von Baeyer, 2011) and when used in conjunction with other distraction techniques (Inal & Kellici, 2002a; 2002b). To optimize the distraction techniques, Eliza's mother was encouraged to be in the room during procedures. Prior to this, the play therapist coached Eliza's mother in ways to help Eliza while present. Eliza was given the choice of a few different ways to sit on her mother's lap, and her *distraction kit* included a new *I-spy* book that she had not seen before. When introducing a distraction kit, therapists should only do so immediately before the procedure to maximise interest.

Eliza's book was useful to block her vision of the procedure, which she did not want to see. During the procedure, the therapist and mother engaged Eliza with the book, and Eliza was able to tolerate IV insertion. Her fear of medical procedures decreased as she and the therapist continued identifying coping strategies. Play therapy continued weekly for two months after she returned to school. Her teacher noted that her academic performance had improved and, most importantly, she was playing and engaging more with her peers. Her parents and teacher recalled that she seemed happier and more carefree now that she could tolerate difficult emotions and medical procedures more successfully.

CONCLUSION

A mobile play therapy service takes into account the many systems affecting a child by being portable between divergent hospital and school settings and involving a multidisciplinary team of educators, medical personnel, and mental health clinicians. Play therapists are in the central position to provide psychosocial and mental health treatment to children with chronic illness while hospitalized. These children benefit from a positive therapeutic relationship, relaxation techniques, developmentally appropriate procedural distraction suggestions, and physical comfort to help them endure invasive medical procedures and frequent hospitalizations. Through individual play therapy and coaching of parents, teachers, and hospital staff, play therapists support children during painful and frightening procedures while assisting health care teams in providing the care needed for children to maintain physical health.

REFERENCES

Artilheiro, A. P. S., Chacon, J. M. F., & De Amorim Almeida, F. (2011). Use of therapeutic play in preparing preschool children for outpatient chemotherapy. *ACTA Paulista de Enfermagem, 24*(5), 611–616.

Axline, V. M. (1969) *Play Therapy*. New York: Ballantine Books.

Baxter, A. L., Cohen L. L., & Von Baeyer, C. (2011) An Integration of Vibration and Cold Relieves Venipuncture Pain in a Pediatric Emergency Department. *Pediatric Emergency Care, 27*(12), 1151–1156.

Baratee, F., Dabirian, A., Yoldashkhan, M., Zaree, F., & Rasouli, M. (2011). Effect of therapeutic play on postoperative pain of hospitalized school age children in pediatric surgical ward. *Journal of Nursing & Midwifery, 21*(72), 57–57.

Bronfenbrenner, U. (1994). Ecological models of human development. In *International Encyclopedia of Education*. Vol 3. (2nd ed) Oxford: Elsevier.

Bronfenbrenner, U. (2001) The bioecological theory of human development. In Smelser, N. J., & Baltes, P. B (Eds.), *International encycopedia of the social and behavioural sciences*. New York, NY: Elsevier.

Bronfenbrenner, U. (2005) *Making human beings human: Bioecological perspectives on human development*. Thousand Oaks, CA: Sage Publications.

Butler, A., Chapman, J., & Stuible, M. (1975). Child's play is therapy. *Canadian Nurse, 71*(12), 35–37.

Cohen, L., Blount, R., Cohen, R., Ball, C., McClellan, C., & Bernard, R. (2001). Children's expectations and memories of acute distress: short- and long-term efficacy of pain management interventions. *Journal of Pediatric Psychology, 26*(6), 367–374.

Cozolino, L. (2006). *The neuroscience of human relationships: Attachment and the developing social brain*. New York, NY: W.W. Norton & Company.

Cunningham, J. C., & Taussig, L. M. (2005). *Adult Cystic Fibrosis*. Retrieved May 9, 2005, from http://medicine.ucsd.edu/pulmonary/cf/aboutCF.htm.

Cystic Fibrosis Australia. *Cystic fibrosis facts*. Retrieved 28th April, 2005, from http://www.cysticfibrosisaustralia.org.au/faqs.shtml.

Cystic Fibrosis Foundation. (2005, May 2004). *Facts about CF*. Retrieved February 22, 2005, from www.cff.org.

Cystic Fibrosis Foundation. (2014). *About Cystic Fibrosis* Retrieved April 10, 2014, from http://www.cff.org/aboutcf/.

D'Antonio, I. (1984). Therapeutic use of play in hospitals. *Nursing Clinics of North America, 19*(2), 351–359.

Dahlquist, L. M., Pendley, J. S., Landthrip, D. S., Jones, C. L., & Steuber, C. P. (2002). Distraction Intervention for Preschoolers Undergoing Intramuscular Injections and Subcutaneous Port Access. *Health Psychology, 21*(1), 94–99.

Doull, I. J. M. (2001). Recent advances in cystic fibrosis. *Archives of Disease in Childhood, 85*(1), 62–66.

Favara-Scacco, C., Smirne, G., Schiliro, G., & Di Cataldo, A. (2001). Art therapy as support for children with leukemia during painful procedures. *Medical & Pediatric Oncology, 36*(4), 474–480.

Gariepy, N., & Howe, N. (2003). The therapeutic power of play: examining the play of young children with leukaemia. *Child: Care, Health & Development November, 29*(6), 523–537.

Grille, R. (2005). *Parenting for a peaceful world.* Alexandria, NSW: Longueville Media.

Haiat, H., Bar-Mor, G., & Shochat, M. (2003). The world of the child: A world of play even in the hospital. *Journal of Paediatric Nursing, 18*(3), 209–214.

Hall, T. M., Kaduson, H. G., & Schaefer, C. E. (2002). Fifteen effective play therapy techniques. *Professional Psychology Research & Practice, 33*(6), 515–522.

Hosseinpour, M., & Memarzadeh, M. (2010). Use of a preoperative playroom to prepare children for surgery. *European Journal of Pediatric Surgery, 20*(6), 408–411.

Inal S., Kelleci M. (2012a). Buzzy relieves pediatric venipuncture pain during blood specimen collection. *American Journal Maternal Child Nursing, 37*(5), 339–345.

Inal S., Kelleci M. (2012b). Distracting children during blood draw: Looking through distraction cards is effective in pain relief of children during blood draw. *International Journal of Nursing Practice, 18*, 210–219.

Khut, G. (2011). *BrightHearts Research.* Retrieved June 1, 2014 from http://georgekhut.com/brighthearts/#1.

Kianifar, H.-R., Bakhshoodeh, B., Hebrani, P., & Behdani, F. (2013). Quality of Life in Cystic Fibrosis Children. *Iranian Journal of Pediatrics, 23*(2), 149–153.

Kuttner, L. (1989). Management of young children's actue pain and anxiety during invasive medical procedures. *Pediatrician, 16*, 39–44.

Kuttner, L. (2009). Treating pain, anxiety abnd sleep disorders with children and adolescents. In D. C. Brown (Ed.), *Advances in the use of hypnosis in medicine, dentistry, pain prevention and management.* Williston, VT: Crown House.

Landreth, G. (2012). *Play Therapy: The art of the relationship.* New York, NY: Routledge.

Levine, P., & Kline, M. (2007). *Trauma through a child's eyes: Infancy through adolecence.* Berkeley: North Atlantic Books.

McGrath, P., Irving, H., & Rawson-Huff, N. (2000). The preferred option: General anaestheic for paediatric lumbar puncture. *Cancer Strategy, 2*, 69–75.

Moon, L. (2004). Determinants of health. In P. Magnus, C. Choi & R. Madden (Eds.), *Australia's health 2004: The nineth biennial health report of the Australian Institute of Health and Welfare* (pp. 122–140). Canberra: Australian Intstitue of Health and Welfare.

Moore, M., & Russ, S. W. (2006). Pretend Play as a Resource for Children: Implications for Pediatricians and Health Professionals. *Journal of Developmental and Behavioral Pediatrics, 27*(3), 237–248.

Nabors, L., Bartz, J., Kichler, J., Sievers, R., Elkins, R., & Pangallo, J. (2013). Play as a mechanism of working through medical trauma for children with medical illnesses and their siblings. *Issues in Comprehensive Pediatric Nursing, 36*(3), 212–224.

O'Connor-von, S. (2000). Preparing children for surgery: An integrative research review. *AORN Journal, 71*(2), 334–343.

Olness, K. (2008). Helping children and adults with hypnosis and biofeedback. *Cleveland Clinic Journal of Medicine, 75*, S39–S43.

Parson, J. (2004, February). *Nursing and procedural play strategies for hospitalised children: A review of the literature.* Paper presented at the 2nd Pacific Rim Conference. Growing, Learning, Healing: Partnerships for children's well-being, Crowne Plaza, Auckland.

Parson, J. (2008). *Integration of procedural play for children undergoing cystic fibrosis treatment: A nursing perspective* (Doctor of Philosophy), Central Queensland University, Rockhampton.

Parson, J. (2009). Play in the hospital environment. In K. Stagnitti & R. Cooper (Eds.), *Play as therapy: Assessment and therapeutic interventions* (pp. 132–144). London: Jessica Kingsley Publishers.

Powers, S. W. (1999). Empirically supported treatments in pediatric psychology: procedure-related pain. *Journal of Pediatric Psychology, 24*(2), 131–145.

Remmington, T., Jahnke, N., & Harkensee, C. (2007). *Oral antibiotics for treating infection with Pseudomonas aeruginosa in people with cystic fibrosis*. Cochrane Database of Systematic Reviews. Retrieved February 5, 2008, from http://www.cochrane.org/reviews/en/ab005405.html.

Robinson, M. J., & Roberton, D. M. (1998). *Practical paediatrics* (4th ed.). Edinburgh: Churchill Livingstone.

Robinson, P. (2001). Cystic fibrosis. *Thorax, 56*(3), 237–241.

Robinson, P. (2004, August 13). *RCH Ward 5 West: Cystic Fibrosis*. Retrieved April 29, 2005.

Roehrer, E., Cummings, E., Beggs, S., Turner, P., Hauser, J., Micallef, N., . . . Reid, D. (2013). Pilot evaluation of web enabled symptom monitoring in cystic fibrosis. *Informatics for health & Social Care, 38*(4), 354–365.

Rollins, J. A., Bolig, R., & Mahan, C. C. (Eds.). (2005). *Meeting children's psychosocial needs: Across the health-care continuum*. Austin, TX: Pro-Ed.

Russell, C., & Smart, S. (2007). Guided imagery and distraction therapy in paediatric hospice care. *Paediatric Nursing, 19*(2), 24.

Salmon, K., Price, M., & Pereira, J. K. (2002). Factors Associated with Young Children's Long-Term Recall of an Invasive Medical Procedure: A Preliminary Investigation. Journal of Developmental and *Behavioral Pediatrics, 23*(5), 347–352.

Schaefer, C. E., & Drewes, A. (Eds.). (2014). *The therapeutic powers of Play: 20 core agents of change*. Hoboken, NJ: John Wiley & Sons.

Shields, L., Munns, A., Taylor, M., Priddis, L., Park, J., & Douglas, T. (2013). Scoping review of the literature about family-centred care with caregivers of children with cystic fibrosis. *Neonatal, Paediatric & Child Health Nursing, 16*(3), 21.

Shopper, M. (1995). Medical procedures as a source of trauma. *Bulletin of the Menninger Clinic, 59*(2), 191–204.

Siegel, D. J., & Payne Bryson, T. (2012). *The whole-brain child: 12 revolutionary strategies to nurture your child's developing mind*. New York: Bantam Books.

Thompson, R. H. (Ed.). (2009). *The handbook of child life: A guide for pediatric psychosocial care*. Springfield, IL: Charles C Thomas.

Tolomeo, C., & Mackey, W. (2003). Peripherally inserted central catheters (PICC's) in the CF population: One center's experience. *Pediatric Nursing, 29*(5), 355–359.

Tottenham, N., Shapiro, M., Telzer, E. H., & Humphreys, K. L. (2012). Amygdala Response to Mother. *Developmental Science, 15*(3), 307–319.

Vessey, J. A., Carlson, K. L., & McGill, J. (1994). Use of distraction with children during an acute pain experience. *Nursing Research, 43*(6), 369–372.

von Baeyer, C. L., Marche, T. A., Rocha, E. M., & Salmon, K. (2004). Children's memory for pain: Overview and implications for practice. *The Journal of Pain, 5*(5), 241–249.

Webb, N. B. (2011). Play Therapy for Bereaved Children: Adapting Strategies to Community, School, and Home Settings. *School Psychology International, 32*(2), 132–143.

Weigold, C. (2011). The use of hyphosis in the management of needle phobia. *Australian Journal of Experimental Hypnosis, 39*(2), 189–195.

West, J. (1996). *Child centred play therapy* (2nd ed.). London: Arnold.

Whelan, T. A. (October 1997). *Parenting a hospitalised child: The views of parents, medical staff and nurses*. Paper presented at the "Getting better together" Partnership in care—a new contract between parents and health professionals, University of Western Sydney.

Wing Lung Alvin, S. (2013). Chronic Disease Management in Children Based on the Five Domains of Health. *Case Reports in Pediatrics*, 1–5.

Yetwin, A. K. (2012). *Heart rate variability biofeedback therapy for children and adolescents with chronic pain* (Unpublished doctoral dissertation), Alliant International University, Los Angeles, CA.

Zahr, L. K. (1998). Therapeutic play for hospitalised preschoolers in Lebanon. *Pediatric Nursing, 23*(5), 449.

III

Clinical Applications for Psychosocial and Developmental Issues

Chapter Eight

The Use of Psychometric Play-Based Assessment to Inform Research-Supported Treatment of Children with Autism

Karen Stagnitti

Play is a complex behavior, although it appears deceptively simple. With no agreed-on definition of play available, the development of assessments of children's play behavior has been hindered and controversial (Bergen, 2013). Notwithstanding the debate about what constitutes play, the development of reliable and valid play assessments is critical to informing research-supported treatment of children, as assessments are used to measure the efficacy of interventions and can act as the basis for planning a targeted, play therapy program.

The Child-Initiated Pretend Play Assessment (ChIPPA) is a standardized assessment of a child's quality of self-initiated, pretend play. A reliable and valid assessment of a child's self-initiated play provides the therapist with insight about how a child processes play and how it relates to adaptive functioning. The development of the ChIPPA, as well as the related Learn to Play program (Stagnitti, 1998, 2009), is rooted in both research, clinical work, and professional literature. It was designed for use with children aged three years to seven years who are experiencing developmental issues. This chapter outlines both the ChIPPA and the Learn to Play program, and includes a case study of a child diagnosed with an autism spectrum disorder.

RESEARCH SUPPORT

The term *assessment* is "an objective and standardized measure of a sample of behavior" (Anastasi & Urbina, 1997, p. 4). When measuring behavior, researchers strive to understand the relationship between *raw data* (i.e., the child's actual scored items on the assessment), the *underlying constructs* they represent (e.g., play ability), and the *extraneous variables* that affect the person's score (e.g., not feeling well). The relationship between these three factors underlies the concepts of *reliability*, the consistency of measurement, and *validity*, whether or not an assessment measures what it is supposed to measure.

Step One

The development of the ChIPPA followed the steps of the *classical measurement model* (Anastasi & Urbina, 1997; DeVellis, 1991). The classical measurement model takes the raw score, the underlying construct, and the extraneous variables into account in the development of new assessments. First, the reason for the assessment was articulated. This play assessment was designed to assess a child's spontaneous pretend play within an early childhood intervention service setting. Therapists with large caseloads can benefit from an assessment that captures a child's ability to spontaneously play. To determine essential aspects of play to be captured within an assessment, a review of the pretend play literature and play assessments was conducted. See table 8.1 for a summary of the pretend play assessments available during the development of the ChIPPA.

The Test of Pretend Play (Lewis & Boucher, 1997) was the only clinically viable, reliable, and valid assessment for preschoolers that measured attributes of pretend play. However, the Test of Pretend Play was originally designed as a language assessment and does not assess self-initiated play or formally assess conventional imaginative play and symbolic play in the same session. Thus, the need for a pretend play assessment that provided detailed information about the child's imaginative conventional and symbolic play skills in one single assessment was clear.

Step Two

The next step in the process required that play be clearly defined. By defining play, there is a decrease in the problems associated with play measurement, such as the lack of boundaries, various definitions of play, and the subjectivity of play (Kielhofner & Barris, 1984). A definition of play is bound to theoretical assumptions, and in this case, the theoretical assumptions underlying the ChIPPA are based on the work of Axline (1947) and the cognitive

Table 8.1. Features of Pretend Play Assessments

Name of assessment	McCune Nicolich Symbolic Play Levels (McCune Nicolich, 1977, 1981)
Age range	14–31 months
Play format	Observation of a child playing and interacting with his/ her mother in the home
Play materials	A standard set of 36 toys (list is available from the author)
Play items	Episodes of play are identified and placed into Piagetian play stages of Prior to Stage VI (presymbolic scheme), Stage VI (autosymbolic scheme), Type I A (single scheme symbolic games using a doll), and Type I B (pretending at activities of other people, objects). McCune Nicolich added to Piaget's stages the following levels: Combinatorial symbolic games (several actors are involved in one pretend scheme, e.g., child feeds doll, feed mother), Multischeme combinations (several schemes are related in sequence, e.g., cooking food and feeding a doll).
Time taken to administer	Not given
General comments, including cross-child comparisons	Available through articles and books. Developed because there was no cognitive development assessment for children between the sensorimotor stage and concrete operations tasks. Small sample of 5. Play levels derived from a longitudinal research study. No score is obtained. Cross-child comparisons cannot be made.
Name of assessment	Westby Symbolic Play Scale (Westby, 1991)
Age range	8 months–5 years
Play format	Children are observed playing in a large play room with five sets of toys representing different developmental levels. Initially the child may be left to play on their own, however, for expediency, the examiner may direct the child to play with materials within the room that are age-appropriate for the child. To elicit play, the examiner can give play suggestions to the child. If the child does not respond, the examiner models pretend activities and invites the child to join in the play.
Play materials	The five sets of play areas include: (a) infant stimulation toys; (b) familiar high-realism toys including a home area, shop area, and small representational toys; (c) low-realism toys on familiar and unfamiliar themes, e.g., Batman, airport; (d) a gross motor area; (e) specific theme play area, e.g., bakery, restaurant.

Play items	Child's play is observed and rated on the developmental level of play observed. Developmental levels are as follows: Presymbolic levels—object permanence, means-ends/problem solving, object use, and communication. Symbolic levels—decontextualization, thematic content, organization (i.e., scripts/schemas), self-other relations, and language. If the item is carried out spontaneously the item on the scale is marked S, if the child joins the play of another the item is marked J, if the item is imitated it is marked I.
Time taken to administer	Not given
General comments, including cross-child comparisons	Available through articles and books. Developed as a guide to children's concept development and the children's understanding and use of language. By 1991 the assessment had been used with 600 children in New Mexico. No score is given, Cross-child comparisons cannot be made.
Name of assessment	Doll Observation Scheme (Jeffree & McConkey, 1976)
Age range	18–41 months
Play format	Three 15-minute play segments each with a predetermined sets of play materials. For each 15-minute segment the child is encouraged to play with the play materials for the first five minutes. The examiner models play actions in a random manner for the second five minutes. In the final five minutes, the child is encouraged to play.
Play materials	Doll, bed, mattress, sheet, chair, comb, spoon, cup, large box, small box, tin, tea-towel, two cloth dolls, a stick, flat piece of wood, plastic cone, and duster.
Play items	(a) Percentage of imaginative actions; (b) percentage of elaborate imaginative actions; (c) percentage of imaginative time; (d) number of different imaginative actions
Time taken to administer	45 minutes
General comments, including cross-child comparisons	Available through a journal article. Developed by the authors as a replicable method of recording pretend play. Cross-child comparisons cannot be made.
Name of assessment	Symbolic Play Test (Lowe & Costello, 1988)
Age range	0–36 months
Play format	A warm up period is permitted. Standard presentation of four sets of toys to the child. The child is encouraged to play with the toys and no instructions are given. No time limit is given except to move onto the next set of toys when the child appears bored or has verbalized he/she has finished.

Play materials	(1) large girl doll, saucer, spoon, cup, brush, comb; (2) bed pillow, blanket, small girl doll; (3) chair, table, tablecloth, fork, small boy doll, knife, plate; (4) trailer, man doll, tractor, logs.
Play items	Items are based on directly observed behavior. Items relate to: placement of the toys (e.g., child relates spoon to cup or saucer, or relates doll to table) and, the play actions of the child (e.g., feeds, combs or brushes doll, puts doll to bed).
Time taken to administer	Child allowed all the time needed to complete the test.
General comments, including cross-child comparisons	Commercially available since 1976. The primary purpose of the assessment is an assessment of language potential. The child's total raw score can be compared to an age-equivalent score.
Name of assessment	Test of Pretend Play (Lewis & Boucher, 1997)
Age range	1 year–6 years 1 month
Play format	Part 1 (optional): Observation of child's free play over a 20-minute play session in a familiar environment with familiar toys and people. Part 2: A structured play condition with set play materials. A warm up period is mandatory where the child must produce or model an object substitution. Following instructions on the test form, the examiner elicits play or models play or gives instructions for play. If spontaneous play actions occur they are scored more highly than other play actions.
Play materials	Warm-up toys: unisex doll, bath, cup, saucer, green fur, material, cube, perspex. Play materials: box, counter, felt, tub, stick, cotton, box, board, reel, unisex doll, bowl, spoon, teddy, brown top.
Play items	Instances of elicited pretend play and whether the child refers to his/her body are recorded. Items relate to the child's appropriate conventional use of objects. Play materials items relate to object substitution, reference to an absent object, and property attributions. Scripted play (e.g., the child produces a series of actions in response to the examiners instructions) is the highest level item.
Time taken to administer	Part 1: 20 minutes. Part 2: 20-30 minutes.
General comments, including cross-child comparisons	Commercially available since 1998. Developed as a language assessment and for gaining information about a child's development. It is recommended to be used with the Symbolic Play Test and other language tests. The child's raw score can be compared to an age-equivalent score.
Name of assessment	Singer's Imaginative-ness Scale and Play Interview (Singer, 1973)

Age range	Children 5 years and over for Play Interview
Play format	Imaginativeness Scale—observation of the child during free play in a familiar environment. Play Interview—children are interviewed
Play materials	No play materials needed.
Play items	Imaginativeness Scale: the child is rated on a Likert Scale of 1 to 5. Play Interview: The child is required to state favorite games, and the kinds of games preferred when alone.
Time taken to administer	Imag. Scale: min. of 4 x 10 minute sessions. Interview—time not given.
General comments, including cross-child comparisons	Available through books and articles. Cross-child comparisons cannot be made with the Scale or Interview.
Name of assessment	Lunzer's Scale of Organization of Play Behavior (Lunzer, 1959)
Age range	2 years 2 months–6 years 1 month
Play format	Children are observed in a familiar play environment
Play materials	Toys and play materials are from the environment.
Play items	Adaptiveness of use of materials: The child is graded from 1 to 5 with 5 being use of material in a highly insightful manner and transcending the context. Integration of behavior: The child is graded from 1 to 5 with 5 indicating the highest level of integration including a complex project, with sub-activities carried out in a coherent sequence. The two scores are then added.
Time taken to administer	2 hour minimum observation
General comments, including cross-child comparisons	Available through books and articles. Developed to ascertain a child's cognitive development in relation to play organisation and integration. A child's level of organisation of play related to the child's pretend play skills maturity. Cross-child comparisons cannot be made.

developmental theorists. Assumptions include that (1) pretend play is the mature form of play for the preschool child; (2) pretend play is important in and of itself; (3) play is a voluntary activity undertaken by the child; (4) pretend play is a spontaneous, self-initiated activity of the child which has meaning for the child; (5) the child is a capable being; and (6) pretend play reflects cognitive skills of the child and is important to learning. Pretend play increases in complexity as children develop; therefore, the preschool child prefers pretend play because it is more interesting and challenging than simple forms of play such as the manipulation and exploration of objects.

Pretend play, as defined in the ChIPPA, includes both symbolic play and conventional imaginative play. *Symbolic play* includes substitution of one object to represent another, the attribution of a property to an action or object (e.g., the doll is hungry), and reference to an absent object (e.g., the wave of an arm represents a doorway; Lewis, Boucher, & Astell, 1992). Symbolic play occurs when the child uses an object (e.g., a stick) or a conventional object (e.g., a shoe) in an unconventional way by pretending the object is something else. For symbolic play to occur, the child is required to transcend reality. For example, when a child pretends a shoe is a car, the reality of the shoe is suspended while the child "drives" the shoe.

The conventional use of objects, such as placing a doll in a bed, is defined as *conventional imaginative play* in the ChIPPA. Conventional imaginative play occurs when the child uses conventional toys to pretend, for example, the doll is asleep or the truck is filled with "gasoline." Conventional imaginative play is play that reflects reality. Some authors refer to conventional imaginative play as *functional play* because the child relates the objects functionally; for example, the chair is placed at the table (Casby, 1992; Lewis & Boucher, 1997). However, the attributes of symbolic play can also be observed in conventional imaginative play. For example, a doll can be sick (i.e., property attribution), and a wave of the arm can refer to a large ocean (i.e., reference to an absent object).

The definition of pretend play in the ChIPPA assumes that children can self-initiate their play. Self-initiation of a play action is considered a more complex behavior than when a child is requested to model another in play (Van der Kooij, 1989). A spontaneous child-initiated play assessment evaluates a child's ability to function adaptively without the organization of a supervising adult (Power & Radcliffe, 1991), which has been advocated as "vital for the normal growth and development of children" (Missiuna and Pollock, 1991, p. 882).

Step Three

The ChIPPA was designed to be used in specialist settings where children with developmental difficulties were assessed and treated. Therefore, it was important that the ChIPPA be able to discriminate between those children who could play and those children who could not play, as well as those children who could play *well* and those who could not. An expert panel was consulted early in the development of the ChIPPA in regards to the concept of the assessment, the play materials, scoring and administration, with standardization as a primary goal (Bonder, 1989). Standardization ensures that assessment conditions are always the same (Anastasi & Urbina, 1997), and allows the measurement of true differences between children or children's reactions.

ChIPPA Items

Items were chosen based on the definition of play, the theoretical assumptions underlying the ChIPPA, and important behaviors of play discussed in the literature. For example, authors such as Casby (1992) discussed the importance of a child's ability to sequence of their play actions logically. Items of pretend play assessments that were already available can be found in table 8.1. The following criteria were identified for the selection of ChIPPA items:

• The assessment measures attributes of pretend play such as object substitution, attribution of properties, reference to absent objects, scheme sequencing, and decentration (i.e., reference to something outside of the self).
• Conventional imaginative play and symbolic play are both assessed in the same time frame.
• Play materials include both conventional toys as well as unstructured objects (e.g., a stick, box).
• Self-initiated play indicates a child's ability to function adaptively.
• The assessment is suitable for a clinical setting.
• The assessment can be standardized.

The items chosen to assess the latent variable of pretend play on the ChIPPA included:

Percentage of elaborate play actions: the ability to elaborate play by logically sequencing play actions; includes scheme sequencing, reference to absent objects, and property attributions
Number of object substitution: use of symbols in play
Number of imitated actions: whether or not the child could initiate his/her own play or imitated the modeled play actions of the assessor

Administration

Because the ChIPPA is a child-initiated assessment, children must feel relaxed. The administration of the ChIPPA involves setting up a "house" made by throwing a sheet over two adult chairs. The child and the assessor sit on the floor in front of the house, and the child is presented with a set of conventional toys and invited to play whatever he/she would like. The play materials of the ChIPPA are supplied, constant, predetermined, gender neutral, and developmentally appropriate (Stagnitti, Rodger & Clarke, 1997; Stagnitti, 2007), allowing for comparison between the play of children (Fewell & Glick, 1993). The assessor sits to the side of the house and can move further away from the child if the child is anxious. The assessor can also be involved in the play if the child directs him/her to play. For children aged four to seven years, eleven months, the ChIPPA is administered in two, fifteen-minute sessions (total of thirty minutes). Fifteen minutes of observation is an adequate length of time to obtain a degree of clinical validity (Czerniecki, Deitz, Crowe, & Booth, 1993), with some studies finding that ten minutes of free play with a predetermined set of toys was adequate for play observation (Mayes, 1991).

In the *imaginative–conventional session*, the child is presented with conventional toys and invited to play freely for five minutes. Over the next five minutes, the assessor models five play actions as often as possible without destroying the child's play scene; it is in this section that the Number of Imitations score is recorded. The modeled actions are the same for all children and tailored to age and play materials. For the four- to seven-year eleven-month children the play actions for the conventional–imaginative play session include doll "walks," doll "waves," doll "drives" truck, doll "fixes" fence with a wrench, and doll "pats" cow. For the final five minutes, the assessor is passive once again and encourages nondirective play (i.e., does not give the child any ideas). In the second session, the child is provided with unstructured objects such as, boxes, cloth, and pebbles for the *symbolic play session* of the ChIPPA. The administration format is the same as for the conventional–imaginative play session with three five-minute segments.

ChIPPA scoring

The method of scoring the items was determined to be continuous, which allows scoring to capture a range of responses and discriminate between behaviors of groups of children (DeVellis, 1991). Scoring for the *elaborate play actions,* which captures the process of a child's self-initiated play as well as the level of organization and complexity, is based on the percentage of the elaborate play actions over total actions for each session of the ChIPPA:

$$e \times 100 / (B + f + R + e + \text{imitated actions})$$

Every action of the child is scored using the following coding system: $B =$ behavioral nonplay actions, such as lying on the floor; $f =$ functional play actions where the child relates objects together in a single, nonsequential manner; $R =$ repetitive actions; and $e =$ elaborate play actions. The *Number of Object Substitutions* score is the number of times a child uses an object as a symbol in play, and the Number of Imitated Actions is the number of times a child imitates the examiner. Elaborate play, object substitution, and number of imitated actions are scored three times in the ChIPPA, once for the conventional–imaginative play, once for the symbolic play sessions, and once as a combination of the two play sessions.

In addition to these scores, a *clinical observations form* captures qualitative aspects of the child's play where a number would be less useful. For example, scoring the number of play scripts (i.e., stories during the play) could result in a score of one. A child with a long story would score one, while a child with a short story with many repetitive actions would also score one. The ChIPPA clinical observations form allows the assessor to indicate whether the item was a typical indicator of play or a deficit of play rather than just the presence or absence of the play. Examples of items on the clinical observations include: time spent in play, use of the doll, play scripts, development of a narrative, and engagement with the assessor.

Step Four

The ChIPPA identifies play dysfunction and strengths and interprets play with respect to a child's development and ability to learn. The final version is a norm-referenced, standardized assessment of the quality of a child's ability to initiate pretend play, meaning that children's data can be compared against other children from the population for whom the assessment was devised (Gyurke & Prifitera, 1989). A summary of the psychometric properties of the ChIPPA, including reliability and validity is available (see table 8.2).

The ChIPPA's Impact on Play Assessment

Developing a norm-referenced, standardized assessment of pretend play is in direct contrast and conflict to how many people perceive play. Bergen (2013) noted that much of children's pretend play occurs away from adult direction and supervision, challenging the notion that aspects of play can be captured when an adult is present or directing the scenes. Although the ChIPPA does involve an adult's presence, some children become so involved in their play that they forget that the assessor is there. Additionally, the child is the director of the session, and adults only become involved if the child directs him/her to be involved. Finally, a measure such as the ChIPPA has the potential to highlight the potential impact of environment on changes in children's pretend play (see Reynolds, Stagnitti & Kidd, 2011).

In the literature, there is still debate about defining play and how it should be measured (see Bergen, 2013; Lillard et al., 2013; Skolnick Weisberg, Hirsh-Pasek, & Golinkoff, 2013). Parents, teachers, and other health professionals typically refer children for assessments to determine whether or not there are developmental problems and if so, what to do about them. For therapists working with children with developmental difficulties, there is a need for reliable and valid assessments of the quality of a child's play. Without such assessments, play behavior is often analyzed and described as a functional outcome of a child's lack of motor, sensory, or visual perceptual skills, or as a description of developmental level. That is, play is regarded

Table 8.2.   Psychometics of the Child-Initiated Pretend Play Assessment

Psychometric Reliability	Paper	Sample	Findings
Interrater reliability	Stagnitti, Unsworth, and Rodger, 2000	82 children aged 4 to 5 years. 41 were identified as being at risk for preacademic problems 41 were typically developing. Interrater analyzed by video analysis.	Kappa for Percentage of Elaborate Play Actions: .96-.98 Kappa for Number of Object Substitutions: 1.00-.97 Kappa for Number of Imitated Actions: 1.00-.98
Interrater reliability	Swindells and Stagnitti, 2006	35 typically developing children	Kappa = .7
Interrater reliability	Pfeifer, Pacciulio, Abrao dos Santos, Licio dos Santos, and Stagnitti, 2011	20 children with cerebral palsy aged 37 to 71 months Interrater analyzed by video analysis	ICC (type2,1) .64 (95% CE = .35-.84)
Intrarater reliability	Pfeifer, Pacciulio, Abrao dos Santos, Licio dos Santos, and Stagnitti, 2011	20 children with cerebral palsy aged 37 to 71 months Intrarater analyzed by video analysis	.ICC (type 2,1) = .73 (95%CI: .46-.87)
Internal consistency	Pfeifer, Pacciulio, Abrao dos Santos, Licio dos Santos, and Stagnitti, 2011	20 children with cerebral palsy aged 37 to 71 months	Cronbach's alpha = .73
Test–retest reliability	Stagnitti and Unsworth, 2004	38 children aged 4 to 5 years. Typically developing sample.	ICC (2,1) Elaborate play .73-.85 Object substitution .56 Imitated action 84.2% agreement

Validity

Discriminative validity	Stagnitti, Unsworth and Rodger, 2000	82 children aged 4 to 5 years. 41 were identified as being at risk for pre-academic problems 41 were typically developing.	Eigenvalue = .83 Significant difference between groups for PEPA combined, $F(1,80)$ = 47.56, p<.0001. A significant difference between the groups for Object Substitution NOS combined, $F(1,80)$ = 41.53, p< .0001.
Concurrent validity with social competence and involvement in classroom	Uren and Stagnitti, 2009	41 children aged 5 to 7 years.	Elaborate play with both play materials and the Penn Interactive Peer Play Scale (PIPPS), interaction scale r = .35, p < .05 Elaborate play with both play materials and the Involvement Scale r = .473, p < .01 Number of object substitution and the Penn Interactive Peer Play Scale, Disruption scale r = -.32, p < .05
Concurrent validity with social competence	McAloney and Stagnitti, 2009	53 children aged 4 to 6 years. Researcher assessed children with ChIPPA, teachers scored children on the Penn Interactive Peer Play Scale. Blind to each other's scores.	Elaborate play with conventional imaginative session and (PIPPS) r = .43, p < .01, r^2 = .185 Number of Object Substitutions and PIPPS disruptive scale r = .34, p < .05, r^2 = .113. Effect size moderate.
Validity with clinical groups	Fink, Stagnitti and Galvin, 2012	3 children with ABI	No children completed the time, suggesting cognitive fatigue.

Validity with clinical groups	Pfeifer, Pacciulio, Abrao dos Santos, Licio dos Santos, Stagnitti, 2011	20 children with cerebral palsy	Level of motor involvement was associated with level of play ability
Predictive validity	Stagnitti and Lewis, under review	48 children in follow up study. Assessed with 3 to 5 years after ChIPPA with the School Age Oral Language Assessment.	Complexity of a child's ability to logically sequence their play actions predicted 23.8% of a child's semantic organization for up to 5 years. NOS combined (number of object substitutions with toys and unstructured objects) (β = .281) was more than four times stronger than Age (β = -.065) and was approximately a seventh stronger again than PEPA conventional (logical sequential pretend play actions with toys) in predicting narrative retell up to 5 years.

secondarily, an approach that strongly underestimates the importance of play itself.

OVERVIEW OF VULNERABLE POPULATION

In 2013, the fifth edition of the Diagnostic and Statistical Manual of Mental Disorders (DSM-5) was released (American Psychiatric Association [APA]), and the diagnosis of autism spectrum disorder (ASD) received a lot of attention. The decision to subsume Asperger's Disorder into ASD may be *the* most controversial change in the new text (Reichenberg, 2014). In the DSM-5, children with ASD will be diagnosed on a severity continuum based on significant and persistent impairments in the areas of social/communication and restricted and/or repetitive behavior. Researchers and clinicians have argued that the DSM-5 diagnosis will do a disservice to children with severe symptoms as well as those higher functioning children that will no longer meet criteria (Turygin, Matson, Beighley & Adams, 2013a; Turygin, Matson, Adams, & Belva, 2013b). Those in support of the changes to the ASD diagnosis counter that the dimensional approach will grant service access to those who might have been otherwise denied (APA, 2013). Currently, the incidence of ASD is approximately 1/166 children in the United States of America, with the rate of diagnosis rising (Overton, Fielding, & Garcia de Alba, 2007). Although the presentation of ASD may vary, common features include difficulties in social interaction, understanding social interactions, literality, and flexibility (Nabor et al., 2008). Sensory and motor difficulties have also been reported (Baranek, 2002).

Difficulties in pretend play have been long cited in children with ASD (Baron-Cohen, 1996). Children with autism have been reported to play with fewer objects compared to typical peers and can become intensely preoccupied with parts of an object or toy (Charman & Baron-Cohen, 1997; Nabor et al., 2008). They also spend less time playing, tend to be repetitive in their play, and rarely, if ever, engage in spontaneous, self-initiated, pretend play (Charman & Baron-Cohen, 1997; Nabor et al., 2008). Charman and Baron-Cohen (1997) found that children with ASD were literal in response to play prompts and only produced functional play with prompting (e.g., moving the spoon to the doll after being asked, "What can you do with this?"). In symbolic play, the authors found that children required very specific prompting, such as "Let's pretend. Give the dolly a drink of juice," in order to produce an object substitution which reflected the real object. This level of exchange would be considered early in the process of developing object substitution, as there is a high level of physical similarity between the intended object and substituted object (Stagnitti, 1998). Children with ASD may present with an inability to sequence pretend play actions, engage in role play and social interactions, use dolls or stuffed animals as someone outside of themselves, or create unique play scripts (Stagnitti, 1998).

INTEGRATIVE PLAY THERAPY TREATMENT PLANNING AND PROTOCOL

Children are referred for play assessments in research settings from specialist services, caregivers, early childhood teachers, or health professionals for an assessment of their play ability. Often, children have a developmental difficulty and many may already carry a diagnosis of ASD. A phone intake prior to the assessment allows parents to discuss their child and their concerns. Prior to the ChIPPA assessment, the "house" is set up and the conventional–imaginative play materials are laid out on the floor. The child is greeted separately from the caregiver and told that there are toys in the room with which they may play.

The child enters the room and once the therapist gauges that he/she is comfortable, the assessment may begin. The therapist sits on the floor, invites the child to sit across from him/her, and shows the toys to the child. The child is told, "You can play whatever you would like with the toys and after a little bit of time, I will show you some other toys." The therapist does not tell the child what to do, although he/she may ease shyness or anxiety by asking general questions such as, "Did you come in a car?" "Do you have a dog at home?" The therapist may also move further away from the child to give more space, using clinical judgment about what would make the child comfortable. After five minutes, the therapist brings in a second doll, walks the doll toward the child, and waves the doll's arms. Depending on the child's reaction, the therapist will leave the doll on the floor or respond to the child's direction. The therapist models five separate play actions as often as possible during this middle five-minute period. In the last five minutes, the therapist returns to his/her nondirective stance, only encouraging the child to continue playing. If it is clear that the child is finished playing, the therapist may offer, "Would you like to finish? Let's pack these toys away."

The therapist gets the play materials for the symbolic play session of the ChIPPA and introduces them to the child: "These toys are really different. You can do lots with these toys." The therapist then introduces play materials. After five minutes, the therapist brings out a second cloth "doll" shape, waves the doll's "arms," and "walks" the doll. The therapist models five play actions with the cloth doll as many times as he/she can without destroying the child's play or play scenes. In the final five minutes the therapist encourages the child to continue playing. When the assessment is over, the therapist tells the child, "That's all the time we have to play. It's time to pack up." The ChIPPA is scored while the child plays.

After the assessment, the therapist completes the clinical observations form of the ChIPPA and meets with the child's caregivers to explain the assessment results, putting emphasis on the child's play ability and strengths. Key features of the child's play are highlighted as well as play attributes that need further development. The child is typically present, and the therapist may include the child in the discussion, if appropriate. In cases where a parent may be highly negative of the child, the discussion is postponed to another day when the child is not present.

Following the ChIPPA assessment, the therapist has a profile of the child's play as well as an indication of how the child's play ability compares to his/her peers. While there is no set profile of play on the ChIPPA for a child with ASD, children with ASD usually score below their peers in elaborate play scores with both types of play materials and may or may not use object substitutions. If they do, the object substitution is at an early level of development (e.g., using the pebbles as food or the box for a bed). During the conventional–imaginative play session they rarely use the doll in the play or establish a narrative. They may or may not demonstrate any imitated actions. Often, the actions exhibited during the symbolic play session became repetitive and functional.

The ChIPPA scores, combined with overall performance and parental concerns, can assist therapists in determining if the child requires treatment sessions. The treatment intervention based on the ChIPPA is the Learn to Play program, which begins with the child's strengths and builds on them to increase play ability.

RELEVANT INTERVENTION

The Learn to Play program aims to increase a child's spontaneous ability to initiate pretend play (Casey & Stagnitti, 2011; Stagnitti, 1998, 2004a, 2009). Learn to Play was developed after the author recognized a need in children engaged in early intervention services, many of whom were scoring more than two standard deviations below the mean on the ChIPPA (Stagnitti, 2007). Optimal candidates for this program include children who are at a developmental level of twelve to eighteen months or higher and have at least one meaningful word or gesture. The child's chronological age is not as important as these two factors; however, for older children with little or no pretend play, the play activities are altered. For example, instead of playing on the floor, miniature play sets may be set up on a table.

The assumptions of the Learn to Play program are (1) children are capable beings and will respond if accepted for who they are; (2) the ability to engage in pretend play is beneficial for a child's health and social–emotional well-being; and (3) children need to build their skills individually before they can join a group/peers. In the Learn to Play program, therapists work individually with children to build their play abilities. Goals include self-initiating play, understanding the play of peers, and knowing how to play with toys. There are several key principles for therapists utilizing the Learn to Play program:

1. Get the child's focused attention before playing with toys. This may not be direct eye contact but often involves looking at the therapist's hands or toys.
2. Begin at the child's developmental play level and choosing developmentally appropriate play activities.
3. Use vocal, facial, and bodily signs of enthusiasm to encourage the child to join in the play. This may be the therapist's role in the first several sessions, as children who do not know how to play are not typically interested in play.

4. Allow the child to join when he/she is ready and accept the child's decision not to join the play.
5. Repeat play activities with variation for as long as the child is engaged. If one of the activities is having a tea party, for example, the therapist will continue the tea party until the child is no longer interested. Despite the repetition of the play, the therapist varies each cup of tea slightly so that he/she has a drink, blows on the cup, stirs the cup, gives a drink to a teddy bear, spills the cup of tea, and so on.
6. Preselect the toys for the play session as opposed to the child choosing the toys off the toy shelf. As the play changes with the child's lead, the therapist gets out other toys to continue the play's movement. When a child's play is developmentally below three years of age, too many toys are overwhelming for him/her. Increase the number of toys in the play sessions only when the child starts to understand and engage in the play.
7. Do not assume the child knows how to use the toys. Using descriptive language, describe how to use the toys while playing with the child. An example of this might be, "The teddy is in the truck, I am pushing the truck, the teddy is in the truck" (Stagnitti, 2009). As the child's play ability becomes more complex, the therapist's language changes to add property attributions and context, such as, "Teddy is having a ride in the truck. Teddy is going fast because he is a racing car driver."
8. Talk about the play as it occurs to model language, social interaction, and pretend play ability.
9. Be flexible if the child disengages from the play. Simplify the play activity and bring him/her back, or finish that play activity and start a new activity.
10. Watch the energy levels of the child and know when to stop the session. Learning how to play can be tiring, as the skills are new to the child and he/she will be working hard during the sessions.
11. Become more nondirective as the child increases in his/her play skills. Signs of this will include adding logical play actions to the play, introducing object substitution to the play, developing short stories in the play. Continue cofacilitating at times to increase the complexity of play by adding small problems, then larger problems. Children add problems to their play because it is challenging to them and strengthens intellectual skills as well as play skills.

Many children will begin the Learn to Play program with play skills at a level of twelve months to two and a half years. The therapist chooses five play activities that match the child's developmental level of play and aims to engage the child in the play. For many children on this level, play begins simply, at the one action–one toy level, with activities such as feeding the doll, putting the doll to bed, pushing a truck, throwing the ball to a large doll with big arms, and playing hide and seek with the doll. Each play activity is introduced separately, and the therapist only has the exact toys and objects out that are needed in the play.

Children with ASD who are involved in the Learn to Play program have demonstrated increases language utterances (i.e., more words in sentences), ability to take turns in social situations, time spent in spontaneous play, use of symbols in play, and developing stories in play (Stagnitti, 2009; Stagnitti & Casey, 2011). Additionally, these children generalize their skills from the therapy room to other environments such as home and daycare settings. The Learn to Play program has also grown to include a parental component, the Parent Learn to Play program (Stagnitti, 2014), in which the parent learns about play ability skills and is shown how to interact with their child in play. The school version of the Learn to Play program involves playing with groups of children (see O'Connor & Stagnitti, 2011; Stagnitti, O'Connor & Sheppard, 2012). Both the parent and school versions of Learn to Play are currently being researched.

CASE STUDY

All details in this case example have been altered to protect client confidentiality. James was four years old and referred to the Learn to Play program for twelve sessions. During the ChIPPA assessment, he could not play for very long and his actions were functional and repetitive. He demonstrated no pretend play, did not use symbols, and was having difficulty with language and social skills.

James came in for his first session with his mouth turned down, his arms crossed, a frown and his eyes fixed firmly on the floor. The therapist greeted him but did not receive a response. James screamed as soon as he walked into the room and soon began kicking. The therapist, unsurprised by this reaction, waited for James' parents to calm him down without providing any additional intervention. Once James had calmed, the therapist told him and his parents that she would start with having a cup of tea with the teddy. James remained on the floor with his head under his mother's chair, unwilling to move. The therapist set up the tea party and invited one of the teddy bears to have a drink, reassuring James' parents that James would participate when he was ready. The therapist drank and stirred the tea, offering cups to James' parents. James remained on the floor.

After about ten minutes, the teddy bear "saw" James' foot. The teddy bear "climbed" off the chair and went to lie near James while the therapist continued drinking cups of tea. The teddy bear reported back to the therapist that he saw something but was not sure what. They continued their cups of tea and the therapist noticed that James had turned his head and was looking up occasionally to track the play. The therapist and teddy bear began making some "food" out of Play-Doh; James moved onto his side so he could see. The therapist did not make eye contact; rather, she continued to play with the teddy bear. James' mom helped the teddy bear to go and find James, who had now moved to a sitting position but did not come any further. James slowly moved to his mother's lap and put his arms around her neck while he watched; the therapist and teddy bear continued playing. Suddenly, the teddy bear fell off his chair, and James giggled. He was now involved in the play! The therapist asked the teddy bear why he had fallen off the chair, and James giggled again. The therapist and teddy bear offered James some Play-Doh food to "eat" and "drink." They played for eight more minutes before it was time for James and his parents to leave.

In the next session, James sat on his mother's lap upon entering the room. It appeared to the therapist that James felt more comfortable, so she began with an active play activity involving a doll hiding under a large cloth. The therapist hid the doll, and then tried to find her but was unsuccessful. James smiled and giggled as the therapist continued searching for the doll. He got off his mother's lap without speaking, went to where the doll was "hiding" and pulled off the cloth enthusiastically. "Aha!" the therapist said, "You found her! I couldn't find her anywhere." The doll hid again, followed by James and his mother. James continued moving further away from his mother. By the end of the session, he and the therapist were cooking with PlayDoh at the other end of the room. At the start of the third session, James came straight into the room and put the doll under the cloth. The therapist and James played "hide and seek" with the doll and "catch" with the doll and a ball. The therapist introduced the trucks, and James gave the teddy bear a ride in the truck. James was engaged for the full session, which was fifty minutes.

In the fourth session, the therapist introduced object substitution by handing James a block. She and James' mother also had one block each, and the therapist explained that the block was a phone that she was going to use to call him. James insisted that it was a block, and told the therapist that he would show her how to use it properly. The therapist demonstrated how James could hold the block to his face and talk into it like a phone; she went to the other side of the room and "called" him. James' mother encouraged him, saying, "Your phone is ringing! Quick! Answer it." James answered it. By the end of the session, James had made the transition from "It's a block," to "The block can be a phone." From then on, the therapist introduced a new object substitution each session.

Over the next seven sessions, James engaged fully in the play and was happy to come to sessions. Sometimes he arrived quacking like a duck, or skipping, and once his mother said he clapped in the car when he realized he was coming to the play session. He engaged freely and spontaneously with the toys, and he knew how to use them. By the completion of his sessions, James could logically sequence up to twenty actions in play spontaneously, substitute objects, use the doll as if alive, and take on the role of shopkeeper, train driver, and parent. In object substitution, he used increasingly more abstract and less physically similar objects to the intended object. In the same play session, James used a row of chairs for a train, a large cloth over a chair for a mountain, and a block as a phone, pillow, and part of a bridge. He was more flexible and could tolerate the introduction of problems into his play. In one play scene, the teddy bear fell from the mountain and could not walk. The therapist could not find the keys to the ambulance. James came up with an alternative solution of using a truck that belonged to another teddy and the teddy bear was able to get to the doctor.

James also began putting problems into the play. Once, during a scene in which people were riding a train to the zoo, James had a lion roar and start to jump around on the other animals. The people became scared and ran back onto the train, which started to move away from the zoo. James made one of the male dolls jump off the train and become the lion tamer. In this same example, James tolerated taking turns as the therapist continued to take the train around the room while James waited for it to return. Outside of the playroom, James was speaking more, using more words in his sentences. His mother and preschool teacher commented that he was understanding turn taking in social interactions with his peers. He was also less disruptive to the play of others.

On the last session, the ChIPPA assessment was readministered. Scores demonstrated that while James was still below the normal range in conventional–imaginative play (75, with normal range being 85 to 115), he was within normal range for symbolic play (90). James was able to play for the duration of the ChIPPA, use the dolls, use property attributions and absent objects through his play; he was also beginning to develop a narrative in his play.

CONCLUSION

Pretend play requires a child to bring together many skills. The development of the ChIPPA as a norm-referenced, standardized assessment of pretend play led to the development of the Learn to Play program which focuses on helping children with developmental difficulties, including ASD, increase their pretend play abilities. Through play, children are able to explore and understand more of their world and begin to engage with peers and the world around them.

REFERENCES

American Psychiatric Association. (2013). *Diagnostic and statistical manual of mental disorders* (5th ed.). Arlington: VA: American Psychiatric Publishing.

Anastasi, A., & Urbina, S. (1997). *Psychological testing*. New Jersey: Prentice-Hall Inc.

Axline, V. (1947). *Play therapy*. New York: Penguin Group.

Baranek, G. (2002). Efficacy of sensory and motor interventions for children with autism. *Journal of Autism and Developmental Disorders, 12*(5), 397–422.

Baron-Cohen, S. (1996). *Mindblindness. An essay on autism and theory of mind.* London: MIT Press.

Bergen, D. (2013). Does pretend play matter? Searching for evidence: comment on Lillard et al. (2013). *Psychological Bulletin, 139*(1), 45–58.

Bonder, B. (1989). Planning the initial version. In L. J. Miller (Ed.), *Developing norm-referenced standardized tests* (pp. 15–42). Binghamton: The Haworth Press, Inc.

Casby, M. W. (1992). Symbolic play: development and assessment considerations. *Infants and Young Children, 4,* 343–48.

Charman, T., & Baron-Cohen, S., (1997). Brief report: prompted pretend play in autism. *Journal of Autism and Developmental Disorders, 27*(3), 325–332.

Czerniecki, J. G., Deitz, J. C., Crowe, T. K., & Booth, C. L. (1993). Attending behavior: a descriptive study of children aged 18 through 23 months. *American Journal of Occupational Therapy, 47,* 708–716.

DeVellis, R. (1991). *Scale development. Theory and applications.* Newbury Park, CA: Sage Publications.

Fewell, R. R., & Glick, M. P. (1993). Observing play: an appropriate process for learning and assessment. *Infants and Young Children, 5,* 35–43.

Gyurke, J., & Prifitera, A. (1989). Standardizing an assessment. In L. J. Miller (Ed.), *Developing norm-referenced standardized tests* (pp. 63–90). Binghamton: The Haworth Press, Inc.

Jeffree, D. M., & McConkey, R. (1976). An observation scheme for recording children's imaginative doll play. *Journal of child Psychology, 17,* 189–197.

Kielhofner, G., & Barris, R. (1984). Collecting data on play: a critique of available methods. *The Occupational Therapy Journal of Research, 4,* 151–180.

Lewis, V., Boucher, J., & Astell, A. (1992). The assessment of symbolic play in young children: a prototype test. *European Journal of Disorders of Communications, 27,* 231–245.

Lewis, V., & Boucher, J. (1997). *The Test of Pretend Play Manual.* London: Psychological Services.

Lillard, A. S., Lerner, M. D., Hopkins, E. J., Dore, R. A., Smith, E. D., & Palmquist, C. M. (2013). The impact of pretend play on children's development: A review of the evidence. *Psychological Bulletin, 139*(1), 1–34.

Lunzer, E. A. (1959). Intellectual development in the play of young children. *Educational Review, 11,* 205–224.

McAloney, K., & Stagnitti, K. (2009). Pretend Play and Social Play: the concurrent validity of the Child-Initiated Pretend Play Assessment. *International Journal of Play Therapy, 18*(2), 99–113.

McCune Nicolich, L. (1977). Beyond sensorimotor intelligence: assessment of symbolic maturity through analysis of pretend play. *Merrill-Palmer Quarterly, 23,* 89–99.

McCune Nicolich, L. (1981). Toward symbolic functioning: structure of early pretend games and potential parallels with language. *Child Development, 52,* 785–797.

Mayes, S. D. (1991). Play assessment of preschool hyperactivity. In C. Shaefer, K. Gitlin & A. Sandgrund (Eds.), *Play diagnosis and assessment* (pp. 249–281). New York: John Wiley & Sons Inc.

Nabor, F., Bakermans-Kranenburg, M. J., van IJzendoorn, M. H., Swinkels, S., Buitelaar, J., Dietz, C., van Daalen, E., & van Engeland, H. (2008). Play behavior and attachment in toddlers with autism. *Journal of Autism and Developmental Disorders, 38,* 857–866.

O'Connor, C., & Stagnitti, K. (2011). Play, behavior, language and social skills: The comparison of a play and a non-play intervention within a specialist school setting. *Research in Developmental Disabilities, 32,* 1205–1211.

Overton, T., Fielding, C., & Garcia de Alba, R. (2007). Differential diagnosis of Hispanic children referred for autism spectrum disorders: complex issues. *Journal of Autism and Developmental Disorders, 37*, 1996–2007.

Reichenberg, L. (2014). *DSM-5 essentials: The savvy clinician's guide to the changes in criteria.* New York: Wiley.

Reynolds, E., Stagnitti, K., & Kidd, E. (2011). Play, language and social skills of children aged 4–6 years attending a play based curriculum school and a traditionally structured classroom curriculum school in low socio-economic areas. *Australian Journal of Early Childhood, 36*(4), 120–130.

Singer, J. E. (1973). *The child's world of make-believe.* New York: Academic Press.

Skolnick Weisberg, D., Hirsh-Pasek, K., & Golinkoff, R. (2013). Embracing complexity: re-thinking the relation between play and leraning: comment on Lilllard et al. (2013). *Psychological bulletin, 139*(1), 35–39.

Stagnitti, K. (1998). *Learn to play. A practical program to develop a child's imaginative play skills.* Melbourne: Co-ordinates Publications.

Stagnitti, K. (2004a). Occupational performance in pretend play; implications for practice. In M. Mollineux (Ed.) *Occupation for Occupational Therapists.* (pp. 103–121). Oxford, UK: Blackwell Science.

Stagnitti, K. (2004b). Understanding play: implications for play assessment. *Australian Occupational Therapy Journal, 51*, 3–12.

Stagnitti, K. (2009). Play intervention: the *Learn to Play* program. In K. Stagnitti and R. Cooper (Eds.) *Play as Therapy: Assessment and therapeutic interventions.* (pp. 176–186). London: Jessica Kingsley Publishers.

Stagnitti, K. (2014). The Parent Learn to Play program: building relationships through play. In E. Prendiville and J. Howard (Eds.). *Play Therapy Today.* (pp. 149–162). London, England: Routledge.

Stagnitti, K., & Casey, S. (2011). Il programma *Learn to Play* con bambini con autismo: considerazioni pratiche e evidenze. *Autismo Oggi, 20*, 8–13.

Stagnitti, K., O'Connor, C., & Sheppard, L. (2012). The impact of the Learn to Play program on play, social competence and language for children aged 5–8 years who attend a special school. *Australian Occupational Therapy Journal, 59*(4), 302–311.

Stagnitti, K., Rodger, S., & Clarke, J. (1997). Determining gender-neutral toys for play assessment with preschool children. *Australian Occupational Therapy Journal, 44*, 119–131

Stagnitti, K., & Unsworth, C. (2004). The test-retest reliability of the Child-Initiated Pretend Play Assessment. *American Journal of Occupational Therapy, 58*, 93–99.

Stagnitti, K., Unsworth, C., & Rodger, S. (2000). Development of an assessment to identify play behaviors that discriminate between the play of typical preschoolers and preschoolers with pre-academic problems. *Canadian Journal of Occupational Therapy, 67*, 291–303.

Swindells, D., & Stagnitti, K. (2006). Pretend play and parents' view of social competence: the construct validity of the Child-Initiated Pretend Play Assessment. *Australian Occupational Therapy Journal, 53*, 314–324.

Turygin, N., Matson, J. L., Beighley, J., & Adams, H. (2013a). The effect of DSM-5 criteria on the developmental quotient in toddlers diagnosed with autism spectrum disorder. *Developmental Neurorehabilitation, 16* (1), 38–43.

Turygin, N., Matson, J. L., Adams, H., & Belva, B. (2013b). The effect of DSM-5 criteria on externalizing, internalizingm behavioral and adaptive symptoms in children diagnosed with autism. *Developmental Neurorehabilitation*, 1–6, early online.

Uren, N., & Stagnitti, K. (2009). Pretend play, social competence and learning in preschool children. *Australian Occupational Therapy Journal, 56*, 33–40.

Van der Kooij, R. (1989). Research on children's play. *Play & Culture, 2*, 20–34.

Vygotsky, L. (1997). *Thought and language* (A. Kozulin, Trans.). Massachusetts: The MIT Press.

Westby, C. (1991). A scale for assessing children's pretend play. In C. Schaefer, K. Gitlin & A. Sandrund (Eds.), *Play Diagnosis and Assessment* (pp. 131–161). New York: John Wiley & Sons Inc.

Chapter Nine

Play Therapy with Children Affected by Obsessive Compulsive Disorder

Amie C. Myrick and Eric J. Green

Obsessive compulsive disorder (OCD) is a complex psychiatric phenomenon that involves both *obsessions,* recurring thoughts, impulses, or images that exceed typical worries about real-life problems (American Psychiatric Association [APA], 2013) and *compulsions,* repetitive behaviors or thoughts that an individual feels compelled to execute in response to an obsession (APA). Compulsions are performed in an effort to prevent or reduce the distress associated with a negatively anticipated event. They may or may not be connected in a realistic way with the event they are designed to neutralize. OCD was recently removed as an anxiety disorder from the *Diagnostic and Statistical Manual of Mental Disorders, Fifth Edition* (DSM-5; APA, 2013) and placed into its own category which also includes body dysmorphic disorder, hoarding disorder, trichotillomania, and excoriation (skin-picking) disorder. This controversial decision reflected research demonstrating similar phenomenology, comorbidity, neurological symptoms, genetics, and treatment response between OCD and the other obsessive compulsive disorders (see Hollander, Braun, & Simeon, 2008).

Children with OCD experience a wide range of clinical presentations, including fears of contamination, obsessive worries about the safety of themselves or their loved ones, and repetitive checking, counting, arranging, or touching. Such obsessions and compulsions may cause distress for the child and significantly interfere with normal functioning because they are lengthy in terms of time they take to complete and misunderstood by others. Clinicians can incorporate play activities into existing evidence-based treatments to ameliorate the symptoms associated with OCD. A case study is presented to demonstrate the integration of play-based activities into the evidence-based treatment protocol for pediatric OCD.

RESEARCH SUPPORT

The developmental course of OCD symptoms is not well understood, although retrospective reports of adults with OCD suggest that symptoms begin in childhood, increase in frequency and intensity into adolescence (Costello, Egger, & Angold, 2005), and continue changing over time (Besiroglu, Uguz, & Ozbebit, 2007). Similarly, the causes of pediatric OCD are still largely understudied. Neurobiological and genetic studies have found differences between children with and without OCD in the right orbitofrontal cortex, and thalamus, and basal ganglia (Woolley et al., 2008), as well as specific alterations of the neurotransmitter glutamate that respond to treatment for OCD (MacMaster & Rosenberg, 2009). Other biological studies have examined the roles of serotonin dysregulation (Fineberg & Gale, 2005) and genetics (Nestatd et al., 2000) in the development of the disorder. Behavioral theorists, on the other hand, point to learned behavior and the negative reinforcement provided by compulsions (Albano, March, & Piacentini, 1999). When a child's attempts to minimize or eliminate the discomfort associated with intrusive obsessions are successful, this theory posits that the probability of repeating the soothing compulsion is increased.

The cognitive theory of OCD is largely supported in the understanding of adult OCD (Frost & Steketee, 2002) and suggests that the interpretation of intrusive thoughts is interpreted differently in OCD patients than non-OCD individuals. According to this theory, those with OCD appraise their thoughts as being indicative of a level of blame or responsibility, leading to increased discomfort and increased attention toward the thoughts themselves (Salkovskis, 1996). This anxiety-provoking, exaggerated assessment of risk largely drives the use of compulsive rituals, which serve to ameliorate the anxiety and minimize the responsibility for the feared negative outcome (Academy of Adolescent and Child Psychiatry [AACAP], 2012; Salkovskis, 1996). Studies have also suggested that children with OCD process information in a way that is different from those children without OCD, with greater beliefs about personal responsibility for negative outcomes and higher concerns about the probability and severity of harm (e.g., Barrett & Healy, 2003).

OVERVIEW OF VULNERABLE POPULATION

Pediatric OCD affects 1 percent to 3 percent of children in the United States (Zohar, 1999), and comorbidity with pediatric anxiety and mood disorders is common (AACAP, 2012; Geller, Biederman, Griffin, Jones, & Lefkowitz,

1996). Like children with other psychiatric disorders, children with OCD experience a lower quality of life than children without OCD (Lack et al., 2009), possibly due to the academic difficulties, poor peer interactions, and limited recreational activities that accompany the disorder (Sukhodolsky et al., 2005).

Pediatric OCD symptoms can mimic those of other psychiatric concerns, such as tic disorders (Eapen, Fox-Hiley, Banerjee, & Robertson, 2004), disruptive behaviors (Lehmkuhl et al., 2009), pervasive developmental disorders (Davis, Saeed, & Antonacci, 2008), attention deficit hyperactivity disorder (Gellar et al., 2004), and trichotillomania (Woods et al., 2006). Despite the fact that the unique behaviors and thought patterns in children with OCD may appear psychotic, research has demonstrated that in many cases of pediatric OCD, reality testing remains intact overall and hallucinations are absent (AACAP, 2012). Careful assessment and attentiveness to the core issue surrounding the obsessive thoughts or compulsive rituals can help the clinician discriminate between disorders. For more information regarding the interplay between pediatric OCD and these comorbid conditions, the reader should consult the AACAP practice parameters (2012).

INTEGRATIVE PLAY THERAPY TREATMENT PLANNING AND PROTOCOL

Behavioral and pharmacological cointerventions have emerged as the most effective treatments for pediatric OCD (POTS, 2004). Pharmacotherapy targets the well-established biological basis for OCD symptoms, and has received support both as an adjunct to talk therapy (Bridge et al., 2007; POTS, 2004; Masi et al., 2009) and a standalone treatment (Geller et al., 2003; Masi et al., 2009). However, only 25 percent to 54 percent of children experience a remission of symptoms (Benazon, Ager, & Rosenberg, 2002; POTS, 2004). Medication and cognitive behavioral therapy (CBT), discussed in detail below, are the only two treatment modalities that have received adequate research support for treating pediatric OCD. Insight-oriented therapies, such as psychodynamic treatment, do not seem to alter the repetitive and intrusive thoughts and behaviors that are central to the diagnosis of OCD (Greist, 1991; Johnston & March, 1992). Likewise, play therapy and family therapy have shown little success as standalone treatment modalities of OCD (Piacentini & Langley, 2004).

Cognitive Behavioral Therapy with Exposure Response Prevention

CBT combined with exposure response prevention (ERP) is recommended as the "gold standard" of treatment for children ages six to seventeen years with mild to moderate intensity of symptoms from OCD (March, Frances, Carpenter, & Kahn, 1997). CBT is utilized as a way to educate children about the way in which thoughts, feelings, and behaviors intertwine to form experience. As this particular CBT treatment model applies to those struggling with OCD symptoms, children are first educated about the obsessive-compulsive cycle. This cycle begins with the obsessive thought, which leads to anxiety that the child attempts to diminish with a compulsive behavior. Children learn that the compulsive behavior allows them to feel relief from the obsessive thoughts, thus negatively reinforcing the continued use of compulsive behaviors (Piacentini, Langley, Roblek, Chang, & Bergman, 2003). An additional component of psychoeducation includes teaching the child adaptive coping skills, such as relaxation techniques, and assigning homework. One example of such a homework assignment might involve a child identifying triggers to obsessive thoughts in between sessions or rating the intensity of the obsessive thought on a numerical scale.

Once the child has mastered the concepts of the interplay between thoughts, feelings, and behaviors, the child collaborates with the therapist to construct both a symptom map and a fear hierarchy to be used in the ERP activities. Symptom maps enable children to create a table in order to see the ways in which experiences trigger obsessive thoughts, which are relieved by compulsive behaviors. These maps then allow children a visual representation of the obsessive-compulsive behaviors that will be targeted during ERP exercises. ERP operates with the idea that anxiety decreases as contact with a feared stimulus increases (Foa & Kozak, 1985; Foa, Stekette, & Milby, 1980). Thus, the child is confronted with feared stimuli and the alleviating compulsive behavior is blocked until anxiety significantly decreases.

CBT/ERP is recognized as an effective treatment for pediatric OCD (Abramowitz, Whiteside, & Deacon, 2005). A large-scale, multisite study which examined the efficacy of CBT/ERP, medication, and combined treatment (POTS, 2004) found that symptom scores significantly decreased over twelve weeks of treatment and that CBT/ERP was more effective than medication alone. Ancedotal data from case reports have also supported this treatment's efficacy (March, 1995). Furthermore, studies have shown that treatment gains are greatest during treatment but successfully maintained at twelve, eighteen, twenty-four, and thirty-six month follow-up intervals (Barrett, Farrell, Dadds, & Boulter, 2005; Shalev et al., 2009).

Including other theoretical approaches may be one way to improve upon treatment. The more engaging treatments are for the children and adolescents who receive them, the higher the likelihood that they will both participate in and respond to them (Shelby & Berk, 2009). The educational literature suggests that games and activities are useful ways to teach new concepts, particularly when attempting to explain concepts that are advanced. Age-appropriate activities may help clarify cognitive–behavioral ideas that are confusing to youth. Therefore, despite its lack of efficacy as a solitary treatment (Gold-

Steinberg & Logan, 1999), play therapy may be beneficial when integrated with CBT/ERP treatment.

Play-Based Integrative Treatment Approach

Through play therapy and the accepting nature of the play therapist, youth are provided with the environment necessary to grow and change (e.g., Landreth, 2002). They begin to internalize the unconditional positive regard of the therapist and become more self-accepting and reliant. Thus, incorporating play therapy into an empirically validated treatment such as CBT/ERP meets children's developmental needs and creatively engages them in treatment. Play activities can be used as tools for assisting children in learning necessary coping skills and promoting a positive memory of remembering (Podell, Martin, & Kendall, 2009); however, few games and treatment activities are suggested in the most commonly used treatment manual for OCD (i.e., *OCD in Children and Adolescents: A Cognitive-Behavioral Treatment Manual;* March & Friesen, 1998).

Therapeutic Alliance

Despite the fact that treatment manual compliance correlates to positive outcome (Luborsky, Woody, McLellan, O'Brien, & Rosenzweig, 1982), the therapeutic relationship also contributes to treatment success. Moreover, such a relationship can suffer if a therapist follows a manual too closely and fails to exhibit empathic understanding of the child and presenting issues. One study found that therapist skills such as empathy and warmth, rather than directive interventions, contributed to treatment outcome (Nalavany, Ryan, Gomory, & Lacasse, 2005). In their pediatric OCD treatment manual, March and Friesen (1998) devote a chapter to addressing treatment pitfalls, which include developmental considerations and therapist variables. Many of the difficulties described, however, can be addressed simply through the compassionate, genuine nature of play therapists. The play therapist's willingness to accept a child unconditionally, for example, may assist in alleviating feeling pressured to improve or desiring to "bail out" (p. 164) of exposures.

March and Friesen suggest that while CBT can be implemented with young children, the therapist may need to be flexible in the presentation of concepts. Again, play therapy operates directly on this concept. Play therapists have the ability to address pediatric OCD in an empirically based but unique way by incorporating creative activities, children's interests, and nondirective play. While nondirective play is not specifically addressed in this chapter, its incorporation into sessions can reduce reassurance seeking, promote self-esteem, and foster mastery in children. These skills can supplement manualized treatment and further engage children in the process.

Externalization of OCD

A substantial component of CBT treatment for OCD involves skills building, the first of which addresses externalization of OCD as the problem. Younger children are even encouraged to give OCD a nickname in order to personify it as a separate entity. This idea parallels a basic premise in narrative therapy that theorizes that the externalization of difficult thoughts and feelings through written expression can bring about psychic healing (Vetere & Dowling, 2005). Narrative therapy views problems as separate from people while also assuming that people have many skills and abilities that are critical to who they are and useful in assisting them to make changes in their lives (e.g., Morgan, 2000). One playful approach to externalizing the problem sometimes utilized in narrative therapy involves writing a letter to the problem (Vetere & Dowling, 2005).

Creating a Symptom Map and Rating Symptoms

Although compulsive behaviors may be viewed as the problem for many children, the obsessive thoughts are the cause of the repetitive nature of the behaviors. It is important that children are able to identify triggers to such thoughts and rate their intensity. The symptom map allows children to have a visual representation of the trigger → obsession → compulsive behavior pattern that appears in OCD. In March and Friesen's (1998) manual, children write each trigger, obsession, and compulsion in a table format on a sheet of paper, although play therapists are encouraged to utilize creative modalities to further engage their clients. Examples are provided later in this chapter.

Similarly, the way in which children rate their obsessions also lends itself to originality. In the OCD treatment manual (March & Friesen, 1998), ratings are determined using a fear thermometer. This thermometer ranges from zero to eight, with eight representing the highest intensity obsessions. The ability to rate intensity of symptoms is an important skill in CBT treatment and one that children must be willing to practice. Allowing children to draw or decorate their own thermometer allows them to connect with the concept. The authors of this chapter have found that some children prefer using a scale of one to ten and are more likely to rate their obsessions in between sessions when they have a visual representation to display in their rooms or on their refrigerators at home. Displaying rating scales at home can also promote a sense of recognition and acceptance from family regarding the hard work of therapy.

Coping Strategies

Cognitive coping skills are a key component to the successful alleviation of OCD symptoms. Clients are taught that obsessions, like other thoughts, dissipate over time. March and Friesen (1998) teach a four-step process that includes (1) identifying that the thought is obsessive in nature, (2) acknowledging that this is just a reaction in the brain, (3) determining that the obsession will go away without doing the compulsive behavior, and (4) distracting oneself with other activities until the obsessive thought goes away. One example of this process might be, "Hi OCD, I know that it is just you. I know you will go away without my washing my hands. Instead, I'm going to think about/do." While this aspect of treatment is relatively straightforward, creative avenues for practicing and remembering the skills can be included. For example, puppets can be used to practice talking to OCD, where one puppet represents the symptomatic thought, and one puppet represents the coping thought "superhero" that helps the symptom decrease. Playful approaches not only allow for developmentally appropriate learning but also serve as a way for therapists to communicate the notion that, "We are a team, and I support you through this process."

In addition to coping thoughts, the fourth step of March and Friesen's (1998) process involves practicing relaxation strategies. Relaxation strategies include guided imagery and progressive muscle relaxation. Readers are encouraged to consider adopting Koeppen's (1974) relaxation script for children. This script, which is available online, suggests fun ways for youth to practice tensing and releasing various muscles in the body. For example, to release tension in the hands, children are told to imagine that they are squeezing a lemon. For these relaxation exercises, it is also helpful to give children an iPod or MP3 recording so that the skills can be practiced at home.

Exposure–Response Prevention (ERP)

ERP is the final aspect of treatment, following psychoeducation and skills building. The authors frequently use metaphors such as thoughts as clouds floating by in the sky or a train passing through a station to explain the process of naturally decreasing anxiety, but it is often the child's ability to experience this process first hand that solidifies the idea that anxiety will decrease even without a compulsive behavior. The symptom map is converted into a fear hierarchy with which an order of exposures is established. Easier, lower-rated symptoms are addressed first, and the highest rated symptoms are last. Directive therapy activities may be used to role play conquering the compulsive behavior. Likewise, children and parents are encouraged to think of creative ways to represent both the symptom and the conquering of the symptom. Therapists are challenged to find playful ways to confront fears during actual exposures as well. Incorporating favorite activities, such as sports, art, and music, or finding new and interesting locations to practice the exposures can make the difference when a child is struggling to resist compulsive behaviors. For example, a child who enjoys art projects may expose him- or herself to contamination worries while using finger paints rather than brushes while creating a picture.

Rewards and Goal Setting

Rewarding effort is an important aspect of therapeutic work, particularly when it involves practicing activities and tasks outside of psychotherapy. Homework tasks allow children to practice and increase the likelihood that they will master the skills (Hudson & Kendall, 2002). These activities can be anxiety provoking and are less enjoyable than other activities that children do outside of session; thus, rewards can help promote practicing tasks in between therapy sessions (Kendall & Barmish, 2007). Before beginning exposures, it is important that children determine ways in which they will reward themselves after they try to resist the obsessions and compulsions. It is the *effort* that is rewarded, rather than simply the ability to successfully resist the urge to perform compulsive behaviors. Parents are encouraged to be involved in the reward process too. Each week, the goals can be revisited and adjusted depending on new needs or mastered skills.

RELEVANT INTERVENTION

The *symptom map* is perhaps the place in CBT/ERP where a child's proclivity for fun and creativity can be most effectively employed. Instead of simply creating a table, children can create artwork that represents their views of OCD and provides information about symptoms patterns. Therapists can use creative ways to represent the "easy" versus "difficult" symptoms while demonstrating an unconditional acceptance of children's perspectives of their symptoms. One child conceptualized the treatment process of working as walking through a neighborhood. She and the therapist created a symptom map which resembled a neighborhood, with each house representing a symptom she wanted to conquer. The therapist provided the child with green, yellow, and red houses to depict the easy, moderate, and difficult symptoms. For her "red houses," she drew a ladder outside to represent the hierarchy of smaller exposures within the bigger exposure. Once the exposures began, the child was able to cross off houses on her poster; this served as a visual image of her progress.

CASE STUDY

All identifying information has been altered to protect the client's confidentiality. Maria was a fourteen-year-old female who presented to treatment for OCD symptoms. Her list of rituals was extensive, and Maria reported that she engaged in them repeatedly throughout the day. Her symptoms were primarily related to wanting things "just so" (March & Friesen, 1998) and included preferring items in sets of six, taking multiple showers throughout the day, and needing to have electronic systems on even numbers (e.g., the volume on the car radio). Maria was also diagnosed with comorbid social anxiety disorder, and some of her OCD symptoms involved mental rehearsal prior to engaging in social situations such as ordering food at a restaurant, answering the telephone, entering a neighbor's home to babysit, or introducing herself to a new peer. Her symptom severity scores ranged from four to ten on a ten-point scale, with those involving social situations receiving the highest ratings. She had recently begun psychiatric medication but denied any improvement.

Early in treatment, Maria shared the ways OCD had complicated her life and affected her self-esteem. She compared the experience to a former horseback riding instructor, Kathy, who made Maria practice her jumps over and over again, criticizing her constantly without giving her any praise in return. After making this connection, Maria began calling OCD "Miss Kathy" which often made her laugh. Once she began discussing OCD as an external idea, rather than an internal flaw within herself, Maria and the therapist discussed the interplay between her thoughts, feelings, and behaviors.

Despite her hard work in sessions and completion of homework assignments, Maria spoke candidly about frustration over what she viewed as lack of progress in treatment. Her therapist asked her to describe the longest car ride she had ever been in, using it as a metaphor. She explained to Maria that, like a drive from Maryland to Mexico, treatment can be long and slow. One hour into the lengthy drive, it may not feel like any progress has been made; however, the car is one hour closer to the destination. Maria liked this metaphor, and it was revisited in treatment often. In fact, her symptom map was written on a world map, with a long red line from Maryland to Mexico. As treatment progressed, Maria tracked her progress with a green marker, inching the line closer to Mexico with each successful exposure. Maria also drew and colored a thermometer that would come to be involved in all exposures. During the final skills-building aspect of the treatment, Maria chose to think of her of her thoughts as clouds floating past. To continue this image, she created index cards with clouds written on them and coping thoughts inside.

Maria identified goals each week in the exposure phase of treatment, which typically included attempting to resist one or more symptoms in increasing difficulty. She chose small, medium, and large rewards to correspond to the difficulty of the exposures. She practiced in and out of sessions, gradually working her way up to the most difficult exposures. Over time, her symptoms greatly improved, and she no longer met criteria for OCD. She had made it to Mexico on her symptom map! Maria continued meeting with her therapist to discuss current life stressors and lingering social anxiety symptoms for several months after completing the CBT/ERP treatment; however, she continued to be successful at resisting her OCD symptoms.

CONCLUSION

While pharmacotherapy and CBT/ERP for pediatric OCD have the most empirical support, studies demonstrate that many children remain symptomatic at the completion of their treatment. The incorporation of play therapy can increase the success of treatment by applying the concepts in ways that are readily accessible to children. Maria benefited from the CBT/ERP concepts and skills when they were introduced creatively, playfully, and in ways that directly related to interests outside of therapy. Play therapists are encouraged to consider adopting manualized treatment for pediatric OCD so that well-researched skills can be combined with the empathy, genuineness, and unconditional respect found in the playroom.

NOTE

The treatment paradigm in this chapter was originally published as a journal article in the *International Journal of Play Therapy*, under the following citation: Myrick, A. C., & Green, E. J. (2012). Incorporating play therapy into evidence-based treatment with children affected by obsessive compulsive disorder. *International Journal of Play Therapy, 21*, 74–86. It has been republished with expressed permission from the Association of Play Therapy.

REFERENCES

AACAP. (2012). Practice parameters for the assessment and treatment of children and adolescents with obsessive-compulsive disorder. *Journal of American Academy of Child and Adolescent Psychiatry, 51*, 98–113.

Abramowitz, J. S., Whiteside, S. P., & Deacon, B. J. (2005). The effectiveness of treatment for pediatric obsessive-compulsive disorder: A meta-analysis. *Behavior Therapy, 36*, 55–63.

Albano, A., March, J., & Piacentini, J. (1999). Cognitive behavioral treatment of obsessive-compulsive disorder. In R. Ammerman, M. Hersen, & C. Last (Eds.), *Handbook of prescriptive treatments for children and adolescents* (pp. 193–215). Boston: Allyn and Bacon.

American Psychiatric Association. (2013). *Diagnostic and statistical manual of mental disorders* (5th ed.). Arlington: VA: American Psychiatric Publishing.

Barrett, P. M., Farrell, L. J., Dadds, M. & Boulter, N. A. (2005). Cognitive-behavioural family-based treatment for childhood OCD: Long-term treatment outcome and predictors of response. *Journal of the American Academy of Child and Adolescent Psychiatry, 44*(10), 1005–1014.

Benazon N. R., Ager J., & Rosenberg D. R. (2002). Cognitive behavior therapy in treatment-naïve children and adolescents with obsessive-compulsive disorder: An open trial. *Behavioral Research Therapy, 40*, 529–539.

Barrett, P. M., & Healy, L. J. (2003). An examination of the cognitive processes involved in childhood obsessive-compulsive disorder. *Behaviour Research & Therapy, 41*, 285–299.

Besiroglu, L., Uguz, F., & Ozbebit, O. (2007). Longitudinal assessment of symptom and subtype categories in obsessive-compulsive behavior. *Depression and Anxiety, 24*, 461–466.

Bridge, J. A., Iyengar, S., Salary, C. B., Barbe, R. P., Birmaher, B., Pincus, H. A., Ren, L., Brent, D. A. (2007). Clinical response and risk for reported suicidal ideation and suicide attempts in pediatric antidepressant treatment: A meta-analysis of randomized controlled trials. *JAMA, 297*(15), 1683–1696.

Costello, E. J., Egger, H. L., & Angold, A. (2005). The developmental epidemiology of anxiety disorders: Phenomenology, prevalence, and comorbidity. *Child and Adolescent Psychiatric Clinics of North America, 14*, 631–648.

Davis, E., Saeed, S. A., & Antonacci, D. J. (2008). Anxiety disorders in persons with developmental disabilities: Empirically informed diagnosis and treatment: Reviews literature on anxiety disorders in DD population with practical take-home messages for the clinician. *Psychiatric Quarterly, 79*(3), 249–263.

Eapen, V., Fox-Hiley, P., Banerjee, S., & Robertson, M. (2004). Clinical features and associated psychopathology in a Tourette syndrome cohort. *Acta Neurologica Scandinavica, 109*(4), 255–260.

Fineberg, N. A., & Gale, T. M. (2005). Evidence-based pharmacotherapy of obsessive- compulsive disorder. *International Journal of Neuropsychopharmacology, 8*, 107–129.

Foa, E., & Kozak, M. (1985), Emotional processing of fear: exposure to corrective information. *Psychological Bulletin, 90*, 20–35.

Foa, E., Steketee, G., & Milby, J. (1980), Differential effects of exposure and response prevention in obsessive-compulsive washers. *Journal of Consulting and Clinical Psychology, 48*, 71–79.

Frost, R. O., & Steketee, G. (2002). *Cognitive approaches to obessesions and complusions.* Oxford: Elsevier Science.

Geller, D. A., Biederman, J., Faraone, S., Spencer, T., Doyle, R., Mullin, B., Magovcevic, M., Zaman, N., & Farrell, C. (2004). Re-examining comorbidity of obsessive compulsive and attention-deficit hyperactivity disorder using an empirically derived taxonomy. European Child & Adolescent Psychiatry, *13*(2), 83–91.

Geller, D., Biederman, J., Griffin, S., Jones, J., & Lefkowitz, T. R. (1996). Comorbidity of juvenile obsessive complusive disorder with disruptive behavior disorders: a review and a report. *Journal of American Academy of Child and Adolescent Psychiatry, 35*, 1637–1646.

Geller, D. A., Biederman, J., Stewart, S. E., Mullin, B., Martin, A., Spencer, T., et al. (2003). Which SSRI? A meta-analysis of pharmacotherapy trials in pediatric obsessive-compulsive disorder. *American Journal of Psychiatry, 160*, 1919–1928.

Gold-Steinberg, S., & Logan, D. (1999). Integrating play therapy in the treatment of children with obsessive-compulsive disorder. *American Journal of Orthopsychiatry, 69*, 495–503.

Greist, J. (1991). Clinical management of obsessive-compulsive disorder. In M. Jenike & M. Asberg (Eds.), *Understanding obsessive-compulsive disorder.* Toronto: Hogrefe & Huber.

Hollander, E., Braun, A., & Simeon, D. (2008). Should OCD leave the anxiety disorders in DSM-V? The case for obsessive-compulsive disorders. *Depression and Anxiety, 25*, 317–329.

Hudson, J. L. & Kendall, P. C. (2002). Showing you can do it: The use of homework assignments in cognitive behavioral treatment for child and adolescent anxiety disorders. *Journal of Clinical Psychology, 58*, 525–534.

Johnston, H. F., & March, J. S. (1992). Obsessive-compulsive disorder in children and adolescents. In W. M. Reynolds (Ed.), *Internalizing disorders in children and adolescents* (pp. 107–148). New York: John Wiley & Sons.

Kendall, P. C. & Barmish, A. (2007). Show-That-I-Can (homework) in cognitive- behavioral therapy for anxious youth: Individualizing homework for Robert. *Cognitive and Behavioral Practice, 14*, 289–296.

Koeppen, A. S. (1974). Relaxation training for children. *Elementary School Guidance and Counseling, 9*, 14–21.

Lack, C. W., Storch, E. A., Keeley, M. L., Geffken, G. R., Ricketts, E. D., Murphy, T. K., & Goodman, W. K. (2009). Quality of life in children and adolescents with obsessive-compulsive disorder: Base rates, parent-child agreement, and clinical correlates. *Social Psychiatry and Psychiatric Epidemiology, 44*, 935–942.

Landreth, G. L. (2002). *Play therapy: The art of the relationship* (2nd ed.). New York: Brunner-Routledge.

Lehmkuhl, H. D., Storch, E. A., Rahman, O., Freeman, J., Geffken, G. R., & Murphy, T. K. (2009). Just say no: Sequential parent management training and cognitive-behavioral therapy for a child with comorbid disruptive behavior and obsessive compulsive disorder. *Clinical Case Studies, 8*(1), 48–58.

Luborsky, L., Woody, G. E., McLellan, A. T., O'Brien, C. P., & Rosenzweig, J. (1982). Can independent judges recognize different psychotherapies? An experience with manual-guided therapies, *Journal of Consulting and Clinical Psychology, 50,* 49–62.

MacMaster, F. P., & Rosenberg, D. R. (2009). Neuroimaging studies of pediatric obsessive-compulsive disorder: Special emphasis on genetics and biomarkers. In M. S. Ritsner (Ed.), *The handbook of neuropsychiatric biomarkers, endophenotypes, and genes, volume 2: Neuroanatomical and neuroimaging endophenotypes and biomarkers* (pp. 201–213), New York: Springer.

March, J. S. (1995). Cognitive-behavioral psychotherapy for children and adolescent with OCD: A review and recommendations for treatment. *Journal of the American Academy of Child and Adolescent Psychiatry, 34,* 7–17.

March, J. S., Frances, A., Carpenter, D., & Kahn, D. A. (1997). The expert consensus guidelines for the treatment of obsessive-compulsive disorder. *Journal of Clinical Psychiatry, 58* (suppl 4), 11–72.

March, J. S., & Friesen, K. M. (1998). *OCD in children and adolescents: A cognitive-behavioral treatment manual.* New York: Guilford Press.

Masi, G., Millepiedi, S., Perugi, G., Pfanner, C., Berloffa, S., Pari, C., & Mucci, M. (2009). Pharmacotherapy in paediatric obsessive-compulsive disorder: A naturalistic, retrospective study. *CNS Drugs, 23*(3), 241–252.

Morgan, A. (2000). *What is narrative therapy.* Adelaide, Australia: Dulwich Centre Publications.

Nalavany, B. A., Ryan, S. D., Gomory, T., & Lacasse, J. R. (2005). Mapping the characteristics of a "good" play therapist. *International Journal of Play Therapy, 14,* 27–50.

Nestatd, G., Samuels, J., Riddle, M., Bienvenu, J., Liang, K., LaBuda, M., Walkup, J., . . . Hoen-Saric, R. (2000). A family study of obsessive-compulsive disorder. *Archives of General Psychiatry, 57,* 358–363.

Piacentini, J., & Langley, A. K. (2004). Cognitive-behavioral therapy for children who have obsessive-compulsive disorder. *Journal of Clinical Psychology, 60,* 1181–1194.

Piacentini, J., Langley, A., Roblek, T., Chang, S., & Bergman, R. (2003). *Multimodal CBT treatment for childhood OCD: A combined individual child and family treatment manual (3rd revision).* Los Angeles: UCLA Department of Psychiatry.

Pediatric OCD Treatment Study Team (POTS). (2004). Cognitive-behavior therapy, sertraline, and their combination for children and adolescents with obsessive-compulsive disorder. *JAMA, 292*(16), 1969–1976.

Podell, J. L., Martin, E. D., & Kendall, P. C. (2009). Incorporating play in a manual-based treatment for anxious youth. In A. Drewes (Ed.) *The effective blending of play therapy and cognitive behavior therapy: A convergent approach.* New York: Wiley and Sons.

Salkovskis, P. M. (1996). Cognitive-behavioural approaches to the understanding of obsessional problems. In R. M. Rapee (Ed.), *Current controversies in the anxiety disorders* (pp. 103–134). New York: Guilford Press.

Shalev, I., Sulkowski, M. L., Geffken, G. R., Rickets, E. J., Murphy, T. K., & Storch, E. A. (2009). Long-term durability of cognitive behavioral therapy gains for pediatric obsessive-compulsive disorder. *Journal of American Academy of Child and Adolescent Psychiatry, 48,* 766–767.

Shelby, J. S. & Berk, M. S. (2009). Play therapy, pedagogy and CBT: an argument for interdisciplinary synthesis. In A. A. Drewes (Ed.). *Blending play therapy with cognitive behavioral therapy: Evidence-based and other effective treatments and techniques* (pp. 17–40). New Jersey: John Wiley and Sons, Inc.

Sukhodolsky, D. G., do Rosario-Campos, M. C., Scahill, L., Katsovich, L., Pauls, D. L., Peterson, B. S., King, R. A., . . . Leckman, J. F. (2005). Adaptive, emotional, and family functioning of children with obsessive-compulsive disorder and comorbid attention deficit hyperactivity disorder. *The American Journal of Psychiatry, 162,* 1125–1132.

Vetere, A., & Dowling, E. (2005). *Narrative therapies with children and their families.* London: Routledge.

Woods, D. W., Flessner, C., Franklin, M. E., Wetterneck, C. T., Walther, M. R., Anderson, E. R., & Cardona, D. (2006). Understanding and treating trichotillomania: What we know and what we don't know. *Psychiatric Clinics of North America, 29,* 487–501.

Woolley, J., Heyman, I., Brammer, M., Frampton, I., McGuire, P. K., & Rubia, K. (2008). Brain activation in paediatric obsessive-compulsive disorder during tasks of inhibitory control. *British Journal of Psychiatry, 192,* 25–33.

Zohar, A. H. (1999). The epidemiology of obsessive-compulsive disorder in children and adolescents. *Child and Adolescent Psychiatry, 8,* 445–460.

Chapter Ten

Adlerian Play Therapy with Children Affected by Externalizing Behavioral Disorders

Kristin K. Meany-Walen and Terry Kottman

Externalizing behaviors impact many children. Children who exhibit externalizing behaviors often break rules, physically or verbally fight with peers and adults, and destroy property. These behaviors typically interfere in some way with other people, cause difficulties for the children exhibiting them, the other members of their families, school personnel, and peers (Hamre, Pianta, Downer, & Mashburn, 2007; Myers & Pianta, 2008; Ray, 2007), and tend to remain stable without intervention (Barkley, 2007; Webster-Stratton & Reid, 2003). The consequences of failure to intervene early to meet the needs of these children are strained relationships, ongoing behavioral problems, difficulty in school, and poor social skills (Myers & Pianta, 2008). Thus, effective, responsive, and available services are necessary in order to meet the needs of these youth. Although there are no longitudinal studies of the efficacy of play therapy as an intervention with this population, there is research supporting the effectiveness of play therapy as an intervention with children with behavior problems (e.g., Meany-Walen, Bratton, & Kottman, 2014; Ray, 2007; Schottelkorb & Ray, 2009).

In Adlerian play therapy, children have an opportunity to practice socially preferred behaviors and experiment with new thoughts and feelings all within the safety of a secure and supportive therapeutic relationship. The process of play and the therapeutic skill of the Adlerian play therapist allow children to use play, conversation, and/or metaphoric storytelling to rehearse changing perceptions, attitudes, and behaviors (Kottman, 2003; Kottman & Ashby, in press). In outcome studies (e.g., Meany-Walen et al., 2014), Adlerian play therapy has demonstrated success in reducing externalizing behaviors of children and shows promise as an intervention designed to prevent these children's long-term psychosocial problems..

In this chapter, we discuss the importance of recognizing and treating children who have externalizing behaviors. We describe the four phases of Adlerian play therapy and the elements of conceptualizing clients and designing treatment plans from an Adlerian perspective. Last, we include a relevant intervention and a case example to illustrate how Adlerian play therapy can be used in professional mental health practice.

RESEARCH SUPPORT

Play therapy has a rich history of being a developmentally appropriate treatment for culturally diverse children with a variety of presenting problems. Published results of child-centered play therapy demonstrate statistically significant treatment outcomes for children with externalizing behaviors in settings that included school-based counseling (e.g., Garza & Bratton, 2005; Ray, 2007); community/agency counseling (e.g., Ojiambo & Bratton, 2014; Tyndall-Lind, Landreth, & Giordano, 2001), and interventions that utilize parents or teachers as the primary provider of care (e.g., Carnes-Holt & Bratton, 2014; Morrison & Bratton, 2010). Meta-analytic results for play therapy outcome research, which compared multiple play therapy interventions, showed play therapy as an effective intervention for children with a variety of presenting concerns (LeBlanc & Ritchie, 1999; Bratton, Ray, Rhine, & Jones, 2005).

Although the research using Adlerian play therapy as the independent variable is relatively new, it is promising and suggests Adlerian play therapy is effective in reducing problematic behaviors. In a randomized control group trial, Meany-Walen et al. (2014) compared Adlerian play therapy with reading mentoring at reducing children's externalized behaviors and increasing their on-task behaviors. Results of this study revealed statistically significant results with a large treatment effect for Adlerian play therapy. Meany-Walen, Kottman, and Bullis (in review) and Dillman Taylor and Meany-Walen (in progress) separately conducted single-case designs using Adlerian play therapy with elementary students referred to counseling for disruptive classroom behaviors and found encouraging results. Similarly, Meany-Walen, Kottman, and Bullis (in progress) found group Adlerian play therapy to be just as effective as individual sessions for children with externalized behavioral disorders. The results of these studies propose individual and group Adlerian play therapy to be effective interventions for children who exhibit externalizing behaviors.

OVERVIEW OF VULNERABLE POPULATION

Estimates indicate that one out of five children experiences distressing emotional problems, and less than one-third of these children will receive treatment (Mental Health America; MHA, 2009). Reports from The President's New Freedom Commission (2003) and U.S. Public Health Service (2000) have emphasized the need for effective interventions for these children and charged the mental health community with developing strategies to help them.

Externalizing behaviors are usually disruptive to others such as peers, teachers, siblings, and parents and are among the most challenging aspects of children's behavior for adults (Hamre et al., 2007; Myers & Pianta, 2008; Ray, 2007). Specific examples of externalizing behavior may include irritability, intense negative reactions, anger, aggression, rule breaking, distractibility, and an inability to adapt (Sanson, Hemphill, & Smart, 2004). Children who are aggressive, unpredictable, irritable, hyperactive, and/or demonstrate many disruptive behaviors experience difficulty in creating and maintaining positive relationships with others (Myers & Pianta, 2008).

Children with externalizing behaviors often have difficulty getting along with other people. Negative interactions with others confirm their already-held beliefs that they are *bad* and that other people do not and will not like them (Kottman, 2003). Acting as if these beliefs are true, they continue to act out. This develops into a pattern of cyclical interactions between these children and adults in their lives, which in turn reinforces negative behavior. Furthermore, even at young ages, children develop reputations among peers and adults. At school, students and teachers develop opinions of children. Likely, these reputations will follow children throughout the school system, and soon many teachers, administrators, and peers have a preconceived perception of certain children. Children who have reputations of being mean, aggressive, or impulsive have a high probability of maintaining these patterns as they age and progress through their academic years (Persson, 2005).

Externalizing behaviors are typically the result of a more significant, underlying emotional problem. Authors suggest that disruptive behaviors are associated with a child's perception of the social environment (Teisl & Cicchetti, 2008). For example, children who believe the world is dangerous, that others are mean, and that they are not likeable have a higher tendency to react to their environment with aggressive and negative behaviors. Thus, the disruptive behaviors are in response to children's perception of a threat in their social environment. In Adlerian terms, the child is compensating for his or her mistaken beliefs by acting aggressively, impulsively, or disruptively (Kottman, 2003).

Without intervention, these children become isolated, which increases their maladjustment by presenting them with fewer opportunities to learn social skills such as cooperation, boundaries, and intimacy. If these children do not receive mental health services, their externalizing behaviors appear to be relatively stable over time and are typically a precursor to ongoing difficulties later in life such as antisocial behavior, violence, drug abuse, and juvenile delinquency (Barkley, 2007; Webster-Stratton & Reid, 2003). The importance of early intervention to alter a course of increased and more severe behavioral problems is clear.

INTEGRATIVE PLAY THERAPY TREATMENT PLANNING AND PROTOCOL

Adler (1931/1958) focused on the influence of early childhood experiences and family of origin as paramount in individuals' development of their perception of self, others, and the world. Terry Kottman developed Adlerian play therapy based on Alfred Adler's theory of human personality known as Individual Psychology (Kottman, 2003; 2011). Adlerian play therapists use the basic tenets of Adlerian theory as the theoretical foundation for their play therapy practice.

Adlerians believe people are socially embedded and have a need to belong. They discover how they belong, starting in infancy, with their families (Adler, 1931/1958). Adler wrote much about family atmosphere, birth order, and illness and how it impacts a person's unique sense of belonging. Children try different behaviors and attitudes to find a way to belong and have significance in their family. For example, children might gain a place in their families by following the rules, excelling in music, being a leader, getting sick often, creating chaos, or being oppositional. Some ways of belonging might be positive or socially useful; others might be negative or socially useless. As children mature into adulthood, they continue to use the patterns for gaining a sense of belonging in other social groups such as school, friendships, work, community, and romantic relationships (Kottman, 2003). Eventually, this established way of belonging in their families becomes their "lifestyle." *Lifestyles* are the unique lens through which people view and operate throughout life. They are a consistent set of patterns, developed throughout early childhood that helps people to predict and control life. Because young children's cognitive functioning, including logic and judgment, are not fully developed, they often draw erroneous conclusions about themselves, others, and the world. Regardless of the accuracy of their interpretation, children and adults behave as if their interpretations were true.

The counseling process and building of the relationship begins even before the therapist meets the child (Kottman, 2003). Because Adlerian therapists believe that all humans are socially embedded, play therapists seek to understand and help children by gathering information from other significant people in children's lives and trying to improve the social atmosphere of their clients. Consultation with parents and teachers is an integral part of Adlerian play therapy. Adlerian therapists work with parents, teachers, and other important people in the child's life to support changes in attitudes toward the child, expectations of the child, and interactional patterns with the child.

Adlerian play therapy follows the same phases as Adlerian therapy with adults: (a) building an egalitarian relationship, (b) exploring the child's lifestyle, (c) helping the child gain insight into his or her lifestyle, and (d) reorienting/reeducating the child (Kottman, 2003; 2011). The first task of the Adlerian play therapist is to develop an egalitarian relationship with the child. Adlerian play therapists create a relationship in which the child feels a shared partnership, with collaboration, trust, and respect between the child and the therapist. The therapist communicates respect and trust to the child and earns the respect and trust from the child by being consistent, dependable, accepting, caring, and respectful (Kottman, 2003). To cultivate the relationship, the Adlerian play therapist uses tracking, restating content, reflecting feelings, encouraging, asking and answering questions, returning responsibility to the child, actively interacting with the child, cleaning the room with the child, metacommunicating, and setting limits. Although these strategies are part of the first phase of play therapy, they are used typically throughout the length of the play therapy process because the therapist consistently and intentionally works to maintain and strengthen the relationship therapeutic relationship.

The second phase of Adlerian play therapy involves the therapist gathering information about the child's lifestyle (Kottman, 2003; 2011). Adlerian play therapists are more interested in how the child makes sense of the world than the objective events of the child's life (Dinkmeyer, McKay, & Dinkmeyer, 2007; Dreikurs & Soltz, 1964; Kottman, 2003). The therapist can do this by observing the child, playing actively with the child, noticing the child's response to directed activities, and watching the child interact with other people. Talking with parents and/or teachers is an excellent strategy for learning about the child, family and/or school atmosphere, and the important people in the child's life. The purpose of this phase is for the therapist to develop an understanding of the child's lifestyle which he or she can then use to make a treatment plan for guiding the child, family members, or teacher to make changes in their perceptions, emotions, thoughts, and behaviors in later phases of therapy (Kottman, 2003).

Before proceeding to the third and fourth phases of therapy, the Adlerian play therapist formulates a lifestyle conceptualization of the child (and sometimes of the significant adults in the child's life) and generates a treatment plan based on this conceptualization (Kottman, 2003). The lifestyle conceptualization can include information about the child's assets, the impact of the family atmosphere and family constellation on the child, the child's mastery of the life tasks, the child's relationship and problem-solving skills, the child's personality priorities, the goals of the child's misbehavior (Dinkmeyer, McKay, Dinkmeyer, & McKay, 2008; Dreikurs & Soltz, 1964), and the Crucial Cs (Lew & Bettner, 1998; 2000). The play therapist then develops lifestyle hypotheses about children's core beliefs about self, others, and their world.

Based on the information gathered during the second phase, Adlerian play therapists make a list of assets that they want to encourage in the child and assets that might be overused by the client. For instance, with a child who is intelligent, but doubts his or her intellectual capacity, the therapist might emphasize and verbally track the child's demonstration of cognitive abilities during play therapy sessions. However, with an intelligent child who is also creative, musical, and funny but overrelies on intelligence to gain significance, bragging about how smart he or she is, the play therapist could emphasize creativity, musicality, and humor and deemphasize intellectual functioning as an asset.

Adlerians believe family constellation and family atmosphere are important components of a therapeutic conceptualization. Based on observations and conversations during the second phase, the therapist forms a picture of the child's perception of his or her place in the family, usually influenced by birth order (Kottman, 2003). Family atmosphere is created by a number of different factors such as the parents' attitudes toward each of the children and one another, their discipline philosophy and skills, their marital satisfaction, their own lifestyles, family communication and conflict patterns, and the relationships between siblings. The child's perception of the family atmosphere and how it affects the child's beliefs about self, others, and the world is an important part of the lifestyle conceptualization.

Adler (1927/1998) suggested that all behavior is purposive. In *Children: The Challenge* (Dreikurs and Soltz, 1964), the authors described four goals of misbehavior, believing that children universally use these behaviors to meet their perceived needs. The four goals of misbehaviors are (1) undue attention, (2) struggle for power, (3) retaliation and revenge, and (4) complete inadequacy. Typically, children are not aware of how their behavior helps them to reach their goals of belonging, and they use misbehavior because they are discouraged and lack socially useful ways of connecting with others (Dreikurs & Soltz, 1964; Kottman, 2003). Children tend to have a pattern of misbehavior. Part of the conceptualization process is to discern this pattern in order to help them shift their behavior toward more positive goals.

Another factor important to conceptualize is the pattern of the child's personality priorities (Kefir, 1981). Kottman and Ashby (in press) described the priorities of Pleasing, Comfort, Control, and Superiority as a person's reactions and behavioral patterns in interpersonal situations that is based on how the person believes he or she belongs, gains significance, and creates a sense of mastery. Pleasing children establish a sense of belonging and mastery by attempting to please and keep others happy. Comfort children seek pleasure, comfort, and ease; working to avoid stress, expectations, and responsibility. Controlling children work to meet their need for belonging by striving for control over themselves or by demonstrating to others that they cannot control them. Children with a superiority personality priority build a sense of belonging and identity by working very hard—they have high standards of achievement in everything they do in order to gain acceptance from others.

In thinking about children and in consultation with the important adults in their lives, the Adlerian play therapist assesses personality priorities and uses them as a means of custom designing interventions. It is important to consider where a child falls on a continuum from positive, healthy manifestation to destructive, unhealthy manifestation of their personality priority (Kottman, 2003; Kottman & Ashby, in press). For example, children who are in the healthy realm of the personality priority of control like to be in control of themselves, but are still flexible in their thinking and behaving; children who are in the unhealthy realm of control are rigid, controlling of others, and lack spontaneity and creativity. The ultimate goal is to move children who are living out a destructive manifestation of their personality priority toward a more constructive method of interacting and managing their lives.

Five tasks of life exist for all humans and challenge them as they move throughout the lifespan: friendship, work/school, love/family, spirituality, and self (Mosak & Maniacci, 2008). The *friendship life task* is the way in which people cooperate with society. For children, this task is reflected in how they get along with peers in school and other places where they interact with other children (Kottman, 2003). The *work/school task* for children is cooperation and success in school (Dinkmeyer et al., 2007). When working with children, the *love/family task* involves how people handle the close, intimate relationships within a family. This may include how children view their parents' partnership, sibling relationships, and the family atmosphere. The *spiritual realm* is individuals' journey in defining their beliefs about the nature of the universe. Lastly, the *self life task* involves people's tolerance and acceptance of themselves (Mosak & Maniacci, 2008). The Adlerian play therapist assesses children's mastery of each of the life tasks and designs interventions to enhance their mastery of the ones with which they are struggling (Kottman, 2003).

Lew and Bettner (1998, 2000) developed the *Crucial Cs* as a way to help parents identify and encourage particular characteristics of their children. The four Crucial C's are count, connect, capable, and courage. Lew and Bettner believed that children need to master each of the Crucial Cs in order to be successful in society as they grow and mature. Adlerian play therapists use the Crucial Cs to make hypotheses about children's assets and limitations and the ways in which children approaches life (Kottman, 2003). Adlerian play therapists think about the Crucial Cs as a vehicle for examining whether and how children believe they *count* in the world and in relationships with others, *connect* with others, believe they are *capable* of success, and demonstrate the *courage* to be imperfect and attempt new tasks. As a part of the intervention process, the Adlerian play therapist develops strategies for capitalizing on children's stronger Crucial Cs and strengthening their mastery of the Crucial Cs that have been difficult for them.

Based on the conceptualization, the play therapist devises a treatment plan that includes strategies for helping the child capitalize on assets, master life tasks, and improve relationship and problem-solving skills. The child might need assistance in reframing and/or thinking more positively about his or her place in the family and in dealing with other members of the family and the impact of the family atmosphere. If a child is misbehaving, he or she may need help in shifting to more positive goals for his or her behavior. There may also be a need for adjustment in how the child acts out his or her personality priorities, moving toward a more constructive manifestation of his or her priorities. For a child who is struggling with one or more of the Crucial Cs, the therapist would develop interventions designed to help foster connect, courage, count, and capable.

The goal of the next phase, helping children gain insight, is to help them increase awareness of their patterns of thinking, feeling, and behaving. One goal of this phase is for children to develop an understanding of how their behaviors impact others and how their behaviors help them to meet their goals of belonging. Children are then free to make informed decisions about whether they want to change and how they could go about making changes. Because Adlerians believe that thinking, feeling, and behaving are interactive, intervention can occur in any of these areas. The Adlerian play therapist also works with children's social spheres, such as family and school, to help create the most supportive environment for change (Kottman, 2003).

Adlerian play therapists help children and adults gain insight by meta-communicating about their lifestyles and making guesses about their perceptions, attitudes, feelings, and behaviors. A therapist can choose to use immediacy, confrontation, and/or humor depending on the therapist's belief about what the individual child or adult needs in that moment. Adlerian play therapists, at a philosophical level, value play and metaphoric expression as the children's primary means of communication. Therefore, therapists use play, metaphors, storytelling, sand tray, dance and movement, and role-plays (among other activities) to help children gain new understandings of themselves, which can help them take responsibility in the changes they choose to attempt (Kottman, 2003).

The reorientation/reeducation phase emphasizes the need for action. Children begin to generate new ways of thinking about themselves, others, and the world; change the way they feel, think, or behave in various situations; and relate to people differently than they did in the past (Kottman, 2003). Adlerian therapists believe that action is more meaningful than words (Dreikurs & Soltz, 1964). Thus, Adlerian play therapists create opportunities for children to practice these new patterns of thinking, feeling, and behaving both in the playroom and in other settings and relationships. Parents and teachers are also updated on the child's current functioning and progress and are asked to encourage the child in new ways of thinking, feeling, and behaving. During this phase, families, teachers, or friends may even be asked to join in the therapy process in the playroom.

During the reorientation/reeducation phase of therapy, Adlerian play therapists act out their philosophical belief in the child's creative ability to solve problems and make changes (Kottman, 2003). There are endless solutions to problems, and therapists must remain imaginative and open to alternatives. Through the use of toys and play, art, role-play, puppets, games, music and dance, sand tray, brainstorming, and other teaching tools, children can practice new behaviors, more adaptive patterns of thinking, and socially appropriate expression of feelings and thoughts. Therapists are most instrumental with children when they allow themselves the freedom to attempt various interventions with children and families.

Consultation with the important adults in the child's life follows the same pattern as the play therapy with the child (Kottman, 2003, 2011; Kottman & Dougherty, 2013). In working with parents and/or teachers, the Adlerian play therapist builds an egalitarian relationship; explores the lifestyles of the adults and explores the adults' perceptions of the child's lifestyle; helps the adults gain insight into their own lifestyles, the lifestyle of the child, and the interaction between them; and teaches new skills in the reorientation/reeducation phase. Because Adlerian play therapists think systemically, this consultation with parents and teachers is an integral component of the Adlerian play therapy process.

RELEVANT INTERVENTION

Adlerians believe that people reprove what they already believe about themselves by "acting as if" their beliefs about self, others, and the world are true. In order to do this, their behavior almost always mirrors the way that they expect others to perceive them. This is often manifested through their bodies—in their posture, their movement, their gestures, and so forth. Because of this, one of the factors Adlerian play therapists can assess in the second phase of counseling is how children physically walk through the world. According to the way Adlerian play therapists conceptualize clients, many children with externalizing behaviors are "acting as if" they are unlikeable. Because they are acting out—arguing, fighting, being disrespectful to others, and so forth—they are walking, talking power struggles waiting to happen. They usually move through life radiating a combination of aggression and defensiveness because they believe they need to protect themselves based on their assumption that the world is a scary and dangerous place, where others will reject them. Children who exhibit externalizing behaviors often believe that they must overpower others in order to keep themselves from being overpowered. There are many ways children with externalizing behaviors can walk through their lives. Two examples of this might be walking with their heads down, shoulders hunched, making little or no eye contract or walking with an aggressive stance, staring others down, pushing them out of their way. However they are walking, they move through the world broadcasting their expectation that others will try to control them and sending the message that they cannot be controlled. This attitude and the physical manifestation of this attitude often evokes exactly what the children were expecting—rejection and hostility from others.

One technique focusing on helping children change their behaviors used in the third and/or fourth phase of Adlerian play therapy is titled *Walk This Way*. The purpose of this intervention is to help children practice new, more socially appropriate ways of physically moving through the world. The Adlerian play therapist can help children who are walking through their lives like they are expecting to have to overpower others by encouraging them to consider the possibility that they could ambulate in a more positive and inviting way. The Adlerian play therapist can help them experiment with walking a different way as a vehicle for transmitting a different message to those they encounter.

The therapist creates interventions used in the third and/or fourth phase of Adlerian play therapy based on what he or she learns about children in the second phase. In this case, the therapist keeps looking for an alternative (hopefully more constructive) way the child would like to be perceived and tries to plant a seed that the child could shift toward having a more positive impact on others. For example, some children would like to be popular, others would like to be important, and others would like to be considered leaders. When designing this intervention, the play therapist tries to incorporate these goals so the process involves walking as if the child is popular, important, a leader, and so on. The play therapist might model the way the child currently walks and then model a new and different way of walking. Then the play therapist engages the child in practicing his or her usual way of walking and the alternative way of walking, perhaps with a conversation about how he or she feels (emotionally and physically) in the contrasting ways of ambulating. When possible, it is also helpful for the child to practice the new way of walking through the world outside the play therapy session. With children who are developmentally able to verbally process abstract concepts (older elementary children and adolescents), it is helpful to suggest that they notice the reactions of others when they move in a different way. As they consider the possibility that walking a different way might have a more positive impact on the way others perceive and react to them, there is often a shift in the ways they think about themselves, others, and the world.

Because many children who exhibit externalizing behavior are resistant to an overtly directive approach and the idea that they could deliberately shift their "acting as if" to a something less aggressive is often a foreign concept, it is often more effective to present the idea tentatively. One strategy would be to ask children if they might be willing to help with an experiment the play therapist is conducting, rather than making a direct suggestion that they should work on moving through the world differently.

CASE STUDY

Graham, a nine-year-old boy in the third grade, lived with his mother, Emily, and his maternal grandmother, Gertrude, in a small town in the southwestern region of the United States (all details have been altered to protect client confidentiality). Graham's parents had never married, and Emily reported that his father, Tom, was a "deadbeat." He had been in incarcerated outside of the local area for most of Graham's life, and Graham had experienced limited contact with him. Over the years, Emily had had a series of paramours who had abused her, and she had a history of alcohol and cannabis abuse. Emily had been to rehab several times and was, at the time of Graham's play therapy process, not using any substances. During the times she was in rehab, Graham had lived with Gertrude, his grandmother. After Emily left rehab, she usually moved in with Gertrude and Graham until such time as she entered into another relationship and she moved in with the man she was currently seeing. Depending on the willingness of the paramours, Graham had moved in with them. When they were uninterested in coparenting, Graham has stayed with his grandmother.

At the beginning of Graham's play therapy, he was living with both Emily and Gertrude. At the request of Ann, Graham's play therapist, they both came to the initial session without Graham so that the play therapist could begin to build a relationship with them and gather information related to Graham's development and his lifestyle. In this initial session, they both reported that Graham was "out of control." He argued with them, refused to follow rules, was rude and disrespectful to both of them, and had regular temper tantrums. Emily and Gertrude alternately blamed Graham and blamed one another for this behavior. They reported that his teacher said he was "a bit bossy," but overall well behaved and cooperative at school. He was above grade level in most subjects.

By the end of this consultation, Ann had formed the beginning of her conceptualization of Graham's lifestyle and was starting to think about how to build a relationship with him. She told his mother and grandmother that she would like to meet with them during each session to continue to explore their perceptions of Graham and begin to help them move toward a more harmonious relationship with him. She mentioned that she believes that when a child is struggling, the entire family system (and sometimes the school system as well) have a share in the problem and that everyone needs to work as a team to make the changes necessary for improvement in the situation. Although they both expressed a desire for Ann to "just fix" Graham, Emily and Gertrude agreed to participate in ongoing consultation.

"I hate you. I hate my mom and my gram. I hate my teacher. I hate the kids in my class. I hate everybody I know. And they all hate me too. I don't have to do what you tell me to do, no matter what you say. I never do what anybody tells me to do. I bet you hate me and you don't even know me yet!" In Graham's opening salvo of his first session of play therapy, he gave Ann additional information about his lifestyle. Although he actually seemed happy to be in Ann's office and eagerly accompanied her to the play room, Graham started every one of their first few sessions with a similar declaration—each beginning was filled with tirades about (a) how much he hated his mother and grandmother, (b) how angry he was at the other children in his class, (c) how unfair it was that his father was never around, and (d) how much he hated coming to play therapy, and so forth. After this initial flourish, each session proceeded along a similar path. Graham had the army men fighting with one another, ending in the death of both the "good guys" and the "bad guys." While the "bad guys" always beat up on the "good guys," they all died in the end. He would then move to the superheroes and villains. He would describe the superheroes as "jerks" and "idiots" and the villains as the "only smart ones around." The villains would battle the superheroes, ultimately defeating them, with only after experiencing heavy casualties. He would occasionally threaten to break the toys, but never follow through with this, though when Ann set limits he tended to argue with her about whether breaking toys should be against the playroom rules. At the end of every session, he would tell Ann that he never "worked as a team" and he was NOT going to help clean up the play room at the same time he was picking the toys up and putting them away. Then he would tell her he was never coming again, right before he refused to leave the playroom and move into the waiting room of her office.

Because this was the first phase of the Adlerian play therapy process, Ann used tracking, restating content, and reflecting feelings to begin to build a relationship with Graham in these sessions. In response to her comments,

Graham argued with her about what he had said and what he was doing in sessions, even when she kept her remarks generic. He consistently told her to stop tracking and restating content, "I already know what I am doing and what I am saying. Why do you keep repeating it? Are you some kind of a weirdo?" He had an even stronger negative reaction to her reflecting feelings, telling her that he was NOT angry, excited, sad, or happy when she used feeling words in her guesses about his affective state. Ann metacommunicated about his negative reactions to her interventions and informed him that it was her job to pay attention to what he was doing and saying so she would need to continue to make comments about what was happening in the play room. Over time, his argumentation seemed to settle down—during his fourth session, he even said, "Well, I give up. If you want to say stupid things, I can't stop you. Go ahead and say stupid things." As his initial resistance to the process lessened, Ann introduced the other components of the first phase: encouragement, returning responsibility to the child, and asking questions. She made encouraging comments about his creativity, his ability to stay on task, his willingness to do things even when he said he wasn't going to do them. When Graham asked her to make decisions about what he was going to do (which did not happen very often), Ann returned responsibility to him, saying things like, "In here, you get to decide that." She asked him questions about his relationships with family members, neighborhood children, and teachers and classmates, about difficulties reported by his mother and grandmother, about ideas he had about how to solve problems encountered by the characters in his play. While he usually seemed to ignore her questions and never answered them directly in words, he almost always answered metaphorically in the play, with characters acting out relationship issues and problem situations.

Ann was conceptualizing Graham's lifestyle from the first interaction with his mother and grandmother, gathering information about his assets, the impact of the family atmosphere and family constellation on him, his mastery of the life tasks, his relationship and problem-solving skills, his mastery of the Crucial Cs, his personality priorities, the goals of his misbehavior, and his ideas about self, others, and the world. She already had ideas about many of these factors because of her interactions with the various family members and her observation of his behaviors in the playroom. However, after the initial five sessions, as they moved steadily into the second phase of therapy, she began a slightly more formal investigation into his lifestyle. With consent from Emily, Ann contacted Graham's teacher, Mr. Strauss, who reported that, while Graham was somewhat controlling with peers, he had several close friends and was doing well academically. Mr. Strauss said that, while Graham's initial reaction to suggestions or feedback that he should do things differently was usually negative, when adults or peers waited patiently rather than getting into a power struggle, Graham always complied and was cooperative.

In their sixth play therapy session, Ann asked Graham to draw a picture of his family. Initially, of course, he declined to draw the picture. When Ann chose not to engage in a power struggle with him about his refusal, he said, "All right. If you really want me to, I will." He drew a picture of himself in the middle of the paper, significantly bigger than the pictures of his mother and grandmother, who were located on either side of him, with their arms reaching out to him. He told Ann, "I am going to draw my dad now" and drew a small dot on the back of the piece of paper. In response to Ann's request that he describe what each person was doing, he told her that his mother and grandmother were doing "what I want them to do" and that his father was doing "nothing. He isn't really even here." For session eight, Ann asked Gertrude and Emily to come to a family session. She asked the family to use some newsprint and masking tape to build a tower. Both Emily and Gertrude deferred to Graham and his ideas about how to build the tower. As he told them what to do, they constructed the tower. When they questioned some of his ideas, Graham yelled at them to, "Just shut up and do it." Instead of stopping the action and giving him corrective feedback, Emily and Gertrude worked harder to comply with Graham's demands. By their tenth session, Ann had a good grasp of most the elements of Graham's lifestyle (and a general idea about the lifestyles of Emily and Gertrude and how they related to the parenting task and their relationships with Graham). The following is a summary of the lifestyle conceptualization:

Assets: Graham was intelligent, determined, and articulate. He had clear ideas about what he wanted and a successful strategy for getting what he wanted from others.

Impact of the Family Atmosphere and Family Constellation: Being an only child with two women who were both trying to please him had resulted in Graham being spoiled. His expectation was that he would get to be the boss in every situation. Because his mother and grandmother expected him to act like his father, who they perceived as irresponsible and difficult, Graham had decided that this was his role in the family. The inconsistency of discipline and Emily and Gertrude's conflict about this subject was confusing to Graham, who took advantage of the resulting chaos.

Mastery of Life Tasks: Graham seemed to have mastered the life tasks of friendship and school, but was struggling with the tasks of love/family and self. The family was not overly religious or spiritual, so there was limited information on the task of spirituality.

Relationship and Problem-Solving Skills: These skills were actually well developed in his relationship with people outside the family. Although he struggled with the relationship with Emily and Gertrude, he quite often got his way, albeit through negative behaviors. There was little motivation for him to change his patterns with the other members of his family, though, because his behavior was working for him, and he was getting what he wanted.

Crucial Cs: Graham connected with people outside his family in mostly positive ways, but tried to dominate his mother and grandmother, which made his connection with them predominantly negative. He seemed to lack courage in most situations, being hesitant to try new things without a guarantee of success. He felt capable at school and at home, but he seemed to believe that the only way he counted was he was in control and dominating others. This might have had something to do with the absence of his father, the efforts of his mother and grandmother to placate him, and the inconsistency in the parenting role and function.

Personality Priorities: Based on his interactions with others and with Ann, Graham seemed to have control as his primary personality priority and superiority as his secondary personality priority, with both of them tending toward the unhealthy side of the continuum. He seemed to need to control others and outdo them, which negatively affects his relationships.

Goals of Misbehavior: Pretty consistently, the goal of Graham's misbehavior was power.

Ideas about Self, Others, and the World: Graham seemed to believe that he must be in control, especially in his relationships with his mother and grandmother. He appeared to believe that others were not to be trusted and would try to control him and his behavior if he would let them. The world seemed to be an unpredictable, inconsistent place in which he needed to protect himself.

It was important for Ann to understand the impact the lifestyles of Graham's mother and grandmother and the intrapersonal and interpersonal dynamics of the family having on Graham. Because Emily and Gertrude's personality priorities were both comfort and pleasing, they were letting him have too much power in the family. The inconsistency in parenting had exacerbated his need for control because the family atmosphere was often chaotic. One of the reasons Graham felt that he needed to be in control was that he perceived that the family was out of control.

Ready to move to the third phase of play therapy, Ann based her treatment plan on these conceptualizations. She wanted to help Graham get insight into his patterns so that he could make shifts into more positive, productive ways of interacting with others and getting his needs met, and she wanted to teach Emily and Gertrude more consistent strategies for parenting him. She used metacommunication to make guesses to Graham about his goals of misbehavior; his mastery of the life tasks; his methods of solving problems; his acquisition of the Crucial Cs; the manifestation of his personality priorities; and his ideas about self, others, and the world. She used encouragement to point out his strengths, his efforts to change his thinking and behaving, and his progress toward more positive ways of relating to others, and meeting his own needs. She used the soldiers and the super heroes to "spit in his soup" about negative patterns and suggest new ways of dealing with situations and relationships. They did some cooperative art projects and played games in which Graham could not control everything, like Uno Attack and Sorry. This phase of play therapy lasted ten sessions before they moved into the final phase.

During the conjoint sessions consulting with Emily and Gertrude, Ann worked with them on understanding the intrapersonal and interpersonal dynamics that had created the negative patterns in their family interactions. Ann shared her ideas about Graham's development and maintenance of his pattern of externalizing behaviors and made suggestions about how, if things were different in the family, he might learn new ways of interacting. She wanted them to understand the systemic issues so that they were more willing to take ownership of their appropriate share of the family power, setting limits and structure, and meeting Graham's need for consistency and communication.

As he became more comfortable with others being in charge, Ann moved the therapy into the reorientation/reeducation phase. As a vehicle for helping Graham learn to share power and control, they put together puzzles, played cooperative games, made Lego models, and did construction projects using shoe boxes and pipe cleaners. She metacommunicated with Graham about his need for structure and control and suggested that he did not always need to overpower others to feel safe.

Ann invited Emily and Gertrude to join them in several sessions, doing the same kinds of cooperative activities to encourage the family members to practice sharing power in developmentally appropriate ways. By teaching Emily and Gertrude to set logical consequences and encourage Graham for positive behavior and giving them a chance to practice these parenting techniques in session and as homework, Ann guided Graham's mother and grandmother toward making the family atmosphere a safer place for Graham. She also taught them how to consider looking underneath Graham's externalizing behaviors and generating strategies to meet his needs in proactive, positive ways so that he would not feel that he needed to act out to get his needs met.

CONCLUSION

Adlerian play therapists believe that all people are creative and unique. Children with externalizing behaviors may have personality priorities, goals of misbehavior, Crucial Cs, assets, and ideas about self, others, and the world that are similar or quite different from Graham. Importantly, Adlerian play therapists remain open and flexible to understand the children with whom they work and those children's social spheres. Treatment plans, including interventions and goals, are to be specifically designed to meet the individual needs of clients. We provided a case study demonstrating how an Adlerian play therapist moved through the four phases of Adlerian play therapy with this particular child. Our hope is for readers to be able to apply the basic notions of Adlerian play therapy with the special and unique children with whom they work.

REFERENCES

Adler, A. (1958). *What life should mean to you*. New York: Capricorn. (Original work published 1931)

Adler, A. (1998). *Understanding human nature*. Oxford, England: Oneworld. (Original work published 1927).

Barkley, R. (2007). School interventions for attention deficit hyperactivity disorder: Where to from here? *School Psychology Review, 36*(2), 279–286.

Bratton, S. C., Ray, D., Rhine, T., & Jones, L. (2005). The efficacy of play therapy with children: A meta-analytic review of treatment outcomes. *Professional Psychology: Research and Practice, 36*(4), 376–390. Doi: 10.1037/0735-7028.36.4.376.

Carnes-Holt, K. & Bratton, S. (2014). The efficacy of child parent relationship therapy for adopted children with attachment disruptions *Journal of Counseling and Development, 4*(12), 121–136.

Dillman Taylor, D. & Meany-Walen, K. K. (in progress). A single case design: Adlerian play therapy with elementary aged children and teachers.

Dinkmeyer, D., McKay, G., & Dinkmeyer, D. (2007). *The parent's handbook: Systematic training for effective parenting* (4th ed.). Bowling Green, KY: STEP.

Dinkmeyer, D., McKay, G., Dinkmeyer, J., & McKay, J. (2008). *Parenting young children: Systematic training for effective parenting (STEP) of children under six*. Bowling Green, KY: STEP.

Dreikurs, R., & Soltz, V. (1964). *Children: The challenge*. New York: Hawthorn/Dutton.

Garza, Y., & Bratton, S. C. (2005). School-based child-centered play therapy with Hispanic children: Outcomes and cultural considerations. *International Journal of Play Therapy, 14*(1), 51–79.

Hamre, B. K., Pianta, R. C., Downer, J. T., & Mashburn, A. J. (2007). Teachers' perceptions of conflict with young students: Looking beyond problem behaviors. *Social Development, 17*(1), 115–136. doi: 10.1111/j.1467-9507.2007.00418.x.

Kefir, N. (1981). Impasse/priority therapy. In R. Corsini (Ed.), *Handbook of innovative psychotherapies* (pp. 400–415). New York: Wiley.

Kottman, T. (2003). *Partners in play: An Adlerian approach to play therapy* (2nd ed.). Alexandria, VA: American Counseling Association.

Kottman, T. (2011). Adlerian play therapy. In C. Schaefer (Ed.), *Foundations of play therapy* (2nd ed., pp. 87–104). New York: John Wiley.

Kottman, T., & Ashby, J. (in press). Adlerian play therapy. In A. Stewart & D. Crenshaw (Eds.), *Guilford handbook of play therapy*. New York, NY: Guilford.

Kottman, T. & Dougherty, M. (2013). Adlerian case consultation with a teacher. In A. M. Dougherty (Ed.), *Psychological consultation and collaboration in school and community settings: A casebook* (6th ed.) (pp. 53–68). Belmont, CA; Brooks/Cole.

LeBlanc, M., & Ritchie, M. (1999). Predictors of play therapy outcomes. *International Journal of Play Therapy, 8*(2), 19–34.

Lew, A., & Bettner, B. L. (1998). *Responsibility in the classroom: A teacher's guide to understanding and motivating students.* Newton Centre, MA: Connexions Press.

Lew, A., & Bettner, B. L. (2000). *A parent's guide to understanding and motivating children.* Newton Centre, MA: Connexions Press.

Meany-Walen, K. K., Bratton, S., & Kottman, T. (2014). Effects of Adlerian play therapy reducing students' disruptive behaviors. *Journal of Counseling and Development, 92*(1), 47–56. DOI: 10.1002/j.1556-6676.2014.00129.x.

Meany-Walen, K. K., Kottman, T., & Bullis, Q. (in review). Adlerian play therapy with children with externalizing behaviors: Single case design. *Journal of Counseling & Development.*

Meany-Walen, K. K., Bullis, Q., & Kottman, T. (in progress). Group Adlerian play therapy with children with externalizing behaviors: Single case design.

Mental Health America. (2009). *Factsheet: Recognizing mental health problems in children.* Retrieved from http://www.mentalhealthamerica.net/farcry/go/information/get-info/children-s-mental-health/recognizing-mental-health-problems-in-children.

Morrison, M. & Bratton, S. (2010), Preliminary investigation of an early mental health intervention for Head Start programs: Effects of Child Teacher Relationship Therapy (CTRT) on children's behavior problems. *Psychology in the Schools, 47*(10), 1003–1017.

Mosak, H., & Maniacci, M. (2008). *A primer of Adlerian psychology: The analytic-behavioral-cognitive psychology of Alfred Adler* (2nd ed.). New York: Taylor & Francis.

Myers, S. S., & Pianta, R. C. (2008). Development commentary: Individual and contextual influences on student-teacher relationships and children's early problem behaviors. *Journal of Clinical Child & Adolescent Psychology, 17*(3), 600–608. doi: 10.1080/15374410802148160.

Ojiambo, D., & Bratton, S. C. (2014). Effects of group activity play therapy on behavior problems of preadolescent orphans in Uganda. *Journal for Counseling and Development.*

Persson, G. E. B. (2005). Young children's prosocial and aggressive behaviors and their experiences of being targeted for similar behaviors by peers. *Social Development, 14*(2), 206–228.

President's New Freedom Commission on Mental Health. (2003). *Achieving the promise: Transforming mental health care in America final report* (DHHS Publication N. SMA-03-3832). Rockville, MD: Department of Health and Human Services.

Ray, D. (2007). Two counseling interventions to reduce teacher-child relationship stress. *Professional School Counseling, 10*(4), 428–440.

Sanson, A., Hemphill, S. A., & Smart, D. (2004). Connections between temperament and social development: A review. *Social Development, 13*(1), 142–170.

Schottlekorb, A. A., & Ray, D. C. (2009). ADHD symptom reduction in elementary students: A single-case effectiveness design. *Professional School Counseling, 13*(1), 11–22.

Teisl, M., & Cicchetti, D. (2008). Physical abuse, cognitive and emotional processes, and aggressive/disruptive behavior problems. *Social Development, 17*(1), 1–23. doi: 10.1111/j.1467-9507.2007.00412.

Tyndall-Lind, A., Landreth, G., & Giordano, M. A. (2001). Intensive group play therapy with child witnesses of domestic violence. *International Journal of Play Therapy, 10*(1), 53–83.

U.S. Public Health Service. (2000). *Report of the surgeon general's conference on children's mental health: A national action agenda.* Washington, DC: U.S. Department of Health and Human Services.

Webster-Stratton, C., & Ried, M. J. (2003). The incredible years parents, teachers, and children training services: A multifaceted treatment approach for young children with conduct problems. In A. E. Kazdin & J. R. Weisz (Eds.), *Evidence-based psychotherapies for children and adolescents* (pp. 224–240). New York, NY: Guilford.

Chapter Eleven

Group Activity Therapy for Physically Disabled Preadolescents Affected by Bullying

Amie C. Myrick, Julia A. Mitchell, and Kelsey A. Stephenson

Bullying is "the intentional, unprovoked abuse of power by one or more children in order to inflict pain or cause distress to another child on repeated occasions" (Dawkins, 1996, p. 603). Between 33 percent and 50 percent of American preadolescents and adolescents are involved in bullying as a bully, victim, or both (e.g., Nansel et al., 2001; Pergolizzi et al., 2011), which can take many forms. Bullying can lead to increases in anxiety, depression, social isolation, and negative views of self (e.g., Marsh, Parada, Craven, & Finger, 2004; Dixon, 2006; Dixon, 2006)

Research suggests that preadolescents with disabilities are the victims of bullying more frequently than their nondisabled peers (Connors & Stalker, 2007; MacArthur & Gaffney, 2001). The focus of this chapter is to provide mental health clinicians with tools to counsel preadolescents with physical disabilities (PD) who are victims of school-based bullying. Children with PD account for 18 percent of the disabled youth population (Child & Adolescent Health Measurement Initiative, 2003) and are diagnosed with conditions that affect their physical self, such as cerebral palsy, coordination disorders, paralysis, and degenerative muscle disorders. An integrative, play-based group therapy for social issues allows play therapists an opportunity to socialize children with and without PD and to enhance skills and self-esteem. A case study involving a preadolescent with a marked coordination disorder who attended such a group for social issues will be discussed.

RESEARCH SUPPORT

Bullying: Defined

Bullying encompasses aggression marked by three key features: (1) the bully intends to harm the victim; (2) the bullying occurs repeatedly over time; and (3) there is an imbalance of power in the bully–victim relationship (Nansel et al., 2001; Olweus, 1993). Bullying may include physical, psychological, relationship, social, or sexual aggression (e.g., Crick & Grotpeter, 1995; Galen & Underwood, 1997; Olweus, 1978; Ross, 1996). Bullying is not gender specific, although boys more commonly use physical aggression (e.g., Nagin and Tremblay, 2001) and girls use relational aggression (e.g., Coyne, Archer, & Eslea, 2006) to bully peers.

The Bullying Process

Bullying is a social activity and group process (Bjorkqvist, Ekman, & Lagerspetz, 1982). There are almost always youth who assist or encourage bullies and/or bear witness to bullies' stories, causing bullying situations to escalate easily. Roles include the *bully* who initiates the bullying; the *victim;* the *assistant* who is an active participant in the bullying; the *reinforcer* who encourages the bully and assistant by laughing; the *outsider* who remains removed from the bullying situation; and the *defender* who attempts to defend the victim (Salmivalli, Lagerspetz, Bjorkqvist, Osterman, & Kaukiainen, 1996).

Empathy and Perspective Taking

Empathy is a child's ability to understand and share in another person's feelings, and *perspective taking* refers to a child's ability to understand another person's thoughts, feelings, motives, and objectives (Feshbach, 1997). In general, those children who have high levels of empathy are less likely to become involved in bullying (Endresen & Olweus, 2001) and followers of bullies (i.e., assistants and reinforcers) have low empathy (Sutton, Smith, & Swettenham, 1999). Researchers have also found that children who were repeatedly bullied did not arouse the same type of empathy that their typically nonvictimized peers did (e.g., Peets, Hodges, & Salmivalli, 2011; Perry, Williard, & Perry, 1990).

Perspective taking is can be associated with healthy social adjustments or aggression. Bullies often have strong social skills (see Bronson & Merryman, 2009) and effectively use their perspective taking skills to anticipate and manipulate others' thoughts and behaviors. One study concluded that bullies had higher perspective taking skills than assistants, reinforcers, defenders, and victims (Sutton et al., 1999).

GROUP ACTIVITY THERAPY FOR SOCIAL ISSUES

Play is an integral component of child development and fosters emotional, social, cognitive, and physical growth. Play encourages independence, collaborative problem solving, and creative expression. All children play, regardless of their physical, intellectual, emotional, or environmental circumstances (Hughes, 2009). Play therapy maintains various perspectives of operation, two of which include "nondirective" and "directive." In *nondirective* play therapy, the goal is to facilitate a safe relationship through empathy, unconditional positive regard, and respect for the child. Therapists do not plan any specific activities for the sessions, allowing children to lead the way to their own healing. In contrast, therapists select activities to target symptom reduction in *directive* play therapy.

Group activity therapy (GAT) is a developmentally appropriate, group therapy module that combines play activities to encourage self-expression and teach important skills (Bratton & Ferebee, 1999; Packman & Bratton, 2003; Sweeney, Baggerly, & Ray, 2014). This approach is different than more traditional group talk therapy, which tends to target specific goals through discussion, verbal communication, and structured encounters (Gladding, 1999). The structure of GAT involves both nondirective, free play and a predetermined, directive activity to assist children in meeting the developmental milestone of feeling valued and accepted by peers, understanding that other youth their age share their thoughts and feelings, and developing and practicing skills within the context of peer relationships (Akos, Hamm, Mack, & Dunaway, 2007). GAT has also demonstrated effectiveness in significantly reducing internalized and externalized problems, including depressive and anxious symptoms (reviewed in Bratton, Ceballos, & Ferebee, 2009).

OVERVIEW OF VULNERABLE POPULATION

Children with PD have "congenital, accidental, or disease related" conditions that result in physical limitations (Thurneck, Warner, & Cobb, 2012, p. 873). Causes often include genetics, prenatal factors, accidents, or infections, although sometimes PD occur spontaneously and without a known reason. Because of the many illnesses and injuries that are encompassed by the term physical disability, children with PD vary greatly.

Individual Mental Health Concerns in Children with PD

Mental health concerns among children with PD are common. Although age of onset, current age, severity of the PD, gender, and social support greatly influence self-worth (see Antle, 2004), a high percentage of children with PD struggle with feelings of inadequacy, rejection, and low self-esteem (e.g., Shields, Murdoch, Loy, Dodd, & Taylor, 2006). They are more prone to experience disciplinary violence (e.g., Sullivan & Knutson, 2000), internalizing and externalizing symptoms (e.g., Lavigne & Faier-Routman, 1992), and poor social relationships (e.g., Child & Adolescent Health Measurement Initiative, 2003). They are also more likely to participate in risky behaviors, such as substance use, suicide attempts, and early sexual experiences (e.g., Blum, Kelly, & Ireland, 2001). Antle (2004) proposed that higher-than-average levels of self-esteem may be needed to offset barriers experienced due to social stigma and physical limitations.

Bullying and Social Concerns of Children with PD

Preadolescents with PD are subject to stereotypical beliefs, stigmatization, and prejudice (Llewellyn, 1995). They feel less accepted by their peers (Llewellyn), experience loneliness and exclusion at school (Curtin & Clarke, 2005), and they are less likely to participate in physical education classes and games on the playground (Bedini & Anderson, 2005). While children with PD may be regarded more positively than children with intellectual disabilities (e.g., Nowicki, 2006), they often still feel ostracized. Nikolaraizi and de Rebekiel (2002) suggest that nondisabled children may feel protective or act in socially polite ways toward physically disabled peers but are ultimately uncomfortable developing a close friendship. Other research has found that nondisabled children perceive themselves as dissimilar to those with PD with respect to interests and level of functioning (Brown, Ouellette-Kuntz, Lysaght, & Burge, 2011).

Youth with PD are twice as likely as nondisabled peers to be victims of bullying (Dawkins, 1996) and have identified emotional and physical bullying among the greatest barriers to educational success. In addition to easily identifiable conditions that leave them exposed to name-calling and teasing (Heary, Hennessy, & Swords, 2014), some children with PD lack the social awareness that would enable them to recognize a bullying situation (Unnever & Cornell, 2003). Other potential risk factors for children with PD include lack of social skills (Hughes, 2009), physical appearance, number and quality of friends, lack of social inclusion, and frequent absences from school (House of Commons, 2007). Finally, Dawkins (1996) identified receiving extra help at school, playing alone, having few close friends, and male gender as predictors for bullying in children with PD.

Play Profiles of Children with PD

Children with PD play less effectively than their typically developing peers, their level of physical activity is lower (Bedini & Anderson, 2005), and they are less likely to explore their environments or engage in meaningful social play (Hughes, 2009). Children's capacities and willingness to play signifies healthy emotional development and is an important factor in establishing creativity and connection with the world around them (Takatori & Bomtempo, 2007). Unfortunately, some adults may not encourage free play in children with PD, mistakenly believing that they are unable to engage in physical play. Some children with PD associate only with other disabled children, and many are involved in programs that emphasize academic skills more than free play and socialization (Hughes, 2009).

Play Therapy for Children with PD

Studies approximate that between 14 percent and 38 percent of children with PD who have poor psychosocial functioning engage in mental health treatment services and only about 10 percent receive outpatient treatment (see Hunt, 2009). Lack of coordination between family members and physicians, uncertainty about typical behavior for children with PD, and lack of sufficient services serve as barriers for these children receiving mental health treatment (Hunt).

Play therapy has demonstrated effectiveness in children with various disabilities, including physical disabilities (Carmichael, 1993), learning disabilities (Packman & Bratton, 2003), vision impairments (Filaccio, 2008), and developmental disabilities (Matson & Fodstad, 2010). Play can assist children with PD in achieving goals such as autonomy, increased communication, and management of emotions (Takatori & Bomtempo, 2007). Through nondirective and directive play, children explore the *I Am* and *I Can* aspects of their identities (Carmichael, 1993), with *I Am* representing self-esteem and *I Can* representing feelings of competence and control.

INTEGRATIVE PLAY THERAPY TREATMENT PLANNING AND PROTOCOL

The social model of disability suggests that children with PD are more affected by their social experiences than their disabilities (see Antle, 2004). A sense of achievement and inclusion are essential in order for children with disabilities to be protected from mental health difficulties (Connors & Stalker, 2003). Group therapy provides children with new opportunities to establish interpersonal relationships while also experiencing new perspectives and skills. Furthermore, in a study utilizing GAT with preadolescent children, researchers found that empathy and interpersonal skills increased (Packman & Bratton, 2003). Therefore, a group play model, such as GAT, where children with PD can engage with peers in a developmentally appropriate way, is an effective way to administer treatment for social issues, including bullying.

GAT aims to assist preadolescents with social issues by addressing a number of relevant variables. Having a psychoeducation component for children can raise awareness and provide youth with terminology to describe bullying behaviors and the effects of bullying. Once children understand the bullying process, the target of GAT becomes strengthening empathy skills, assisting children in seeing others' points of view, learning and practicing prosocial skills, and increasing children's self-esteem. Bullies and victims may have more in common than they even realize, as both groups can be disliked and rejected by their peers. Bullies may be disliked if they appear to lack empathy, whereas victims may have poor social skills or struggle to fit in with peers (e.g., Hafen, Laursen, Nurmi, Salmela-Aro, 2013). Despite this similarity, however, victims and bullies often experience teasing encounters differently, with bullies more likely to view the exchanges as funny, perceive others as liking them, or possibly feel guilt for their behavior (Kowalski, 2000). GAT allows children in all bullying roles to come together.

Participants

Preadolescents with and without PD should be included in GAT for social issues. In general, children with PD miss opportunities for meaningful contact and relationships with friends (Prellwitz & Tamm, 2000), and studies suggest children with PD have more varied and complex play when they are included with typically developing peers (Buysse, Goldman, & Skinner, 2002; Guralnick, 1999). To facilitate meaningful member interactions, groups should remain small in number, generally between four and six preadolescents (Bratton & Ferebee, 1999). The group outlined below is designed for youth in middle school, although the topics and activities could be revised for use with older or younger children as well.

Session Structure

Fifty-minute sessions occur weekly for six weeks and follow a similar format: check-in (five minutes), nondirective play (fifteen minutes), skills building (twenty minutes), and self-esteem building/check-out (ten minutes). Through the nondirective segment, children have the opportunity to make decisions and practice self-control and coping skills including teamwork, empathy, perspective taking, accepting responsibility, and initiating new relationships. Recommended toys for nondirective play include art supplies, sporting equipment, building materials, figurines, and board games (Bratton & Ferebee, 1999). As therapists watch group members play freely, they can also reflect members' feelings and behaviors or point out connections and similarities between the children (Paone, Packman, Maddux, & Rothman,

2008). The skills-building period of each session is focused on a particular topic targeting the goals outlined above and is summarized in table 11.1.

Session 1: Introduction to Group

All sessions begin with a brief check-in; in the first session, this may be largely led by the play therapist who can ask each member to introduce him/ herself and share something that happened over the last week. Play therapists may also pose an open-ended question to the group, such as, "Tell the group one thing that happened that made you feel included," or "Tell the group one thing that made you laugh this week" to engage the members meaningfully. During this first group, the play therapist will explain the structure of the sessions. Play therapists are encouraged to set minimal limits during nondirective play, and may simply say, "Each week, you will all have time to play with any of the materials in this room in most of the ways you would like. You may play together or alone. I will tell you when there are five minutes left." During the session, the play therapist comments on the activities the members are choosing and make connections between members.

Table 11.1. Summary of GAT Sessions

Session	Topic	Goals of Session	Example of Play Activity
1	Introduction	Group members meet Structure of group explained Group rules established	Group rules sign
2	The process of bullying	Introduce participant roles in bullying Discuss bullying experiences	Group art activity Operation Bully Bucket
3	Feelings and empathy	Feelings identification Strengthening of empathic understanding of peers	Group poem
4	Strengthening social skills	Identifying social skills strengths and weaknesses Perspective taking	Social experience self-report
5	Assertiveness and limit setting	Understanding own limits Establishing limits with peers	Role-plays
6	Goodbye celebration	Summarization of sessions Completion of self-esteem activity Termination and goodbye	Mailbox

Start of each session: Check-in and nondirective play. End of each session (sessions 1–5): Self-esteem activity and check-out (session 6: check-out only).

Next, the play therapist assists group members in cooperatively developing a list of group rules. Group rules typically include intangible expectations such as respect and turn taking but may also be quite literal (e.g., no food during group; cell phones off). Finally, the play therapist will introduce a long-term activity aimed at increasing self-esteem. One such activity is the *self-esteem tree* (adapted from KidsPlayandCreate, 2014) that addresses self-esteem building in a way that encourages group members to assist one another in identifying positive traits about themselves. Therapists provide children with a "tree trunk" template and blank "leaves." During the first week, children write three things that they like about themselves on the leaves and attach them to the tree trunk. Each week, group members assist each other in adding another leaf to the tree. The self-esteem tree is an easy and fun way to bring the *I Am* and *I Can* aspects of each child's personality into focus weekly.

Session 2: The Process of Bullying

Play therapists can utilize any number of activities to educate children about bullying, but two examples are a group drawing and modified game activity. In the *group drawing activity*, the play therapist provides a roll of paper and art supplies, explaining that the group is going to create a story about bullying together. One child begins the story by drawing a person or item. Each child takes turns adding items until the story is completed. The only rules are (1) the child's addition must contribute to the story, (2) the child may not negate anything another child has done (i.e., crossing out a drawing), and (3) the story must be about bullying in some way. This activity allows the therapist to see how each child views bullying, including antecedents, actions of characters in the story, and consequences. Once completed, the group members discuss the story and their experiences with bullying. The therapist adds information about bullying roles and adverse effects where necessary.

The therapist is the target of bullying in a modified version of a frustration-inducing game such as *Operation* (adapted from Frey, n.d.). In this game, the therapist attempts to remove plastic ailments from the game board without touching the edge of the cavity opening, and group members tease the therapist as he/she works. When the game is finished, the group talks about the teasing that was used, how members felt when partaking in the bullying, and how the therapist may have felt while being teased. This activity can introduce topics such as bullying roles, adverse effects, and reasons children bully.

Session 3: Feelings and Empathy

Feelings identification is an important aspect of any bullying protocol. Children who have been bullied may feel helpless, sad, excluded, and fearful while bullies may admit feeling powerful, remorseful, or guilty. Strengthening empathic understanding in the bullying process can have a long-term effect on the use of bullying; one study found that greater empathy was directly associated with decreased bullying up to one year later (Batanova & Loukas, 2011).

Poetry increases empathy in children (see Sassen, 2012). As a group, children identify feelings that are associated with bullying such as hurt, sad, funny, powerful, and helpless. Each preadolescent is assigned one of the feelings and asked to write one line for a poem related to the feeling. Prior to beginning, participants can discuss ways to give constructive feedback, rather than teasing or mocking. Some group members may even share negative feedback experiences they have had in other group settings. Children create and read their line of the poem to the group—the other members comment—and the play therapist adds the line to the group's poem. At the end of the exercise, the group reflects on the poem.

Session 4: Strengthening Social Skills

The research on social skills training suggests that merely teaching new skills to children does not mean that the skills are used long term or result in greater peer acceptance (O'Donnell, 2002). GAT not only teaches social skills but, through nondirective play, provides an opportunity for group members to practice and engage in positive interactions while receiving reinforcement and feedback from the therapist and other group members. There are several aspects of social skills that can be addressed during this fourth session, including giving and receiving compliments, problem solving, and perspective taking. Group leaders may incorporate all or some of these, depending on presenting issues and participation levels. The *social experience self-report* (Kuzma, 2008) asks each participant to take a self-inventory of their social skills. After identifying their strengths and weaknesses, the group members choose one or more skill to improve upon and identify an activity to assist them. Bibliotherapy, art, games, and role-playing can all be suggested and used effectively.

Session 5: Assertiveness and Limit Setting

Throughout the six weeks, children are exposed to limit setting by the therapist. Using the A-C-T model of limit setting (Landreth, 2012), the therapist reflects feelings while setting therapeutic limits to keep members safe. Setting limits also assists children in learning and practicing self-control. In A-C-T, the "A" stands for *acknowledge the feeling,* "C" stands for *communicate the limit*, and "T" stands for *target an alternative.* An example of an A-C-T limit might be, "John, I know you are really excited to roll the dice, but in this group, we take turns. You can choose to wait quietly, or you can cheer

Sam on while he takes his turn." Session five allows group members to experience and discuss effective limit setting. Preadolescents identify their own limits when it comes to physical space, verbal communication, and topics of conversation and consider these with their fellow group members. These limits may be written in the shape of a stop sign and discussed by group members.

Session five also includes a discussion of assertiveness, aggressiveness, and passivity. Group members learn the importance of making eye contact, using a firm, loud, tone of voice and a stern expression, and making an "I" statement, such as, "I don't like it when you throw my book bag on the ground" to assert themselves. Role-playing situations supplied by the group members is one way to playfully practice these skills. One member acts as the bully, while three other members are the aggressive responder, the assertive responder, and the passive responder (adapted from Vernon, 2009).

Session 6: Goodbye Celebration

The final, termination session involves closure from the group and the therapeutic process. Group sessions are summarized, children's hard work is celebrated, self-esteem trees are completed, and members say goodbye. The group can also complete a *mailbox* activity, where children put statements about one another in envelopes to take home. Each child finishes three prompts for each of his/her fellow group members, such as, "I'm glad you were in this group because _____"; "Next time I see you in class, I will _____"; and "I did not realize we had _____ in common!"

RELEVANT INTERVENTION

The *bully bucket* acts as a physical representation of the effect that bullying has on victims. Members take turns choosing rocks from a large container to represent times that they have been bullied. They write one word to describe the incident on the rock and place it in the bucket. The significance of this activity is that all group members, whether they have predominantly been victims or bullies, will have rocks to add to their buckets. The buckets act as symbols; that is, the more members experienced bullying, the more they have been affected or "weighed down" by it. To extend this activity further, members can think of times when someone said/did something kind or caring toward them. These, in contrast to the rocks, can be written on a light object, such as a ping pong ball. Group members can discuss the ways in which kindness can make them feel "light" but also acknowledge that these words and actions do not replace the rocks. Instead, they get mixed in with the rocks, with both having effects on feelings, thoughts, behaviors, and self-esteem. Finally, the group can discuss ways to help "carry" the heavy bucket of unkind, bullying messages to relieve their effects on others.

CASE STUDY

The names and identifying details have been changed to protect the privacy of individuals. Billy, a ten-year-old African American male, was referred to the GAT group for social issues after his mother witnessed an increase in depressive symptoms. She told the therapist that Billy had been a victim of bullying for many years and had matriculated through three elementary schools. Billy was born with Neurofibromatosis type 1 (NF1), a genetic condition that disturbs cell growth in the nervous system causing tumors to form on nerve tissue. Additionally, Billy was diagnosed with Congenital Pseudoarthrosis (CP), a common ailment in those with NF1. CP resulted in Billy having one leg growing faster than the other; he had a significant limp and endured multiple surgeries to correct the deformity.

Prior to the start of the group, Billy was failing several subjects in school, despite presenting as articulate and intelligent. He was being bullied regularly because of his physical limp, academic struggles, family's financial limitations, and mother's history of substance abuse. Billy appeared much younger than his chronological age. He stated that he had no friends and that no one liked him. His mother found letters that he had written expressing how sad and unhappy he was. In these letters he stated that he hated the people that bullied him. Billy exhibited low self-esteem, and his mother told the therapist that she felt "at a loss" for managing the bullying. Unfortunately, she kept him home from school to protect him. This only compounded the problem, however, as Billy's grades declined. He also became more isolated.

In the first session, Billy appeared timid and reserved. During free play, he removed himself from his peers, building Legos in corner alone. He participated in the creating of rules by suggesting "no teasing," but the therapist noticed that he mostly listened to the other members. Although he played alone again during free play in session two, he appeared slightly more comfortable in session two, where he participated in the group art project readily and laughed along with the other group members as the therapist failed to extract pieces from during Operation. During the poetry activity in session three, Billy received the feeling word "lonely" and contributed to the group's poem by writing, "Lonely is when no one likes you." Interestingly, the group tried to change Billy's perspective on loneliness, chiming in with their own stories about times when they were lonely but not necessarily disliked. The therapist noted that the group was trying to help Billy feel better, and reflected this to him.

At the start of session four, the therapist noticed that Billy was again playing with the Lego blocks in the corner; however, she observed that another group member had joined him. She commented reassuringly, "Chris and Billy, I notice you are playing together." Billy smiled. In session five, the boys again played together, and the therapist noticed that Billy was participating more and more each week in the skills-building part of the group as well. He even answered another member's question about his disability without appearing ashamed. The therapist reinforced the member's empathy as she asked the question, and Billy's kind responsiveness rather than defensiveness. Finally, during the termination session, Billy shared that he was going to miss the group and that he liked everyone in the room. He seemed to enjoy writing statements for everyone's mailboxes and smiled as he read what others had written to him.

After the group had ended, the therapist continued seeing Billy for individual therapy, and assisted Billy in identifying his strengths and improving his self-esteem. She helped Billy get involved in the school's building club, where he was exposed to other children who enjoyed creating using blocks and Legos. Billy told her that he liked participating in an activity that was not affected by his disability. Although bullying did not completely dissipate for Billy, he reported that it was bothering him less, especially because he had made a couple friends in his building club and still occasionally talked to Chris from the group.

CONCLUSION

Bullying is a reality for most preadolescents. Children with PD may be at increased risk for victimization and often struggle to fit in with nondisabled peers. GAT for social issues is a group, play-based treatment paradigm that addresses many aspects of bullying through connectedness with peers, psychoeducation, and skills building. Through the use of free play and structured activities, preadolescents can become more aware of the role that thoughts, feelings, and behaviors play in bullying, and those with PD gain an opportunity to integrate with their peers in a supportive, therapeutic environment.

REFERENCES

Akos, P., Hamm, J. V., Mack, S., & Dunaway, M. (2007). Utilizing the developmental influence of peers in middle school groups. *Journal for Specialists in Group Work, 32*(1), 51–60.

Antle, B. J. (2004). Factors associated with self-worth in youth people with physical disabilities. *Health and Social Work, 29*(3), 167–175.

Batanova, M. D., & Loukas, A. (2011). Social anxiety and aggression in early adolescents: Examining the moderating roles of empathic concern and perspective taking. *Journal of Youth and Adolescence, 40*(11), 1534–1543.

Bedini, L. A., & Anderson, D. M. (2005). I'm nice, I'm smart, I like karate: Girls with physical disabilities' perception s of physical recreation. *Therapeutic Recreation Journal, 39*(2), 114–130.

Bjorkqvist, K., Ekman, K., & Lagerspetz, K. M. (1982). Bullies and victims: Their ego picture, ideal ego picture, and normative ego picture. *Scandinavian Journal of Psychology, 23*, 307–313.

Blum, R. W., Kelly, A., & Ireland, M. (2001). Health-risk behaviors and protective factors among adolescents with mobility impairments and learning and emotional disabilities. *Journal of Adolescent Health, 28*(6), 481–490.

Bratton, S. C., Ceballos, P. L., & Ferebee, K. W. (2009). Integration of structured expressive activities within a humanistic group play therapy format for preadolescents. *The Journal for Specialists in Group Work, 34*(3), 251–275.

Bratton, S. C., & Ferebee, K. W. (1999). The use of structured expressive art activities in group activity therapy with preadolescents. In D. S. Sweeney & L. E. Homeyer (Eds.), *The handbook of group play therapy, How to do it, how it works, whom it's best for* (pp. 192–214). San Francisco: Jossey-Bass.

Bronson, P., & Merryman, A. (2009). *Nurtureshock: New thinking about children.* New York, NY: Twelve.

Brown, H. K., Oullette-Kuntz, H., Lysaght, R., & Burge, P. (2011). Students' behavioural intentions toward peers with disability. *Journal of Applied Research in Intellectual Disabilities, 24*, 322–332.

Buysse, V., Goldman, B. D., & Skinner, M. (2002). Setting effects on friendship formation among young children with and without disabilities. *Exceptional Children, 68*(4), 503–517.

Carmichael, K. D. (1993). Play therapy and children with disabilities. *Issues in Comprehensive Pediatric Nursing, 16*(3), 165–173.

Child and Adolescent Health Measurement Initiative. (2003). *2003 National Survey of Children's Health,* Data resource center for child and adolescent health website. Retrieved June 1, 2014, from www.nschdata.org.

Connors, C., & Stalker, K. (2003). *The views and experiences of disabled children and their siblings: A positive outlook.* London, England: Jessica Kingsley Publishers.

Connors, C., and Stalker, K. (2007). Children's experiences of disability, Pointers to a social model of childhood disability. *Disability & Society, 22*(1), 19–33.

Coyne, S. M., Archer, J., & Eslea, M. (2006). "We're not friends anymore! Unless . . . ": The frequency and harmfulness of indirect, relational, and social aggression. *Aggressive Behavior, 32*(4), 294–307.

Crick, N. R. & Grotpeter, J. K. (1995). Relational aggression, gender, and social psychological adjustment. *Child Development, 66*(3), 710–722.

Curtin, M., & Clarke, G. (2005). Listening to young people with physical disabilities' experiences of education. *International Journal of Disability, Development and Education, 52*(3), 195–214.

Dawkins, J. L. (1996). Bullying, physical disability and the paediatric patient. *Developmental Medicine and Child Neurology, 38*, 603–612.

Dixon, R. (2006). A framework for managing bullying that involves students who are deaf or hearing impaired. *Deafness and Education International, 8*(1), 11–32.

Endresen, I. M. & Olweus, D. (2001). Self-reported empathy in Norwegian adolescents, Sex differences, age trends, and relationship to bullying. In A. C. Bohart & D. J. Stipek (Eds.), *Constructive & destructive behavior* (pp. 147–165). Washington, DC: American Psychological Association.

Feshbach, N. D. (1997). Empathy, The formative years implications for clinical practice. In A. C. Bohart & L. S. Greenberg (Eds.), *Empathy reconsidered. New directions in psychotherapy* (pp. 33–59). Washington, DC: American Psychological Association.

Filaccio, M. D. (2008). *Child-centered play therapy for children with low vision: A multiple case study* (Published doctoral dissertation). University of Northern Colorado, Colorado.

Frey, D. E. (n.d.). Creative strategies for the treatment of anger. Retrieved June 11, 2014 from http://www.lianalowenstein.com/anger_frey_edited.pdf.

Galen, B. R. & Underwood, M. K. (1997). A developmental investigation of social aggression among children. *Developmental Psychology, 33*(4), 589–600.

Gladding, S. T. (1999). *Group work: A counseling specialty.* Upper Saddle River, NJ: Merrill.

Guralnick, M. J. (1999). The nature and meaning of social integration for young children with mild developmental delays in inclusive settings. *Journal of Early Intervention, 22*(1), 70–86.

Hafen, C. A., Laursen, B., Nurmi, J. E., & Salmela-Aro, K. (2013). Bulllies, victims, and antipathy: The feeling is mutual. *Journal of Abnormal Child Psychology, 41*, 801–809.

Heary, C., Hennessy, E., & Swords, L. (2014). Stigma associated with disease and disability during childhood and adolescence: A developmental approach. In P. W. Corrigan (Ed.), *The stigma of disease and disability: Understanding causes and overcoming injustices* (pp. 205–222). Washington, DC: American Psychological Association.

House of Commons—Education and Skills Committee. (2007). *Bullying HC 85, third report of session 2006–07, report, together with formal minutes, oral and written evidence.* London, England: The Stationary Office.

Hughes, F. P. (2009). *Children, play, and development.* Los Angeles, CA: Sage Publications.

Hunt, S. M. (2009). *Patterns of psychosocial functioning and mental health service utilization in children and adolescents with chronic health conditions or physical disabilities* (Published doctoral dissertation). Utah State University, Utah.

KidsPlayandCreate. (2014). Me tree: Self-esteem. Retrieved June 4, 2014 from http://www.kidsplayandcreate.com/me-tree-self-esteem-character-building-arts-and-crafts-project-for-kids/.

Kowalski, R. M. (2000). "I was only kidding!" Victims and perpetrators' perceptions of teasing. *Personality and Social Psychology Bulletin, 26*(2), 231–241.

Kuzma, J. (2008). *Social experience self report.* Retrieved June 15, 2014 from http://jillkuzma.files.wordpress.com/2008/09/social-experience-self-report.pdf.

Landreth, G. L. (2012). *Play therapy: The art of the relationship (3rd ed.).* New York, NY: Routledge.

Lavigne, J. V., & Faier-Routman, J. (1992). Psychological adjustment to pediatric physical disorders, A meta-analytic review. *Journal of Pediatric Psychology, 17*(2), 133–157.

Llewellyn, A. (1995). The abuse of children with physical disabilities in mainstream schooling. *Developmental Medicine and Child Neurology, 37*, 740–743.

MacArthur, J., & Gaffney, M. (2001). *Bullied and teased or just another kid? The social experiences of students with disabilities at school.* Wellington, New Zealand: Council for Educational Research.

Marsh, H. W., R. H. Parada, R. H., Craven, R. G. & Finger, L. (2004). In the looking glass: A reciprocal effects model elucidating the complex nature of bullying, psychological determinants, and the central role of self-concept. In C. E. Sanders and G. D. Phye (Eds.), *Bullying implications for the classroom* (pp. 63–106). New York, NY: Elsevier Academic Press.

Matson, J. L., & Fodstad, J. C. (2010). Teaching social skills to developmentally delayed preschoolers. In C. E. Schaefer (Ed.), *Play therapy for preschool children* (pp. 301–333). Washington, DC: American Psychological Association.

Nagin, D. S., & Tremblay, R. E. (2001). Parental and early childhood predictors of persistent physical aggression in boys from kindergarten to high school. *Archives of General Psychiatry, 58*(4), 389–394.

Nansel, T., Overpeck, M., Pilla, R. Ruan, W., Simons-Morton, B., & Scheidt, P. (2001). Bullying behaviors among US youth: Prevalence and association with psychosocial adjustment. *Journal of the American Medical Association, 285*(16), 2094–2100.

Nikolaraizi M. & de Rebekiel N. (2002). A comparative study of children's attitudes toward deaf children, children in wheelchairs, and blind children in Greece and in the UK. *European Journal of Special Needs Education, 16*(2), 167–182.

Nowicki E. A. (2006). A cross-sectional multivariate analysis of children's attitudes toward disabilities. *International Journal of Disability, Development, and Education, 50*(Pt 5), 243–265.

O'Donnell, A. S. (2002). *Implementation and evaluation of a treatment program for relational aggression and victimization with preadolescent girls* (Published doctoral dissertation). Alliant International University, California.

Olweus, D. (1978). *Aggression in schools.* Washington, DC: Hemisphere.

Olweus, D. (1993). *Bullying at school: What we know and what we can do.* Oxford: Blackwell.

Packman, J., & Bratton, S. (2003). A school-based group/play activity therapy intervention with learning disabled preadolescents exhibiting behavior problems. *International Journal of Play Therapy, 12*(2), 7–29.

Paone, T. R., Packman, J., Maddux, C., & Rothman, T. (2008). A school-based group activity therapy intervention with at-risk high school students as it relates to their moral reasoning. *International Journal of Play Therapy, 17*(2), 122–137.

Peets, K., Hodges, E. V. E., Salmivalli, C. (2011). Actualization of social cognitions into aggressive behavior toward disliked targets. *Social Development, 20*(2), 233–250.

Pergolizzi, F., Pergolizzi, J. III, Gan, Z., Macario, S., Pergolizzi, J. V. Jr., Ewin, T. J., & Gan, T. J. (2011). Bullying in middle school: Results from a 2008 survey. *International Journal of Adolescent Medical Health, 23*(1), 11–18.

Perry, D. G., Williard, J. C., & Perry, L. C. (1990). Peers' perceptions of the consequences that victimized children provide aggressors. *Child Development, 61*(5), 1310–1325.

Prellwitz, M., & Tamm, M. (2000). How children with restricted mobility perceive their school environment. *Scandinavian Journal of Occupational Therapy, 7*, 165–173.

Ross, D. M. (1996). *Childhood bullying and teasing: What school personnel, other professionals, and parents can do.* Alexandria, VA: American Counseling Association.

Salmivalli, C., Lagerspetz, K., Bjorkqvist, K., Osterman, K., & Kaukiainen, A. (1996). Bullying as a group process: Participant roles and their relations to social status within the group. *Aggressive Behavior, 22*(1), 1–15.

Sassen, G. (2012). Drums and poems: An intervention promoting empathetic connection and literacy in children. *Journal of Creativity in Mental Health, 7*, 233–248.

Shields, N., Murdoch, A., Loy, Y., Dodd, K. J., & Taylor, N. F. (2006). A systematic review of the self-concept of children with cerebral palsy compared with children without disability. *Developmental Medicine and Child Neurology, 48*, 151–157.

Sutton, J., Smith, P. K., & Swettenham, J. (1999). Social cognition and bullying: Social inadequacy or skilled manipulation? *British Journal of Developmental Psychology, 17*(3), 435–450.

Sullivan, P. M., & Knutson, J. F. (2000). Maltreatment and disabilities: A population based epidemiological study. *Child Abuse and Neglect, 24*(10), 1257–1273.

Sweeney, D. S., Baggerly, J. N., & Ray, D. C. (2014). *Group play therapy: A dynamic approach.* New York, NY: Routledge.

Takatori, M., & Bomtempo, E. (2007). The implications of Winnicott's theory of play for the work of occupational therapy's observation with children with physical disabilities. *European Journal of Special Needs Education, 22*(1), 47–61.

Thurneck, D. A., Warner, P. J., & Cobb, H. C. (2012). Children and adolescents with disabilities and health care needs, Implications for intervention. In D. T. Brown (Ed.), *Counseling and psychotherapy with children and adolescents* (pp. 844–914). Hoboken, NJ: Wiley.

Unnever, J. D. & Cornell, D. G. (2003). Bullying, self-control, and ADHD. *Journal of Interpersonal Violence, 81*(2), 129–147.

Vernon, A. (2009). *More what works when with children and adolescents: A handbook of individual counseling techniques.* Champaign, IL: Research Press.

Chapter Twelve

Integrating Expressive Arts and Research-Supported Play-Based Interventions with LGBTQI Adolescents

Linda Goldman

The acquisition of a unique and genuine self-identity is an integral part of the developmental work of young adults. Adolescents experiment and assimilate learning in their social, educational, family, and societal arenas to formulate what is comfortable for them as they navigate their ever-changing emotions and thoughts. Myers (2005) defined adolescence as the "life between childhood and adulthood. It starts with the physical beginnings of sexual maturity and ends with the social achievement of independent adult status" (p. 124). As adolescents develop and strengthen their needs for interpersonal intimacy and the creation of close emotional ties, many turn to peers. Often they question, "Who am I?" "What will I be?" and "What are my values and beliefs?" The following are important developmental tasks for young people:

- Accepting one's body as it is and creating more mature relationships with others their age
- Seeking to become responsible members of society and identifying evolving values
- Preparing for a future of economic success, marriage, and family life (Goldman, 2008, p. 94)

Experts often view adolescence as the most difficult developmental epoch through which to matriculate. The prodigious struggle that young people face to achieve goals and *find themselves* can be complicated by marginalization because of their diverse sexual orientation and variable gender identity. Lesbian, bisexual, gay, transgender, queer, questioning, and intersex (LGBTQI) youth face more complex psychosocial issues than their heterosexual peers. The long road from between childhood and maturity can be fraught with struggles of stigma, shame, secrecy, abuse, rejection, abandonment, and bullying. A natural by-product of these conditions is difficulty in achieving the developmental tasks of adolescence—often resulting in significant loss or grief issues. Too many LGBTQI youth experience challenges associated with adolescent development, coupled with and overwhelmed by additional complexities arising from exposure to stereotyping, hidden agendas, sexual orientation and gender identity conflicts, and problematic concerns from peers, parents, and society. Therapeutic goals in working with this population are threefold: (1) to recognize this is a societal and systemic issue that needs to be addressed comprehensively, (2) to help LGBTQI adolescents process their myriad feelings with the recognition of their sexual orientation or gender identity as valid and normal, and (3) to create safe home, schools, and communities for LGBTQI adolescents.

This chapter explores the complex issues that LGBTQI adolescents face when *coming out* (i.e., telling friends and family about their sexual orientation or gender identity) as lesbian, bisexual, gay, transgender, queer, intersex, or questioning youth. Through drama, art, music, journaling, and poetry, the exploration of the unspoken can be incorporated into a counseling framework. Expressive arts- and play-based interventions such as drama and role-play resonate with many adolescents as they naturally seek creative outlets for self-expression. Further, these tools can assist with discovery and acknowledgment of information for LGBTQI adolescents that may be otherwise too difficult to verbalize within the mental health context. A case study illustrates the way in which this integrated therapy modality can be utilized with LGBTQI adolescent clients.

RESEARCH SUPPORT

In the current social justice literature, educators and mental health professionals are called to design a new level of social awareness to help LGBTQI youth recognize, overcome, and integrate psychosocial challenges to optimize their mental health. Adolescents continuously refine their moral judgment, focus disproportionately on their peers' appraisal, and experience a turbulent gamut of emotions as a part of their daily life. Due to the internalization of societal judgment and the sexual prejudice often projected from heterosexuals who maintain a bigoted heterosexist attitude, LGBTQI youth often become an "at-risk" group. These factors converge to accelerate psychological conditions such as depression, low self-esteem, suicide ideation, drug and alcohol abuse, anxiety, panic disorders, and greater likelihood of being harmed by weapons, often culminating in homelessness, hate crimes, and peer and parental rejection. "Healthy identity development and self-worth can substantially diminish for young people living in a culture where they are rejected, judged, and hated because of behaviors, sexual orientation, or gender identity" (Goldman, 2013, p. 49).

There is a research base in the current literature to substantiate the psychological distress associated with being LGBTQI. One study involving 350 gay adolescents between the ages of fourteen and twenty-one reported that 54 percent made their first suicide attempt before coming out to others, 27 percent made the attempt during the same year they came out, and 19 percent made the attempt after coming out (Kitts, 2005). LGBTQI young adults who reported high levels of family rejection during adolescence were 8.4 times more likely to report having attempted suicide, 5.9 times more likely to report high levels of depression, 3.4 times more likely to use illegal drugs, and 3.4 times more likely to report having engaged in unprotected sexual intercourse, compared with peers from families that reported no or low levels of family rejection (Ryan, Huebner, Diaz, & Sanchez, 2009). The emotional isolation, rejection, and complete withdrawal from parents that many LGBTQI youth face can ultimately lead to depression, substance abuse, and homelessness. LGBTQI youth experience a higher prevalence rate of being thrown out of or opting to leave their homes than their heterosexual peers. Goldfried (2001) reported, "1 out of 3 was verbally abused by family members; 1 out of 10 was physically assaulted by a family member" (as cited in Kitts, 2005, p. 625). The fear of potentially experiencing this rejection and abuse is a significant psychosocial stressor.

Ploderl and Fartacek (2005) indicated a higher incidence rate for most suicide-related risk factors with increased psychosocial stress and vulnerability and lack of family support for LGBT youth. LGBT youth who decide to *come out* risk rejection and abuse from parents, friends, family members, and society at large. Goldfried (2001) reported that one out of four [LGBTQI students] had experienced physical abuse at school. Research has demonstrated that adolescents struggling with issues surrounding their sexual orientation who do not receive appropriate therapy and support are at risk for serious psychological difficulties.

The expressive arts is one psychotherapeutic means of using visual and word images to (a) portray the deep emotions, (b) gain control over psychological suffering, and (c) inspire understanding that leads to self-contentment. Bertman (2008) explained, "I would go so far as to suggest that there is an unmistakable synergy between therapeutic and aesthetic competence. Both involve grappling with understanding of ambiguity, nuance, metaphor, and comfort with the inexpressible" (p. 55). There is growing evidence in support of a relationship between personal creative expression and sexual identity, as well as between creativity and psychological health (Pelton-Sweet & Sherry, 2008). Fraser and Waldmen (2004) presented art therapy work with gay and lesbian young people who were challenged by sexuality gender identity, homophobia, depression, coming out, and shame. They clarified that for some young people art creations allowed them to make visible the invisible, hidden and secret, to bear witness to pain, and to celebrate courage.

Many art therapy interventions are ideally suited for clients struggling with identity. Techniques discussed included *Inside Me, Outside Me* with two self-portraits, single self-portraits, puppets to project emotions or be the speaker, a collage used as a representation of themselves in society with key words, and phrases to initiate discussion. Fraser and Waldman (2004) concluded that art making has been used by many art therapist with LGBT clients to explore issues such as sexual identity, bigotry, internalized homophobia, trauma and abuse, gender identity, depression, and coming out. The researchers go on to say that by clinicians nurturing and assisting with the expression of the imagination, adolescents may be able to protect their physical and emotional health while learning more about, and ultimately becoming, their authentic selves.

OVERVIEW OF VULNERABLE POPULATION

LGBTQI young people are more at risk for major depression, anxiety disorder, drug and alcohol dependency, low self-esteem, being harmed by a weapon, being abused or rejected, becoming homeless, or dropping out of school. This at-risk stature sometimes can be associated with additional stress from marginalization or disenfranchisement from peers, family, and society, and their inability to see the same future with economic success, political success, marriage, and children. LGBTQI students attempt suicide at least twice as much as other teens, and have a much greater chance of bullying and harassment.

These additional pressures in school and family have created a marginalized segment of adolescents that often exist as a stigmatized minority. In a *Los Angeles Times* article, "Gay and Homeless: In Plain Sight, a Largely Hidden Population," Alexandra Zavis (2010) reported that every year, hundreds of gay youths end up alone on the streets of Los Angeles County, where they make up a disproportionate share of the at least 4,200 people under twenty-five who are homeless on any given day. LGBTQI teens are "more likely to be harshly punished by schools and courts than their straight peers" (Brody, 2011). The following are a few of the many statistics that enlarge the scope of the challenges our LGBTQI young people face:

- Lesbian, gay, or bisexual youth who reported high levels of family rejection in adolescence were 8.4 times more likely to have attempted suicide (Ryan, 2009).
- The Massachusetts Youth Risk Survey (2009) states that lesbian, gay, and bisexual youth are up to four times more likely to attempt suicide than their heterosexual peers.
- As many as 20 percent of the runaway and homeless youth population identifies as lesbian, gay, bisexual, transgender, or questioning (LGBTQI; Federal Policy Brief, 2012, p. 1.)
- Two million U.S. teenagers were reported in 2001 as having serious problems in school because they were taunted with antigay slurs.
- According to the National School Climate Survey, 52.9 percent of LGBT students were harassed or threatened by their peers via electronic mediums, often known as cyber-bullying (GLSEN [Gay, Lesbian, Straight Educational Network], 2010).
- GLSEN's 2009 School Climate Survey reported nine out of ten LGBTQI students experienced harassment at school. The following statistics give a mirror of the world our LGBTQI teens live with in their educational environment.
- Nearly two-thirds (61.1 percent) of students reported that they felt unsafe in school because of their sexual orientation, and more than a third (39.9 percent) felt unsafe because of their gender expression (GLSEN, 2010, p. 3).
- LGBT students missed a class at least once was 29.1 percent and 30.0 percent missed at least one day of school in the past month because of safety concerns, when compared to the general population of secondary school students (GLSEN, 2010, p. 5).
- LGBT students who were more frequently harassed because of their sexual orientation or gender expression had grade point averages almost half a grade lower than for students who were less often harassed (GLSEN, 2010).
- Derogatory remarks such as "faggot" or "dyke" were often heard by 72.4 percent of students at school; 88.9 percent reportedly heard "gay" used in a negative way often or frequently at school; 40.1 percent reported being physically harassed at school because of their sexual orientation; and 18.8 percent were physically assaulted because of their sexual orientation (GLSEN, 2010, School Climate Survey, p. 3).
- Nonheterosexual youth suffer disproportionate educational and criminal justice punishments that are not explained by greater engagement in illegal or transgressive behaviors.

It can be extremely painful for LGBTQI girls and boys to be in a hostile school environment that involves exclusion or ridicule, especially among peers. Many young people are targeted for atypical behavior and coming out as LGBTQI and become victims of bullying and harassment. This distress often culminates in anxiety, depression, suicide ideation, or physical and emotional harm. Additionally, schools settings often contain cliques, with the ostracized left with feelings of silent or unspoken depression, suicidal ideation, anger, and hostility. Withdrawal, vulnerability, low self-esteem, and hopelessness can manifest in any rejected LGBTQI adolescent.

INTEGRATIVE PLAY THERAPY TREATMENT PLANNING AND PROTOCOL

Adolescents are attracted to symbolism, graphic portrayals, and art; therefore, they are more likely to engage by using art as a language than verbal expression (Riley, 2001). In light of the extraordinary issues and obstacles faced by out LGBTQI youth, it is essential to highlight the creative arts as a strong vehicle and immeasurable tool to use in mental health counseling interventions.

One of the most beneficial approaches in allowing LGBTQI youth to process their issues around sexual orientation and gender identity is the creation of an oasis of safety and protection for self-expression (Goldman, 2008). A teen struggling with coming out, a young girl rejected by family for being a lesbian, or an adolescent boy taunted with antigay slurs, can be guided through difficult feelings using art, poetry, music and drama, powerful examples for self expression and creativity. These techniques allow the teens to go beyond limitations of age, ability, and the spoken or written word in order to embrace an inner world more easily liberated through these medias. All too often LGBTQI young people are exposed to outdated thinking and cultural indoctrination that have reinforced stigma around sexual orientation and gender identity. As one young man expressed, "I am not going to change or apologize for who I am. It's the society that needs to change" (Maston, 1997, p. 112).

Through the creative arts young people are given an avenue of expression that may reduce anxiety, increase memory retrieval, and share narratives. Often expression through art creates a psychological safe space to communicate reservoirs of grief in ways that direct conversation may not permit. A simple drawing speaks volumes. As Goodman explains, "therapeutic communication can be easier or more direct through the use of symbols or images rather than the complex world of spoken language" (Webb, 2002, p. 299).

The mental health goal of helping children of all ages is to promote their competence, facilitate their ability to cope, and help them recognize that they are active participants in their own lives (Silverman, 2000). Children, teens, and adults can work toward this goal by the use of artwork, poetry, music, writing, and other forms of journaling allow expression through the creative arts. They help young people release stored, underground notions that become an endless groundswell of turbulence until they can be sorted out and shared. "Direct access to a child's world is often achieved by way of his/her imagination, where thoughts, ideas, and feelings interact freely with facts" (Webb, 2002, p. 299).

Self-Expression Through Artwork

Art allows teens an innovative way to express themselves than verbal interventions alone may not accomplish. LGBTQI young people can solve problems and build self-esteem through art interventions. Two dynamic art interventions are *mask making* and *paper bag self-portraits* (adapted from Moon, 2006). Mask making involves the creation of two masks: one that represents the self seen by society, and one that represents one's inner world. With LGBTQI teens, the differences between the two masks may be greater than that of their heterosexual peers. The therapist asks the teen about each mask and listens to the information without judgment. Similarly, a paper bag self-portrait involves placing objects inside a bag that represent different aspects of the teen's self. This may include pictures of loved ones, allies, pets, music, or book titles. Adolescents' hopes and fears can also be listed on each side of the bag.

The externalization of an issue or internal stress by creating an art object may aid an adolescent through the process of resolving the problem. Riley (2001) suggested asking the adolescent to make a collage that illustrates the psychosocial challenges being brought to therapy. Nathan, an adolescent male, decided to call his collage *Trouble*. He reviewed magazines and websites to find images depicting homophobia and placed them on a large piece of red poster board with a written word highlighted using magic markers on every picture. These words included *gay, marriage, equality, hate,* and many more. Two pictures contained headlines of a fourteen-year-old murdered by another eighth grader for being gay and an eleven-year-old who hung himself after being tortured by antigay slurs. Another headline was the suicide of a college student after his roommate secretly videotaped him kissing another male student and then posted the video on the Internet.

Figure 12.1.   "Junky Words Belong in the Trash Can"—Christopher, Age Eight
Reprinted with permission from GLESN.

"My world isn't safe," Nathan explained when he shared the collage. His artwork enabled him to explain why it wasn't safe through imagery, and allowed enough emotional distance from his personal life to discuss it. As Riley (2001) suggested, art provides "an entrée into a relationship with teenagers by tapping into their creativity and offering a form of communication that is nonthreatening over which the adolescent has control" (p. 2). Only after Nathan shared his work could he and his therapist begin to establish ways they could make his world psychologically and physically safer.

Another example of the healing nature of artwork came from the *No Name-Calling Week Creative Expression Contest*. In this contest, participants aged eight to eighteen submitted original artwork, music, poetry, videos, and essays. These contributions illustrated an intimate understanding of name-calling and its negative impact and displayed valuable insights into the need for compassion, understanding, resilience, and creative problem solving approaches to this challenging problem. Christopher, aged eight, won the grand prize for his mixed media submission, entitled, "Junky Words Belong in the Trash Can" (see figure 12.1). Through his artwork, Christopher explained that hurtful words should be thrown away.

Self-Expression Through Writing

Writing is another integral form of creative self-expression including journaling, questionnaires, and storytelling as practical tools. Writing serves as an avenue for expression, a forum for discussion, and a vehicle to normalize challenging issues with others. The *LGBT Youth Questionnaire* (Goldman, 2008) demonstrates how projective questions can safely convey troubling experiences and private, psychological struggles (see box 12.1). Teens can project (a) what might happen if they *come out*, or what friends and family might say or do when they *come out*; (b) mentors to look up to; and (c) potentially challenging circumstance they see in the future in terms of dating, marriage, children, political rights, religious acceptance, and economic success. The following is an example of a journal response to one of the questions by a fifteen-year-old teen named Sophia. Her response gave her insight into a dialogue with her father, and an impetus to share feelings in the future:

> Question: If you have come out . . . what were your parent's reactions? How did you feel about their reactions? Were they what you expected?

> Response: My mom said she had figured it out a long time ago. My dad said it wasn't the life he would have chosen for me but whatever makes me happy. I really expected both of the reactions.

Box 12.1. LGBT Youth Questionnaire

1. What has helped you the most to accept being gay?
2. What has been the most hurtful?
3. If you have come out . . . what were your parent's reactions?
4. How did you feel about their reactions? Were they what you expected?
5. If you haven't come out, why not?

6. Is there an incident you recall about sexual orientation or gender identity that stands out in your mind?
7. What have you said or done when you heard a prejudicial remark?
8. Where have you felt the most comfortable?
9. What advice do you have for young people who have not yet come out?
10. Is there any TV, movie, or music or art portrayal you found the most offensive? Was their one you found most helpful?
11. Is there any public figure that served as a mentor for you in the LGBT community? (Goldman, *Coming Out, Coming In*, 2008, p. 140)

A month after this journal, Sophia realized that her father's response had actually psychologically hurt her. By journaling and rereading her story, she interpreted his message as meaning that she wasn't good enough. Sophia bravely disclosed her discomfort with his words to him directly. He responded to her in a loving framework: "I'm so sorry. I never meant to hurt you. I love you just the way you are." Journaling incidents in the questionnaire allowed Sophia to recognize hidden hurts, express and process thoughts and feelings, and eventually create a positive experience with her father.

Self-Expression Through Sculpting

Sculpting is another expressive vehicle that can open a path to easier communication and sharing. "Clay has a very calming effect for children (teens and adults) and they can gain a feeling of mastery by . . . pounding, squeezing, pinching, ripping, smoothing, and poking it" (Goldman, 2001, p. 97). Lila, age sixteen, was angry with her parents. She had *come out* to them as a lesbian, and they became enraged. "I won't have a lesbian daughter," Dad screamed. Mom sobbed, "This can't be true!" Lila recreated the scene using clay. Then she took her dad's image and smashed it. She took her mother's image and pounded it, as she cried, "I hate you! I hate you! How could you say those things to me?" Clay represented a safe avenue to express her rage through a play-based experience.

Self-Expression Through Music

Music is an expressive tool that enables young people to go beyond their cognitive mind and feel their feelings in a deep way. Music is the voice of the human spirit: It expresses better than our mere words the passions and emotions that illuminates life (Frohnmayer, 1994). Sometimes not being able to access the perfect words to share tender feelings about a loved one, music serves as a vehicle to express what the griever may not be able to articulate. Songs can serve as an important vehicle for expression of thoughts, feelings, and emotions (Rogers, 2007). Rogers developed several creative exercises involving music that can be adapted for children, adolescents, and adults. One example is a *life review* through a song, with the young person sharing tunes ranging from lullabies, to wedding music, to relaxation melodies. The life review many include songs of different eras, favorite songs, and songs with relatable lyrics. Rogers (2007) also suggests writing a song or modifying self-created words to modify an already existing melody. In working with young LGBTQI teens, music is an effective technique to convey sentiments that weren't easily expressed in conversation.

Alicia was seventeen years old when she came out to her mom as a lesbian. From that point on, her mother appeared emotionally distant, barely speaking and rarely demonstrating affectionate behaviors to her daughter. Feeling the pain of parental rejection, Alicia turned to music as a source of comfort. She identified with a music artist that sung about the freedom to be and the ability for people to let each other "go their own way." She even shared lyrics from an original song called, "Finding My Way Home" that reflected her search for a new home within her self as she struggled with the alienation she experienced from family. As she sang it to her therapist, tears filled her eyes. It was the first time she cried. "I just couldn't talk about it," she explained, "but the song understood my silent thoughts."

Fourteen-year-old Alexa was struggling with her same-sex attraction to girls. She tried many times to express herself about her sexual orientation, but she became tongue-tied and shy, including an inability to sustain eye contact with her therapist. In one particular session, Alexa spontaneously started singing a popular song about a girl kissing a girl. "I think I'll bring in this CD. You might like it." She continued, "Music means a lot to me. It talks about things I can relate to. I don't feel so alone when I listen." She did bring in the song to her next therapy session, played it for the therapist, and they both enjoyed listening to it. The following week Alexa seemed more open and candid in her verbal sharing with the therapist. Qualitative investigations have indicated that the existing relationship between young people and music serves as a platform for connectedness and emotional expression (McFerran, Roberts & O'Grady, 2010). Music therapy can facilitate positive self-concept and improve self-esteem, facilitate communication and self-expression, increase appropriate social behaviors, facilitate relaxation, and reduce reverse tension and anxiety. Music can also create words and feelings that the young person may be unable to access in conversation.

Brandon came out in therapy after spending many sessions leading up to his final disclosure. As he was leaving a session he mentioned to his therapist, "I'm so relieved. I can't wait to tell my parents. I know they will be okay with it." And he closed the door behind him. Brandon came the next week to psychotherapy and sat down motionless. His face was sullen, and it was difficult for him to look maintain eye contact with the therapist. "I told my mom. She cried and cried for days. I can't believe it. I didn't expect that." Too many teens are surprised by the reaction they receive from parents. Preparation for coming out is paramount in aiding their process. The loss of acceptance by parents is all too common for LGBTQI youth after they disclose their sexual orientation or gender identity. The adolescent needs to be educated on common parental responses.

Self-Expression Through Role-Playing

Role-play is a key expressive art therapy technique in identifying problems and issues, imagining real and fictional outcomes, and planning what to expect in situations such as coming out. Tanya's parents were religious and talked openly about their feeling that being gay or lesbian was unacceptable. Tanya confided that she was fearful to tell her parents. In fact, she used the word "terrified." When asked what was so terrifying, Tanya found it too difficult to speak. The therapist handed Tanya a stuffed animal (a plush bear) and said, "Try telling him (him referring to the stuffed animal)." She began sobbing, "I know they'll hate me; they'll kick me out; they will never speak to me again if they find out." And she hugged the bear tightly. As they spoke, the clinician asked Tanya if she was willing to role-play. She could be mom or dad, and the therapist would be Tanya. As her mom, Tanya beginning screaming, "I hate you. I won't have a lesbian daughter. Get out of my house." As they acted out different scenarios, her apprehension grew stronger. They shifted roles, and as the therapist role-played Tanya's parents, she began to recognize how she could respond to them.

The role-plays also initiated a discussion about Tanya's most difficult imaginings. She was able to gain a more realistic appraisal of her situation by considering some of the following questions:

- If you live with your parents, and they kick you out of the house, do you have a place to go?
- Do you have a backup?
- Why do you want to tell your parents?
- Do you have another family member you can come out to first as an ally in case your parents have a strong reaction?

Role-play and psychodrama are critical expressive techniques that address challenging feelings related to sexual orientation, gender identity, loss issues, and rejection or abuse. Young people feel empowered when they can imagine alternative and viable solutions, release feelings, and create dialogue through projective play. Psychodrama allows youth to work through complex issues with their imagination and safely express thoughts and feeling without needing to directly verbalize them. The dramatic arts provide adolescents safe expression to communicate their feelings, wishes, fears, and manage solutions to their problems (Webb, 2002).

RELEVANT INTERVENTION

For some, coming out is the most courageous act of their young lives. Many LGBTQI youth have kept this prospect buried deep inside, under layers of false pretenses and societal conformities until the burden becomes too great to carry and the secret becomes all too consuming. Justin was a high school senior struggling with wanting to share his sexual orientation alongside the terror of being rejected when he did. Justin acknowledged that after this secret was disclosed his life would change, and he would need to begin to live differently. Afraid of the repercussions and psychosocially paralyzed by his fear of rejection, Justin admitted that he felt there was no way out. Justin needed a supportive therapeutic relationship and useful interventions to express his feelings of despair surrounding the secrecy of his sexual orientation, create supports to come out safely, and present resources to aid in his adjustment to being out.

Poetry

Justin often expressed his love for poetry, and he had shared some of his writings with his therapist. The therapist suggested that he might use his love for poetry to express the inner state of weariness with which he seemed burdened. Research substantiates the time before coming out can be the most difficult, with one study finding that 54 percent of adolescents made their first suicide attempt prior to coming out, 27 percent in the year following their coming out, and 19 percent immediately after coming out (D'Augelli, Hershberger, & Pilkington, 2001).

The following poem, *Jail Break*, was Justin's expression of the psychological weight he felt and his perceived inability to find a release from his self-imposed prison. His reflects on a sliver of light, his searching for spirituality, and the hope of escaping from his "cell."

JAIL BREAK

Only in the darkest times of the day,
Can I see where I am?
Grey structures engulfs me,
A constant digestion

A sliver of light comes in from high above,

Only to illuminate the darkness,
It shines in constantly to remind me
That it is my undoing
I can only find sleep in the cold,
Fluorescent glow of my cell,
But, lately, the lights have been
Turned off, and I do not get any sleep.
I stir in discomfort, overwhelmed
By the beam of sunlight above,
I've tried covering it, but I can't reach
I must live with it.
I am so tired. Still afraid of the
Light, but more scared of this
World of darkness
I resolve on change.
My past actions led to this incarceration.
I am not mad at my captures,
Only weary of this suppression from the light.
Where is God?
Where is Allah?
Where is Adonai?

It is time to go. (Goldman, 2008, pp. 146–147)

Justin bravely came out to his friends, family, and teachers. He was suddenly confronted with the shocking realization that his life had forever changed by sharing who he was in the world. Becoming aware of the new journey he had begun, he now felt unsure about where to go and what to do in this unfamiliar territory. Justin expressed his weariness form this experience: "I finally said, 'I'm gay.'" Those words were exhilarating and terrifying for him. "It was the best thing I had ever done and the hardest thing I had ever done." The following poem, *Asylum*, and represented Justin's weariness and inner searching associated with his newfound freedom. His spiritual belief system is evident as a support in maintaining an inner resilience toward a successful integration of sexual orientation.

ASYLUM

At first I am blinded by the light.
Feeling it on my skin is exhilarating.
I float, intoxicated, down the highway.
Suddenly, the road is less defined.
My honesty weighs me down,
And I realize how tired I am.

I sit on a rock off the path,
Light up a cigarette, and look for God.
I sit on this rock for a long time.

The road has moved somewhere else,

And I am lost.
I move to other rocks,
Sometimes I find an old tree stump,
Aimlessly exploring my world
I light another cigarette,
And I see just how big the sky really is,
Brilliant light spreads out before me.
God is everywhere, directionless,
I can go anywhere without moving.
I will just sit where I am. (Goldman, 2008, p. 148)

Drama Therapy

In the next therapy session, Justin shared his newfound freedom. "Now that I can share who I am and how I really feel, I realized I don't know where to go or what to do." Having facilitated his *coming out,* it was now important to facilitate his *being out.* Justin loved the theater, and he had performed in several school productions. Drama through theater is an important creative arts expression that correlates to social issues and common life struggles for young people to explore. Working with other teens through original plays not only supports sharing but promotes forming friendships as well. Justin began participating in a community-based theater for adolescents that eventually helped him bridge the gap from isolation to acceptance. He joined a diverse group of teens that came together as allies and peer support to share life stories.

One of their productions was a choreographed musical made up of scenarios addressing contemporary issues including homophobia. Cast members portrayed roles based on actual peer stories. Justin wrote a story about coming out in a homophobic school. Chase, his good friend, played the role as the boy taunted by gay peers. Although Chase was heterosexual, he reflected that he had learned from acting this part how it felt to be in someone else shoes. Fifteen-year-old Lizzie wrote another scene. Her story depicted a young girl in love with her female best friend, and how difficult it was when her crush was discovered, as she struggled to keep the friendship. Through Lizzie's sharing, Justin said he didn't feel so alone and was comforted that someone else had a same sex crush with a heterosexual peer.

Another scenario centered on a group of students brought together to write an article about teenagers and faith. One young man is "out'ed" as gay, and the group struggles to find common ground in discussing religion and sexuality. Issues surrounding religion and coming out are examined, and the conflict between religion and acceptance of sexual orientation were acted out. This last scene magnified for Justin many conflicts that he had expressed in his poetry as he searched for spirituality in light of his sexual orientation. Realizing this was a societal issue that many shared, Justin was comforted in knowing there were others searching for spiritual meaning as well.

The freedom to express oneself and opportunity to help one another provided by these live stage performances allowed LGBTQI adolescents and their heterosexual peers a platform to share intimate life challenges for public presentations through the arts. The journey of Justin's coming out, being out, and safely integrating his sexual orientation had been deeply tied to the creative arts interventions of writing and drama he had deeply resonated with, resulting in an empowerment to take control over difficult experiences in his life.

CASE STUDY

The following is a case study of a sixteen-year-old named Adam. All details have been altered to protect client confidentiality. Adam was a bright student and gifted artist who often expressed his predilection for painting and the creative freedom it provided him. He yearned for self-expression about his sexual orientation, and he commented often in therapy on the difficulty he encountered when any attempt was made to share his life with friends or parents.

Adam had disclosed that he was gay in a homophobic school environment. His mother and father believed that being gay was unacceptable and against their religious beliefs. "'You're so gay,' 'that's so gay,' is all I hear. There is nowhere I can show affection to my boyfriend, Mathew, without being stared at or taunted," Adam explained. "One of my friends questioned me with a mocking tone, 'How can you kiss another guy? That is so disgusting.'"

"Who are your allies?" his therapist asked during a therapy session. Adam responded that his sister, Carol, and aunt, Joan, were supportive but that he had not disclosed his sexual orientation to them. "No, I don't want to let them in. I'm too scared they will reject me like the others." Realizing Adam needed an avenue for expression, the therapist suggested that Adam share those feelings through his painting. Adam's face lit up. He acknowledged that he had never considered that before and was not sure what he would create. As he left that day he said, "I'll give it a try."

For many weeks, Adam and his therapist worked to create a psychologically safe space in which to share the myriad of challenges related to his sexual orientation. As Adam became more comfortable, his therapist also began offering community resources where he could experience acceptance and meaningful friendships, including a teen support groups for LGBTQI teens and a welcoming religious organization of his faith.

One teen group, *The Rainbow Connection,* was especially beneficial. Having the support of peers was paramount and enabled Adam to create new friendships outside of school, openly discuss dating issues, and share strong feelings and thoughts about prejudice and bigotry. Adam even attended his first high school party with the group as an openly gay youth without fear of reprisal. Local police officers explained what they were doing to keep LGBTQI citizens physical safe in their community. An openly gay teacher and state senator served as mentors to share their life and role models of a future they could see as LGBTQI. Adam was able to form meaningful relationships outside of school based on honesty of self-expression, even volunteering time to advocate for same sex marriage in his state.

Adam sometimes questioned his spiritual belief system. His parents often admonished him: "You are living in sin," was their repeated phrase. Adam internalized this homophobia, asking the question, "Do you think God hates me?" Adam said he was willing to attend a welcoming faith-based peer support group as well. As his experience in this group unfolded, he began to have conversations that seemed to transform past concepts of an angry God to a loving God. "I finally realize that it wasn't God that hated me, it was my parent's ignorance and homophobia." Having an accepting religious peer group helped to release doubts that he had about God and love. He began to reframe his internalized sexual prejudice, separate from it, and see it as a societal issue.

After working with Adam for many months, the therapist was surprised to find him anxiously awaiting an hour early for his appointment, carrying two huge wrapped canvases. "Well," he exclaimed, "I tried." The results of his efforts were two paintings. The first was titled, "The Kiss" (see figure 12.2). His imagery speaks for itself in sharing with all who view the artwork his attraction to men, and manifests his vision of sexuality through the arts.

The second painting was called "Self Reflection" (see figure 12.3). This self-portrait reflects an inner strength evident in the image. Justin's growth from isolation and low self-worth to confidence is personified.

Both illustrations convey the broad canvas of emotions and imagery created by art expression. Adam's paintings are poignant examples of the power of expressive therapy to relieve suffering and promote healing.

CONCLUSION

Rogers (2005) said, "Anything that's human is mentionable, and anything that is mentionable can be more manageable." These words are a useful paradigm for all caring adults working with LGBTQI youth. Allowing young people to acknowledge and express thoughts and feelings involving their sexual orientation and gender identity is imperative and seemingly benefi-

Figure 12.2.   The Kiss Reprinted with permission from Goldman (2008, p. 135).

cial. Through the creative arts clinicians can open a door to an ongoing and integral piece of their counseling process by offering a psychologically safe, nonjudgmental forum for expression.

LGBTQI youth face many challenges, including societal stereotyping and the internalization of homophobia. The sexual stereotyping projected from the heterosexual world often leads to overwhelming feelings of depression

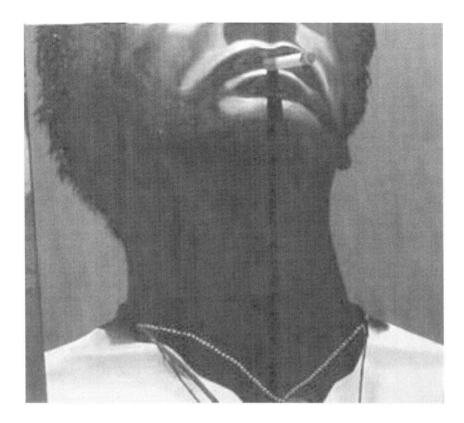

Figure 12.3. Self-Reflection Reprinted with permission from Goldman (2008, p. 135).

and low self-esteem. These difficult feelings converge with adolescents' knowledge that their sexual orientation may impact their futures socially, economically, politically, and spiritually. Often these challenges can be too difficult to speak of out loud or even formulate through words. By opening communication through expressive arts, clinicians can assist youth in accessing inner thoughts and feelings safely throughout the counseling process.

REFERENCES

Bertman, S. (2008). Visual art for professional development. In G. Bolton (Ed.), *Dying, bereavement, and the healing arts* (pp. 51–56). London, England: Jessica Kingsley.

Brody, J. (2011, January 3). Gay or straight, youths aren't so different. *The New York Times*. Retrieved from http://www.nytimes.com/2011/01/04/health/04brody.html.

D'Augelli, A., Hershberger, S., & Pilkington, N. (2001). Suicidality patterns and sexual orientation-related factors among lesbian, gay, and bisexual youths. *Suicide and Life-Threatening Behavior, 31,* 250–264.

Federal Policy Brief (April 19, 2012). LGBTQI youth national policy statement. *National Alliance to End Homelessness.* Retrieved on March 9, 2014, at http://www.endhomelessness.org/library/entry/lgbtq-youth-national-policy-statement.

Fraser, J., & Waldman, J. (2004). Singing with pleasure and shouting with anger: Working with gay and lesbian clients in art therapy. In S. Hogan (Ed.), *Gender issues in art therapy* (pp. 69–91). London, England: Jessica Kingsley.

Frohnmayer, J. (1994). Music and spirituality: Defining the human condition. *International Journal of Arts Medicine, 3*(1), 26–29.

GLSEN. (2010). *2009 national school climate survey.* Retrieved on March 9, 2014, from http://www.glsen.org/cgi-bin/iowa/all/news/record/2624.html.

Goldman, L. (2008). *Coming out, coming in: Nurturing the well-being and inclusion of gay youth in mainstream society.* New York, NY: Taylor and Francis.

Goldman. L. (2013). Young people and gender issues: Living with loss. In B. Deford & R. Gilbert (Eds.), *Living, loving, and loss: The interplay of intimacy, sexuality and grief* (pp. 43–63). Amityville, NY: Baywood.

Kitts, R. (2005). Gay adolescents and suicide: Understanding the association. *Adolescence, 40*(159), 621–628.

Massachusetts Department of Education. (2009). Massachusetts youth risk behavior survey. Retrieved on March 9, 2014 from http://www.mass.gov/clgy/publications.htm.

Maston, A. (1997). *The shared heart: Portraits and stories celebrating lesbian, gay, and bisexual young people.* New York, NY: William Morrow.

McFerran, K., Roberts, M., & O'Grady, L. (2010). Music therapy with bereaved teenagers: a mixed methods perspective. *Journal of Death Studies, 34*(6), 541–565.

Moon, P. (2006). Reaching the tough adolescent through expressive arts therapy groups. VIS-TAS. Retrieved March 9, 2014 at http://www.counseling.org/resources/library/vistas/vistas06_online-only/moon2.pdf.

Myers, D. (2005). *Exploring psychology: Sixth edition in modules.* New York, NY: Worth.

Pelton-Sweet, L., & Sherry, A. (2008). Coming out through art: A review of art therapy with LGBT clients. *Art Therapy, 25*(4), 170–176.

Ploderl, M., & Fartacek, R. (2005). Suicidality and associated risk factors among lesbian, gay, and bisexuals compared to heterosexual Austrian adults. *Suicide and Life-Threatening Behavior, 35*(6), 661–670.

Riley, S. (2001). Art therapy with adolescents. *Western Journal of Medicine, 175*(1), 54–57.

Rogers, F. (2005). *Life's journey according to Mr. Rogers: Things to remember along the way.* New York, NY: Hyperion.

Rogers, E. J. (Ed.). (2007). *The art of grief: The use of expressive arts in a grief support group.* New York, NY: Routledge.

Ryan, C., Huebner, D., Diaz, R. M., & Sanchez, J. (2009). Family rejection as a predictor of negative health outcomes in white and Latino lesbian, gay and bisexual young adults. *Pediatrics, 123*(1), 346–352.

Silverman, P. (2002). *Never to young to know.* New York, NY: Oxford University Press.

Webb, N. B. (2002). *Helping bereaved children: A handbook for practitioners.* New York, NY: The Guilford Press.

Zavis, A. (2010, December 12). Gay and homeless: In plain sight, a largely hidden population. *The Los Angeles Times.* Retrieved on March 9, 2014 from http://articles.latimes.com/2010/dec/12/local/la-me-gay-homeless-20101212.

Subject Index

Author Index

AACAP, 164, 165, 172
Abramowitz, 166, 172
Abramson, D., 108, 121
Adams, H., 154, 162
Adler, A., 4, 180, 193
Ager, J., 165, 172
Akos, P., 197, 206
Albano, A., 164, 172
Alegria, M., 109, 123
American Psychiatric Association, 153, 161, 163, 172
American Psychological Association, 13, 121
Anastasi, A., 142, 147, 161
Anderson, D. M., 198, 207
Anderson, E. R., 175
Antle, B. J., 197, 199, 206
Antonacci, D. J., 165, 173
Archer, J., 196, 207
Arkowitz, H., 5, 20
Artilheiro, A. P. S., 127, 135
Ashby, J.S., 10, 20, 177, 182, 183
Astell, A., 147, 161
Axline, V.M., 116, 121, 129, 135, 142, 161
Ayalon, O., 105, 123

Baggerly, J. N., 66, 81, 108, 109, 113, 115, 120, 121, 123, 197, 209
Bakermans-Kranenburg, M. J., 161
Bakhshoodeh, B., 128, 136
Ball, C., 135

Banerjee, S., 165, 173
Baranek, G., 154, 161
Baratee, F., 127, 135
Barbe, R. P., 173
Barkley, R., 177, 180, 193
Barmish, A., 170, 173
Bar-Mor, G., 127, 136
Barnes, P. M., 13, 20
Baron-Cohen, S., 154, 161
Barrett, P. M., 164, 166, 172
Barris, R., 142, 161
Bartz, J., 136
Bass, J., 122
Batanova, M. D., 202, 207
Baxter, A. L., 134, 135
Beckloff, D., 25, 38
Bedini, L. A., 198, 207
Beggs, S., 137
Beighley, J., 154, 162
Belfer, M. L., 105, 121
Below, R., 105, 122
Belva, B., 162
Benazon, N. R., 165, 172
Bergen, D., 141, 150, 161
Bergman, R., 165, 174
Berk, M.S., 53, 62, 167, 174
Berloffa, S., 174
Bernard, R., 135
Bertman, S., 213, 229
Besiroglu, L., 164, 172
Bettner, B. L., 182, 183, 194

About the Authors

ABOUT THE EDITORS

Eric J. Green, PhD, RPT-S, LPC-S, is associate professor of counseling at the University of North Texas at Dallas and faculty associate at the Johns Hopkins University School of Education in Baltimore, MD. He's the author of *The Handbook of Jungian Play Therapy* and co-editor of *Integrating Expressive Arts and Play Therapy with Children*. Recently, he released two educational DVDs produced by *Alexander Street Press*, "Jungian Play Therapy with Children" and "Expressive Arts with Adolescents." He is a regularly invited keynote speaker and lecturer on the topic of play therapy with children across the United States and internationally. He maintains a part-time, private practice in child psychotherapy in Dallas, TX. For more information, visit www.drericgreen.com.

Amie C. Myrick, MS, LCPC, is a licensed clinical professional counselor whose clinical experience includes work with children, adolescents, adults, and families. She currently treats youth for anxiety, mood, trauma, and self-injurious symptoms as a trauma therapist and general counselor. She completed her graduate training at Johns Hopkins University and completed a post-Masters certificate in play therapy. In addition to her clinical experience, Ms. Myrick has been involved in research for trauma-related disorders for over ten years, and she is currently a research consultant for a large-scale, longitudinal treatment outcome study of adults with dissociative disorders. She has had articles and book chapters published on a range of issues related to play therapy, trauma, and nontrauma treatment with youth.

ABOUT THE CONTRIBUTORS

Marshia Allen-Auguston, LPC-S, is adjunct professor of counseling at the University of North Texas-Dallas. She has over ten years of crisis stabilization experience as an adolescent group and family therapist at Texas Health Seay Behavioral Health Center in Plano, Texas. She is a PhD student utilizing her specialization in play therapy to research the specific impact HIV/AIDS has on family interactions, parenting, and the parent–child relationship.

Brenda Aranda, PhD, is postdoctoral fellow at the Harbor UCLA Medical Center. She has a PhD in clinical psychology from the California School of Professional Psychology (CSPP) at Alliant International University (AIU), San Diego. She has co-authored some peer reviewed journal articles concerning family violence and child custody and book chapters concerning child abuse and custody issues. She has also presented at the International Conference on Violence, Abuse, and Trauma on the topic of child custody evaluations. Dr. Aranda has extensive clinical training in providing psychological services (i.e., individual and group therapy, crisis intervention, and assessment). She has also been an assistant editor for four internationally disseminated journals: *Journal of Aggression, Maltreatment and Trauma*, the *Journal of Child Sexual Abuse*, the *Journal of Child and Adolescent Trauma*, and the *Journal of Emotional Abuse*. She has previously been an editorial assistant for the *Journal of Child Custody*, and the *Journal of Emotional Abuse.*

Lisa Asbill, MA, is a clinical psychology student in Southern California, where she completed externships in the Child Trauma Clinic at Harbor-UCLA Medical Center. She is currently a predoctoral intern at Aurora Mental Health Center in the Child/Family Track.

Jennifer N. Baggerly, PhD, is professor and chair of the Division of Counseling and Human Services at the University of North Texas-Dallas. She is chair of the Board of Directors of the Association for Play Therapy (APT) and the former chair of the APT research committee. Jennifer is a licensed professional counselor supervisor, a registered play therapist supervisor, and a field traumatologist. A recipient of the Outstanding Play Therapist Award from the Florida Association for Play Therapy, she has provided child mental health services locally and disaster relief services internationally, including victims of 2013 Oklahoma Tornados, Hurricane Katrina, and the tsunami in Sri Lanka. Dr. Baggerly's multiple research projects have led to her being recognized as one of the lead play therapy experts in the world. She has over fifty publications, including two books, numerous peer refereed journal articles, many books chapters, and several videos. She is the lead editor of the recently published book *Child-Centered Play Therapy Research: The Evidence Base for Effective Practice* and co-author of *Group Play Therapy: A Dynamic Approach*.

Tracie Faa-Thompson, MA, AASW, PDdipNDPT, DipC.hypno, EAGALA certified, is a specialist social worker in adoption, a nondirective play therapist, clinical hypnotherapist, and is EAGALA certified. Tracie specializes in trauma, attachment, and relationship work with adoptive families. Risë Van-Fleet and Tracie have developed a specialist training course for play therapists using dogs and horses as co-therapists. Risë and Tracie are currently co-writing various articles in the growing field of animal-assisted therapy. Based near the Scottish border, Tracie has a lifetime of working alongside horses and is a member of the classical riding club. Tracie is currently running an equine-assisted research project for at risk teenagers. Tracie is a founder member of the attachment and resilience training consortium and has developed an experiential training course on life story work for carers and social workers.

Jenny A. Gallagher, MA, is a clinical psychology student from Southern California, where she completed externships in the Child Trauma Clinic and the TIES for Families Clinic at Harbor-UCLA Medical Center. She is currently a predoctoral intern at Tulane University School of Medicine in the infant mental health rotation.

Linda Goldman, MS, LCPC, is author of several books, including *Coming out, Coming In: Nurturing the Well Being and Inclusion of Gay Youth in Mainstream Society* and *Life and Loss: A Guide to Help Grieving Children, 3rd Edition*. She has been an educator in the public school system as a teacher and counselor for almost twenty years and has a private therapy practice in Chevy Chase, Maryland. She also teaches as an adjunct professor in schools and universities including Johns Hopkins Graduate School and Kings College.

Terry Kottman, PhD, NCC, RPT-S, LMHC, founded the Encouragement Zone in Cedar Falls, Iowa, where she provides play therapy training and supervision, life coaching, play therapy, counseling, and "playshops" for women. Terry developed Adlerian play therapy, an approach to counseling children, adolescents, and adults that combines the ideas and techniques of Individual Psychology and play therapy. She regularly presents workshops and writes about play therapy, activity-based counseling, school counseling, and life coaching. She is the author of *Partners in Play: An Adlerian Approach to Play Therapy*, *Play Therapy: Basics and Beyond*, *Active Interventions for Kids and Teens*, and several other books.

Kristin K. Meany-Walen, PhD, LMHC, RPT, NCC, is assistant professor of counseling at the University of Northern Iowa in Cedar Falls. She has published and presented on topics such as Adlerian play therapy, expressive arts, counseling preadolescents and adolescents, and working with parents as therapeutic agents of change. Her primary research focus is Adlerian play therapy with elementary-aged children.

Julia A. Mitchell, BSW, MSW, LCSW-C, is a clinical social worker, working for MHM Services in Baltimore, MD, doing clinical assessments on new detainees. She also works part time with inner city families doing individual and family therapy. In 2013, the Harford County Local Management Board awarded her the "Champions for Children and Youth" award for her outstanding service to children and youth in the community. She uses an eclectic approach to her work incorporating play therapy, CBT, solution-focused and strengths-based perspectives to empower her clients to create change often against extenuating circumstances.

Judith A. Parson, PhD, APPTA RPT-S, MA, BN, RN, is a pediatric qualified registered nurse, play therapist, and lecturer in mental health–child play therapy at Deakin University, Australia. Her PhD focused on the integration of procedural play for children undergoing invasive medical procedures for the treatment of cystic fibrosis. While Judi has over twenty years experience working in acute hospital, child and adolescent health units, she now practices play therapy in a community-based clinic on a part-time basis. Judi speaks regularly throughout Australia and has been invited to speak in neighboring Asia-Pacific countries. She is currently researching and lecturing in child play therapy and is the president of the Australasia Pacific Play Therapy Association (APPTA).

Eileen Prendiville is course director for the MA in humanistic and integrative psychotherapy and play therapy, the postgraduate diploma in play therapy, and the diploma in child psychotherapy and play therapy at the Children's Therapy Centre in Co Westmeath, Ireland. Eileen was a founder member, and national clinical director, of the Children at Risk in Ireland Foundation, Ireland's specialist treatment service for children and families affected by child sexual abuse. Eileen holds qualifications in humanistic and integrative psychotherapy, Jungian sandplay therapy, biodynamic psychotherapy, and family law. She is a psychotherapist, play therapist, supervisor, and trainer. Her chapter on "Abreaction" is published in the second edition of Dr. Charles Schaefer's seminal text, *The Therapeutic Powers of Play: 20 Core Agents of Change* co-authored with Dr. Athena Drewes. Her own co-edited (with Dr. Justine Howard) book, *Play Therapy Today: Contemporary Practice for Individuals, Groups, and Parents*, was published in 2014.

Janine Shelby, PhD, RPT-S, is director of the child trauma clinic at Harbor-UCLA and associate professor in the Geffen School of Medicine at UCLA. Dr. Shelby's supervisorial, clinical, training, consulting, academic, and humanitarian relief work focus on the delivery of evidence-based treatments in developmentally and culturally sensitive ways. Inspired by her clinical experiences in both community settings and international humanitarian work, Dr. Shelby has presented widely in this country as well as in dozens of countries abroad.

Cynthia C. Sniscak, LPC, RPT-S, is in private practice in Carlisle, Pennsylvania. She utilizes play therapy and filial therapy to address issues involving a wide range of problems facing families and children. She has a special interest in trauma and attachment issues. Ms. Sniscak also provides training for child-related community organizations, and has been a featured speaker at state, national, and international conferences on adoption, attachment, trauma, domestic violence, and play therapy and filial therapy. She has trained many professionals in CCPT and filial therapy and provides supervision in these methods to other professionals. She is the author of numerous chapters and articles on play therapy and filial therapy and co-authored, with Dr. Risë VanFleet and Dr. Andrea Sywulak, *Child-Centered Play Therapy* (2010). She is the recipient of the Outstanding Contributions to Professional Training in Filial Therapy Award from the Family Enhancement and Play Therapy Center.

Karen Stagnitti, PhD, currently works as professor, personal chair at the School of Health and Social Development at Deakin University, Victoria, Australia. She graduated with a bachelor degree in occupational therapy from the University of Queensland. Over the past thirty-plus years she has mainly worked in early childhood intervention programs in community-based settings as part of a specialist pediatric multidisciplinary team. In 2003 she graduated from LaTrobe University with a doctor of philosophy. Her area of research is children's play. Karen has over seventy national and international papers published as well as fifteen book chapters. Her norm referenced standardized play assessment, the Child-Initiated Pretend Play Assessment has been used in several countries including Australia, Brazil, Canada, the United Kingdom, Japan, Switzerland, Norway, and Finland. There is now an Australian Indigenous version of the Child-Initiated Pretend Play Assessment. From her research work, a play therapy program called "Learn to Play" was developed to encourage play ability in children with developmental issues.

Kelsey A. Stephenson, MS, is professional school counselor and recent graduate of Johns Hopkins University. Her bachelor's degree in psychology was completed at Southern New Hampshire University. Her research and professional interests include educational differentiation for children with disabilities and advocacy in school counseling. Her experiences also concentrate on school reform, at-risk youth, and social justice specifically in urban and/or metropolitan areas.

Anne Stewart, PhD, is professor of psychology, author, and trainer. She teaches, supervises, and conducts play and family therapy each week at James Madison University. She has written and presented about attachment, crisis intervention, supervision, nature and therapy, military families, improv, andresilience around the world. She is the founder and president of the Virginia Association for Play Therapy, chairs the Foundation for Play Therapy, and is a member of the editorial board for the *International Journal of Play Therapy*. She's the recipient of the Association for Play Therapy's Distinguished Service Award and the State Council of Higher Education of Virginia's Outstanding Faculty Award.

Glade Topham, PhD, LMFT, is associate professor of human development and family science at Oklahoma State University, where he serves as the program coordinator for the graduate program in marriage and family therapy. He received his BS and MS at Brigham Young University and his PhD from Texas Tech University. His research and clinical interests are focused on the treatment of parents and children within the context of the parent–child relationship.

Risë VanFleet, PhD, is known internationally for her fun and informative presentations and workshops as well as for her books, articles, and DVDs about the fields of play therapy, filial therapy, and animal-assisted play therapy. Her innovative approaches and stimulating training programs are frequently hailed by participants as among the best they've ever attended. A licensed psychologist (PA), registered play therapist-supervisor, and a certified dog behavior consultant, Dr. VanFleet brings thirty-five years of experience to her seminars, DVDs, and books/articles. The quality of her work has been recognized by eight national and international awards.

Lightning Source UK Ltd.
Milton Keynes UK
UKOW04n0604030615

252811UK00007B/133/P